Max Weber's Method

Si le grain ne meurt.
Gide

Max Weber's Methodologies

Interpretation and Critique

Sven Eliaeson

polity

First published in 2002 by Polity Press in association with Blackwell Publishers Ltd, a Blackwell Publishing Company

Editorial office:
Polity Press
65 Bridge Street
Cambridge CB2 1UR, UK

Marketing and production:
Blackwell Publishers Ltd
108 Cowley Road
Oxford OX4 1JF, UK

Published in the USA by
Blackwell Publishers Inc
350 Main Street
Malden, MA 02148, USA

A catalogue record for this book is available from the British Library.

Library of Congress Cataloging-in-Publication Data

Eliaeson, Sven, 1948–
  Max Weber's methodologies : interpretation and critique / Sven Eliaeson.
    p. cm.
Includes bibliographical references and index.
  ISBN 0-7456-1812-X (hb) – ISBN 0-7456-1813-8 (pb)
  1. Sociology – Methodology. 2. Weber, Max, 1864–1920. I. Title.
  HM511 .E43 2002
  301'.01 – dc21

                                                              2002001669

Typeset in 10.5 on 12 pt Sabon
by SNP Best-set Typesetter Ltd., Hong Kong
Printed in Great Britain by MPG Books Ltd, Bodmin, Cornwall

This book is printed on acid-free paper.

Contents

List of Abbreviations

Weber's Works

E & S   *Economy and Society: An Outline of Interpretive Sociology*, ed. Guenther Roth and Claus Wittich. New York: Bedminster Press, 1968. This is a translation in three volumes (two in the German original) by many translators – including Talcott Parsons and A. M. Henderson – and with an Introduction by Guenther Roth.

GARS   *Gesammelte Aufsätze zur Religionssoziologie.* Tübingen: Mohr-Siebeck, 1920.

GASW   *Gesammelte Aufsätze zur Sozial- und Wirtschafts- geschichte.* Tübingen: Mohr-Siebeck, 1924.

GAW   *Gesammelte Aufsätze zur Wissenschaftslehre.* Tübingen: Mohr-Siebeck, 1922.

GPS   *Gesammelte politische Schriften.* Tübingen: Mohr-Siebeck, 1958, expanded 2nd edn with 'Geleitwort' by Th. Heuss, first German edn 1921.

MWG   *Max Weber-Gesamtausgabe.* Tübingen: Mohr-Siebeck, 1984–.

PW   *Political Writings.* Cambridge: Cambridge University Press, 1994 (this translation is not a complete translation of *GPS*).

WuG   *Wirtschaft und Gesellschaft.* Tübingen: Mohr-Siebeck, 1921–3 (vols I–II).

'Einleitung': in *Die Wirtschaftsethik der Weltreligionen*, in *GARS*.
'Freiburger Antrittsrede': 'Der Nationalstaat und die Volks- wirtschaftspolitik', in *GPS*.
'Vorbemerkung': in *GARS*.

'Zwischenbetrachtung': 'Zwischenbetrachtung: Theorie der Stufen und Richtungen religiöser Weltablehnung', in *GARS*.

The original collections from the early 1920s are reprinted after the latest Johannes Winckelmann editions, in a UTB edition in 1988 (seven volumes in paperback).

Other Abbreviations

AJS	*American Journal of Sociology*
APSR	*American Political Science Review*
Archiv	*Archiv für Sozialwissenschaft und Sozialpolitik*
ASR	*American Sociological Review*
FAZ	*Frankfurter Allgemeine Zeitung*
FZ	*Frankfurter Zeitung*
IJPCS	*International Journal of Politics, Culture and Society*
KZfSS	*Kölner Zeitschrift für Soziologie und Sozialpsykologie*
TdKH	*Theorie des Kommunikativen Handelns*
Verein	*Verein für Sozialpolitik*
ZfP	*Zeitschrift für Politik*
ZfS	*Zeitschrift für Soziologie*

Good bibliographies of Weber's work are those by Käsler (first published 1975 in *KZfSS)* and Riesebrodt (in *MWG*).

For a good bibliography of the secondary literature, see Constance Seyfarth and Gert Schmidt, *Max Weber Bibliographie: Eine Dokumentation der Sekundärliteratur.* Stuttgart: Enke, 1977. It builds on the collection at the Weber archives in Munich.

For a documentation of Anglo-Saxon secondary literature, see Peter Kivisto and William H. Swatos Jr, *Max Weber. A Bio-Bibliography.* New York: Westport, Conn., London: Greenwood Press, 1988. It contains very useful abstracts as well as an overview of the archival material.

Acknowledgements

I have been working on this book for a long time. It is impossible to thank everybody who helped to bring it about, so I restrict myself to listing in alphabetical order those who, one way or another – advice, suggestions and critical comments – left their marks on the final product: Martin Albrow, Ola Agevall, Rita Aldenhoff, Rolf Ahlzén, Hans Henrik Bruun, Robert J. Antonio, Karl-Ludwig Ay, Horst Baier, Niall Bond, Finn Collin, Randall Collins, Agnes Erdelyi, Leah Florence, Anthony Giddens, Dieter Henrich, Horst Jürgen Helle, Wilhelm Hennis, Tapani Hietaniemi, Göran Hydén, Georg G. Iggers, Bjarne Jacobsen, Inger Johansson, Dirk Kaesler, Elisabeth Suzanne Kassab, Peter Kivisto, Jürgen Kocka, M. Rainer Lepsius, Carsten Ljunggren, Thomas Mautner, Cornelia Meyer-Stoll, Wolfgang J. Mommsen, Per Månson, Karl-Heinz Nusser, Kari Palonen, Guenther Roth, Gert Schmidt, Ralph Schroeder, Gerd Schroeter†, Edward Shils†, Ilja Srubar, Richard Swedberg, Friedrich H. Tenbruck, Zoltan Tarr, Göran Therborn, Regina F. Titunik-Yoshikawa, Rolf Torstendahl, Charles Turner, Stephen P. Turner, Lars Udéhn, Arthur J. Vidich, R. Stephen Warner, Sam Whimster, Johannes Winckelmann†, Elfriede Üner and Hans Zetterberg. These names don't exhaust the list of those to whom I am indebted.

However, special thanks are due to Stephen P. Turner. Without his detailed critical comments and encouragement this work would not have been brought to fruition. The same is true of Karl-Ludwig Ay, who on numerous occasions provided me with shelter down at the Weber archives at the Bavarian Academy of Science and in the process taught me a lot about German history. Sam Whimster has given many comments *unterwegs*, on both language and content. Mrs Leah

Florence has left her imprint on the final guise in which this book is cast. I am solely responsible for the final version.

Special thanks are also due to the whole staff of the Weber archives in Munich (Die Arbeitsstelle und Archiv der Max Weber-Gesamtausgabe an der bayerischen Akademie der Wissenschaften) and the staff of the Carolina Rediviva in Uppsala.

Thanks for economic support are due to the following institutions and endowments: HSFR (The Swedish Social Science Research Council), The Tercentenary Fund of the Swedish National Bank, Karlstad University, The Magnus Bergvall Foundation, DAAD (Deutscher Akademischer Austauschdienst), DFG (Deutsche Forschungsgemeinschaft) and SI (The Swedish Institute).

Saxhyttan

Introduction

There are a few notions basic to this book. First, there is no 'essential' Weber. Attempts at an all-inclusive interpretation (the Germans would call it *Gesamtdeutung*), at finding the one and only 'key' to Weber, have not proved convincing thus far. Nevertheless, it is worthwhile to try to interpret Weber's *methodology* as a coherent whole. But, in an effort not to repeat some recurring retrospective misrepresentations, a contextual reconstruction is in order. Too many scholars have seen the Weber they wanted to see, not Weber in his own right.

Weber has been claimed as a founding father of many sociological traditions, but the way in which this genealogy is traced has caused conflicts of interpretation. Many scholars read their own ambitions into Max Weber's *œuvre*; not surprisingly, they find – or believe they find – what they look for. In some cases they even try to tell Weber what he ought to have meant 'had he only fully realized', or think they know what he would have tried to accomplish if he had lived longer. I find that this condescending approach tends to impose something on Weber after the fact, and can lead to an improper interpretation of what he actually tried to communicate. Weber certainly could not foresee the controversies and applications his work would lead to, but if competing methodological paradigms claim his methodology as constitutive, it calls for further elucidation.

Weber's methodological works were in response to his immediate circumstances, but they can still inform us today. He is relevant because he dealt with a central paradigmatic divide: the as yet unresolved problem of values and objectivity in the social sciences. Although the meaning of value-freedom appears obvious now, Weber qualified the concept; he did not argue for value-freedom in the sense of avoiding values, but offered an apparently paradoxical solution in which values could be used to promote objectivity rather than subjectivity.

His qualification of value-freedom (or value-neutrality) toward value-relevance (or value-orientation) has been subsequently misused and misunderstood, mainly because a particular view of Weber has been taken out of context, and he has been retrospectively apprehended as an almost contemporary thinker. It is important to keep in mind – if we wish to avoid 'chronological imperialism' – that the labels we apply to Weber are *our* labels and not his own or those relevant in his day.

In courses on the classics, Weber's work is often introduced as an 'up-to-date theoretical classic in sociology'. But the surviving classics are *also* our constructions, the result of a transcultural encounter between modern readers and classical authors. This book seeks, in an account of Weber's context, a more reliable and less biased interpretation of his methodology, drawing on hitherto little noticed essays as well as neglected parts of his correspondence.

When we try to evaluate Weber as a classical author in the sociological tradition, it is important to keep in mind the unusual history of how he was received. His methodology has predominantly been left in the hands of Anglo-Saxons (American and British), who cut it off from its original context and thereby its meaning. We have to recapture Weber's original context in order to make sense of his thought today.

The 'Olympic Weber' in the pantheon of classical authors probably had to be a reconstructed version, taken out of the context of the *deutscher Sonderweg* (or 'special way', the peculiar route of German history); otherwise his reception would have been even more inhibited. It is doubtful if a genuine image of Weber would have been 'marketable' in the New World; his militant nationalism and lack of inner democratic creed are easily misunderstood in the light of the experience of Hitlerism. It is difficult to explain Weber as simultaneously pioneering parliamentary rule and plebiscitary charismatic (therefore also Nazi) rule.[1]

The violent dispute that erupted at the Heidelberg centenary in 1964[2] clearly demonstrated how deep the controversy over Weber's legacy to political sociology was; it still is. The German Weber – in comparison to the Anglo-Saxon one – is clearly more historical than theoretical. The German attempts at all-inclusive interpretations typically discuss Weber as a historian of Western capitalism and religious ideas. This runs the risk of leaving out his innovative methodological achievements.

Weber did not really have a methodological 'programme'; he rather responded to crucial problems put on the agenda by other scholars. In the end, to the extent that a coherent position may be attributed to Weber, it must be constructed from the critical essays he wrote on his contemporaries. Weber is a master at telling us what is wrong with his colleagues, and he does so forthrightly and in detail; but he was less than forthcoming about his positive views. Moreover, he was not concerned with the accessibility of his writings to a wide audience; he felt that it should not necessarily be any easier to read his texts than it had been for him to write them. Nor was Weber very helpful about explaining what views he considered to be original and what views he simply took over from other scholars. He relied heavily on others, and often wrote as though he were simply defending normal practice. His writings sometimes bordered on plagiarism, but in the end he always added something that made the analysis distinctly Weberian; he borrowed, but was never the unthinking appropriator of his sources.

There is no obvious methodological break between Weber writing in 1894 as a bourgeois activist and Weber defending scientific objectivity in 1909–14 and 1917–19. He had no interest in the philosophy of science for its own sake, yet he wrote a great deal on methodological questions. There is, however, no systematic treatise on methodology and no definitive exemplary text, though some essays are more telling than others. In my view, Weber is fundamentally consistent in his methodological writings.[3]

Weber was provoked to clarify his position on methodological matters – for others as well as for himself. We have some evidence of Weber's own ideas about these writings, for there are a number of letters between him and his publisher that give some indications of what Weber himself wished to include in his *Wissenschaftslehre* (this is untranslatable; it is often rendered in English as 'theory of science' or 'philosophy of science' or even 'metascience').

Weber's work is like a gigantic quarry with many shiny stones to pick up – many concepts and hypotheses to extend, elaborate and transcend. In addition, his 'schizophrenic' or antinomian qualities make him – and especially his methodology – difficult to grasp. For example, on my first visit to the Weber archives in Munich more than twenty years ago, I read an article whose author claimed that Weber was a deeply religious man. A reader had angrily written in the margin: 'Surely not!' Yet, both statements are true. On the one hand, Weber cultivated a 'puritan' lifestyle and he kept in close contact with his deeply religious mother (who lived until October 1919, less than a year before Weber's own death); on the other hand, he himself gave no sign that he was a believer.[4]

It seems that the paradigmatic divides in social science – between history and theory – are the same today as they were 200 years ago, although the positions have been refined. Weber still serves as a *mediator* or way station in the history of ideas; we can turn to him for identity and roots rather than for actual guidance. Even if he is best understood in context, he also plays a role in theoretical discourse beyond his own horizons and has an obvious (omni)presence in today's social science.[5]

He would probably himself be much surprised by some allegedly 'Weberian' present-day applications and 'Procrustean bed' interpretations.[6] I have chosen to focus on Weber's methodological polemics, the essays relating to the controversies of his day, to unfold the continuity and common denominators in his methodology.

Weber could be approached from different time-horizons. In the very longest perspective – over several centuries, from 'early modernity' 500 years ago – he is a manifestation of the 'long line of secularization' and anti-metaphysics,[7] anti-natural law and calculability as core elements and rational economic man as prototype.

In a somewhat shorter perspective – after the Enlightenment – Weber could be understood as being a mediator between positivism and historicism, i.e. theory and history, which is a perennial tension, basically the same today as it was two centuries ago.

In the more immediate perspective Weber could be placed in the context of three interrelated contemporary controversies (*Methodenstreit*, about history *vs* theory; demarcation-controversy, over various arguments to protect the human/cultural sciences from the intrusion of the naturalistic unity of science; and *Werturteilsstreit*, about objectivity and value-intrusion), two currents (neo-Kantianism and marginalism), and one predicament (the theodicy crisis, affecting a lot of German scholars after the death of Weber).

The widespread historicism is part of the general ambience, the importance of the historical dimension taken for granted by most scholars. The problem of objectivity and value-intrusion is present as a dimension within the other two debates but it is also a debate in its own right, a recurrent theme to which Weber contributes.[8]

In chapter 4 I shall also demonstrate the flaws in three prominent 'creative extensions' of Weber's methodology. The competing interpretations of Weber's ideal-type methodology have been caused by the vested interests of the various interpreters who claim his true legacy.

1
The Contexts

German Historicism and the Controversy over Method

There is an aspect of difference in political cultures involved in the controversy over method, where 'Anglo-Saxon' modes of thinking are brought onto the stage belatedly. This is manifested in the marginalism and utilitarianism of the Austrian Menger school, which challenges the dominant younger historical school of Schmoller and his many pupils.

The state, which had originated in medieval taxation structures, had become the focus of post-Renaissance social thought. It was an interesting historical phenomenon, and was also an object of controversy, since the degree of statecraft viewed as desirable varied with the needs of a society's entrepreneurial class: in periods of chaotic civil wars or early nation-building, demand for the state was high; in periods of prosperity and stability, especially if growth occurred independently of state initiatives, the coercive capability of the state was considered more of a threat. In Germany, at the turn of the nineteenth century, most scholars in social science and history were adherents of the broad tradition of historicism.[1] Historicism regarded reality as an historical product and stressed what was historically unique or singular. It was rooted in the early nation-building attempts during the Napoleonic era, in reaction against French intervention, when the Germans tried to reawaken a lost – and partly fictional – creed of a great national past;[2] the transcendentalist philosopher Hegel, who viewed the World Spirit moving through history towards higher and higher levels of self-realization, belonged to this broad camp.[3] With nation-building a particularly pressing task in a fragmented Germany, the historical school was more firmly established there than in England or France; the market for historians was thus created and secured.

In England the state was viewed as a necessary evil to be minimized. The German position was that the state embodied ideals, and its purposes could not be reduced to rational calculation.[4] Members of the older historical school did not consider the theoretical positions of classical British political economy to be generally valid, but as applicable only in particular historical settings where citizens were very liberal and inclined to come under the spell of the idea of 'rational economic actors'. There was, furthermore, an ethical element in their critique. The ideal of state reason (*raison d'état*) was embraced by all thinkers on the historicist side. German historicists considered themselves to be of a higher moral standing than those one would find in England (in their eyes a nation of shopkeepers and materialistic merchants), and political-economy theories were seen as a hypocritical rationalization of self-interest.[5] This is a subdimension in the controversy over method.

Yet, despite its idealist and romanticist background, as part of the *deutscher Sonderweg* and late nation-building in search of roots, historicism also contributed to the furthering of scientific techniques and brought about both a new technical awareness, a 'feeling' for the actual material that historical research works with, and a more critical approach to sources of information. However, an important trademark of historicism was its animosity towards abstract concepts. Historicists felt that reality was either revealed through empirical research or grasped with some sort of empathetic or intuitive act of understanding: either way, one could embrace the essence of the phenomenon under study. The more empirically inclined representatives of the younger historical school even entertained the hope of establishing some kind of 'law', but their basic conceptions complicated their efforts to achieve this goal. The problem was this: on the one hand, historicism programmatically stressed what was historically unique; on the other hand, it tried to pursue the true meaning of history through its study. This inherent contradiction – the relativism required in seeing all phenomena as time-bound while trying to generalize from the unique historical data to eternal laws, norms and principles – put the historicists at a distinct disadvantage, as compared to the theoretical side, in the controversy over method.

The most important aspect of the long historicist hegemony in Germany is that theoretical elements from the increasingly successful natural sciences could not easily, if at all, be assimilated into the social sciences, and the historicists' increasingly eager defence of their territory became the basis for the famous *Methodenstreit* – the controversy over method: the issue was whether a historical or a theoretical approach to the study of the economy should be preferred.[6] The nineteenth century is sometimes spoken of as the century of history, because it was not until then that methodologically aware historical research emerged as a significant phenomenon. It was also the century of natural science. By its end, these two cultures were on a collision course.

The conflict between history and theory began in 1883 with the debate between Gustav Schmoller, the leading personality and main exponent of the younger historicist school, and Carl Menger, the representative of Austrian marginalist economics.[7] As a result of the historicist dominance, classical political economy in its British form had been sadly neglected by German scholars, who were inclined instead towards Schmoller's spirit, captured by the expression from Goethe's *Faust*: 'Grau, treuer Freund, ist alle Theorie, / Und grün des Lebens goldner Baum' (Theory is grey, my friend, only the golden tree of life is green). The controversy over method can in fact be understood as an expression of hostility to the foreign and utilitarian tradition of the theoretical, British-inspired political economy that was making a back-door entrance through Menger's Austrian marginalism.[8] At the same time, many Germans who were ambivalent about England still tried to appropriate some useful elements of successful British science and politics and adapt them to German conditions.

The British simply were successful in areas where their German cousins were late to mature – such as empire-building and parliamentary democracy. There was a certain envy of – and a substantial interest in – the English model.[9] This is a recurrent theme from the days of Friedrich ('Freddy') List onwards, until the First World War, when intellectuals such as Werner Sombart turned against England because of disappointment and as part of their 'war service'.[10]

The methodological quarrel between Schmoller and Menger, the conflict between history and theory, was a manifestation of the late nineteenth-century antagonism between historicism and positivism. A century ago, 'positivism' referred to the search for theoretical laws, in the spirit of Auguste Comte, who coined the term for the social sciences. Today, positivism refers mostly to fragmentary forms of knowledge production and anti-theoretical attitudes, e.g. 'empiricism'; it calls to mind repeated experiments and induction.

The present-day meaning of 'positivism' is thus marked by the impact of logical positivism or logical empiricism. Both the older and the more modern definitions posit the unity of science as an ideal and maintain a sharp distinction between science and metaphysics.[11] Again, the main difference is between the strong theory-building of the 'old' positivism and modern positivism's occasionally (but not as frequently as some have charged) anti-theoretical stance.[12]

It is common practice to distinguish between a deductive-rationalist approach, 'theory from above', and an inductive-empiricist approach, 'theory from below'. The former utilizes classical deductive chains; the latter generalizes on the basis of a thorough study of reality and its regularities. In principle, there is no problem with either approach; they are both trips from different starting points to the same destination. But, as often happens in real life, the two strategies have become methodological opposites rather than alternative paths to establishing scientific laws.[13] Since the central problem in the controversy over method concerned the proper way to establish laws, the historicist position was weakened because it simultaneously insisted on the particularity of history while maintaining a belief in a higher unity of order, a grand narrative.

Schmoller and his followers had not abandoned their ambitions to create theory, but felt it would be the product, the natural outcome of inductive-empirical efforts; and a realistic science of empirical reality – *Wirklichkeitswissenschaft* (see below) – was the proper context in which to pursue induction and theory. In historicist undertakings reality was reproduced, and flesh and blood were described but hardly explained; at least, no theoretical explanations – in which phenomena are subsumed under some general law(s) – were achieved. Schmoller felt that more facts would be needed before such achievements were possible. By contrast, Menger's position could succinctly be characterized as deductive-rationalist; for the marginalist economists, the starting points for economic analyses were clearly defined theoretical concepts, models that allowed for deductions, hypothetical statements and predictions about human acts.

Both sides in the controversy tried to make use of persuasive definitions; the one was 'realist' against 'exact' science or the 'modern' school. By the end of the nineteenth century, however, 'pure theory' of the kind used in classical economics was already regarded as lacking in realism. Some marginalists argued that there is no once-and-for-all given of human nature; the degree of rationality in human action is context-bound and so must vary. Yet, although rational economic actors are a rather simplified model abstracted from reality, they have significant explanatory power. Any position that presupposes a certain anthropology to be generally valid is problematic.

It is difficult to understand our contemporaries, perhaps impossible to understand pre-Enlightenment humans, and when we try to understand those who lived before the Renaissance, we usually resort to some of the basics of life: hunger and reproduction. This poses the epistemological problem that some distinction between concept and reality must be introduced in order to proceed without any trace of metaphysics, namely the problem of concept formation and inter-subjectivity, which Weber and Schutz tried to solve in different ways, as we will see.[14]

Thus, the debate turned on the role of conceptual constructions within the social sciences and the value of theoretical abstraction. The historicists, who thrived on statistics and archival studies, adhered to induction; the patient gathering of historical facts would result not in abstract, anaemic theories but in precise formulations of the rela-tionship between important causal factors that were there 'in reality'. The historicists conceived of abstract laws as a part of reality to be uncovered rather than invented; this 'realist' concept of knowledge implied that other approaches were unrealistic.

One might say that Schmoller and the elder historicists had painted themselves into a corner. The intrinsic weakness in the historicists' position was that their inductive efforts, although predominantly idiographic (interpretative and descriptive, with a focus on narra-tives) in practice, still aimed to be nomothetic (law-building), to establish 'theory' in the long run. These ambitions are not necessar-ily antagonistic; for instance, in the case of Hegel and Marx they coincide. The meaning of history in their case appeared as a devel-opmental scheme – a historical law of the unique and singular, to give it a somewhat paradoxical formulation. The historicists' posi-tion was not strengthened even by their claim to pursue 'real' and not 'abstract' theory. Menger could afford to be more moderate, to consider the value to the scientific process of both theory and history. This position took hold in the German-speaking world[15] and broke the previously exclusive grip of historicism.[16]

Towards the end of the original *Methodenstreit*, however, it became clear that the gulf revealed in the heated debate between Schmoller and Menger was not quite as unbridgeable as its most tur-bulent phases might have suggested. When the turmoil was over, a new *modus vivendi* resulted between history and theory,[17] an aware-ness that they were complementary rather than antagonistic.[18] That the controversy over method never produced any clear winners or losers comes as no great surprise. Academic disputes rarely have immediate and clear-cut consequences, especially in social science, where almost any position can be rescued by *ad hoc* arguments. Rather, the outcome of controversy is usually revealed much later, in the changing patterns of authority within the academic community. In the case of the great *Methodenstreit*, with all its ensuing debates, the peak came early, with Schmoller *vs* Menger, and then gradually

faded away, apparently because the participants became exhausted.[19]
Idiography always has some value in its own right. Moreover, as part
of heuristics and the generation of hypotheses, it is methodologically
necessary to historicize phenomena; genetic problems, for instance,
cry out for historical approaches. Historicism thus became a matter
of appropriate scope and application. Although it survived, its hegemony did not, and historicism, a viable but not very innovative tradition, became one alternative out of many.[20]

In the controversy over method, the marginalist school understood
individual self-interest to be fundamental, and the role of the state
best restricted to enforcing the rules of the game in a free-market
economy. For liberal utilitarianism, the state was a residual institution that should not intrude unnecessarily into the market economy;
because of non-economic motives, the state should work to preserve
and promote free enterprise.[21] This is a telling example of the simultaneously normative and empirical character of social science in the
post-Enlightenment nineteenth century, when both classical liberalism and Marxism sought general principles by which to understand
society.

The rational economic actor represented reality not only as it 'is,'
offering a model for understanding economic life, but also as it
'ought' to be. In the same way, Marxist predictions about growing
contradictions within capitalist economies combined the 'is' (fact)
and the 'ought' (value judgement), a distinction that was not yet
accepted in the nineteenth century.

The Post-Enlightenment Anguish of Polytheism

After the Enlightenment and the so-called Death of God, the field was
open to competing sects in the marketplace of ideas, an inevitable
consequence of modern secular science. The search for a new authority led some to glorify the creative individual in his or her search for
self-realization, a Narcissistic route made possible by the Enlightenment; others embraced collective allegiances in an attempt to regain
the meaning of life that the Enlightenment had deprived them of; and
for many who found it difficult to find any orientation in the ethical
chaos of the post-Enlightenment era, nihilism became yet another
option.

Disillusionment and the anguish of polytheism of values created a
theodicy crisis, a crisis of the meaning of life in the Western world,
as the decline of religious norms led to discontent. In the course
of the loss of the credibility of transcendent goals outside the

individual, the self – the ego – replaced the soul. Weber was himself very well aware of this: 'Many old gods ascend from their graves; they are disenchanted and hence take the form of impersonal forces. They strive to gain power over our lives and again they resume their eternal struggle with one another' (*GAW*: 605). Competing value systems or worldviews have become our destiny. When our anxiety over the confusing array of worldviews is replaced by resignation, we accept being captured in a life of increasing and meaningless rationality; as routinized humans we tend towards utilitarianism or even sheer materialism.[22]

Lebensphilosophie (the philosophy of life) appeared as a way out of the dilemma of competing value-hierarchies, and became for some an escape from the paralysis brought on in the face of the polytheism of values. It peaked later but was 'in the air' in the days of Weber, part of his problem horizon because of his connection with Simmel.

The basic problem was to find some guidance in everyday life, in order to avoid the threat of cultural chaos. The ethical aspect of meaning content – what we call the theodicy problem – aside, *Lebenswelt*, rather than *Lebensphilosophie*, provided a possible solution to the epistemological or methodological problem of intersubjectivity (i.e. that critical observers at least in principle could see the same things, for instance through documentation) and the existialist predicament of humans left alone to choose their God. *Lebenswelt*, specifically on the methodological level, provided tentative solutions to the intersubjectivity problem created within social science in a post-Enlightenment situation of polytheism.[23]

Before being philosophically annihilated by the Enlightenment, the firm believer in God did not have the anguish of choice; neither did the believer in liberalism or Marxism. In this sense, the various political ideologies that arose during the nineteenth century were all children of Enlightenment polytheism, tending either to conceive of themselves as basically scientific (for example, liberalism and Marxism) or reacting against an overemphasis on reason (for example, conservatism). All these products of the Enlightenment provided competing hierarchies of preferences based on norms founded in extrascientific notions like equality and liberty, and the ideologies of liberalism and Marxism can be seen as transitional and paradigmatic manifestations of the secularization of social science.[24]

The Enlightenment and the progress of the natural sciences contributed to a so-called moral crisis, later often conceived of as a 'cultural crisis', and also, in the words of Ernst Troeltsch, the 'crisis of historicism'.[25] Historicism was certainly partly responsible: its habit of regarding all products of culture and its values as context-bound is in keeping with a moral relativism also touched by positivism.[26] Weber would respond to this by insisting that we cannot escape individual responsibility in our choice of values. In the political process we cannot invoke the authority of science to guide us 'all the way'. The value-philosophical basis for this means–ends rationality we call scientific value-relativism (see pp. 25ff and 55ff). Top values in competing hierarchies are not capable of rational proof; however, these hierarchies can become matters for logical analysis in a process of rationalization of value-hierarchies. We still live with value-incommensurability, as a problem of the limits of reason. How to deal with this on a methodological level has been a perennial paradigmatic divide during the last couple of centuries.

Opaque practices in concept formation give leeway for uncontrolled value-intrusion. This is notorious in the pre-neo-Kantian historicist tradition, as in the case of Hegel and his independent conceptual reality, while neo-Kantian nominalism tries to solve a problem, bringing about concepts in a lucid way.[27]

Neo-Kantianism and Nominalism

The attitude in which concepts are considered objectively independent, ready for human exploration rather than construction, had long survived in harmony with the peculiarly German anti-Enlightenment tradition.[28] Then the so-called 'Back-to-Kant' movement, which emerged in the 1860s, gained strength and precipitated a crisis among the historicists. Neo-Kantianism might be considered the first truly secularized modern scientific methodology – a codification of how to proceed in the cognitive process of causal investigation.[29] It represented a new level in scientific development while reviving certain aspects of Kant's philosophy, a renaissance for the critical philosophy of Kant applied to the modern achievements of science. Neo-Kantianism distinguishes between the constructs of the mind and material reality. It explains how one can achieve testable propositions about reality by utilizing lucid conceptual constructs, and it removes the eternal question about the true nature of reality from the sphere of science and situates it instead in the sphere of metaphysics. Neo-Kantian nominalism does not help us in transcendental matters.

This anti-metaphysical creed is evident in the secular view of concept formation we call 'nominalism'. Nominalism holds that concepts are constructions of the human mind; that we ourselves ascribe the meaning our concepts signify. Moreover, one cannot plead for any scientific meaning for concepts other than those that have factual referents. Nominalism claims that scientific attempts to grasp the true meaning of a social phenomenon are in vain. There can be no confusion of concept with reality. Concepts are only *names* we attach to phenomena; conceptual insight as such does not provide any knowledge. Other-worldly problems like the existence of God and life after death cannot be subject to scientific conceptual construction as they refer to phenomena that fall outside the sphere of empirical investigation. Matters of metaphysics are historically and culturally relative. Although perfectly legitimate in their proper context, where magic and religious belief still play a role,[30] the metaphysical notions that obscure scientific practice and the cumulative growth of knowledge are clarified by nominalism.

Kant's distinction between the directly observable surface world of phenomena and *das Ding an sich* ('the thing in itself'), or true essence, could be – and was – developed in two quite different directions. One attempted to capture concrete reality in the manifestations of its essences. The other abandoned efforts to find an essential and eternal truth, and instead accepted concepts as artificial human constructs created for the purpose of knowledge production or classification in an infinite search for truth. This is the core of the nominalism that neo-Kantians adopted and put to methodological use: the world of phenomena is that on which we ultimately rely in our evaluation of the fertility and adequacy of conceptual constructs (although this by no means excludes other analytical criteria or logical consistency).[31]

To the neo-Kantians, in a certain sense, science creates its own objects of knowledge and our knowledge of these is always a product of human activities and thus is never independent of us.[32] Analytically derived concepts do not necessarily have anything to do with reality as such; they are merely the means for increasing our knowledge through instrumental and conventional methodological procedures. The neo-Kantian element is crucial for the understanding of how Weber contributes to the controversy over method.

The unsophisticated notion of deducing 'pure' reality from abstract theory recurred on the positivist side in the *Methodenstreit*. Menger was himself not guilty of such extravagance or ignorance, though: 'In fact, a number of positivistically oriented economists did advance exorbitant methodological claims, culminating in the idea of an abstract theoretical system of economics from which concrete economic life could be *deduced*' (Bruun 1972: 83).[33] But the tendency to identify the concept with the reality it is intended to denote was common to extremists on both the positivist and the historicist sides. The former believed in the possibility of deducing concrete reality from theoretical constructs and premises, and the latter clung to the law-creating potential of *Wirklichkeitswissenschaft*. From a neo-Kantian (and thus anti-Hegelian) standpoint, these positions seem self-contradictory. The two extremes of marginalist theory and his-toricist concreteness nearly coincided in their lack of lucid conceptu-alization; they held the same position on this issue from opposite perspectives.

Schmoller and his adherents actually believed that concepts repre-sented, even *were*, reality, not abstracted aspects of it; that once general concepts were established inductively, one could deductively trace one's steps back to reality.[34] This project was undertaken by the marginalist believers in the basic law of psychophysics. Psychophysics entertained the anthropological belief that we have an inherent ten-dency to act in accordance with the marginalist model of rational economic actors; that is, self-interest is a natural inclination. There are really two issues interwoven here: that of the concept of law in social science and that of the relationship between concept and reality. Essentialism and conceptual realism, as kin doctrines, blur the clear distinction between concept and reality.[35]

Of primary interest here is not whether the so-called 'Back-to-Kant' movement is based on a correct interpretation of Kant's philosophy; the central argument is about the extent to which this neo-Kantian mode contributed to the development of scientific rigour and procedural awareness. The explicit distinction between concept and reality is characteristic of methodological interpretation in neo-Kantianism. In turning against essentialist modes of concept forma-tion and other metaphysical elements, neo-Kantianism was a crucial intermediary in the secularization of German social science.[36] When unreflexive practice is transformed into lucid procedures for order-ing reality, better explanations can emerge, and, at long last, tools for commensurability (allowing for comparisons) – except for ultimate values – become available. Methodologically rational conventions are instrumental in the furtherance of hypothesis generation and theo-retical propositions and their evaluation and testing – a central element in what I call the secularization of social science: the elements of art and magic diminish and rational discourse grows, eventually breaking through static phases of normal science by focusing on tech-nique. Consensus on the standard positions of methodological procedure might vary and develop, but commensurability, as an instrument in the cumulative process of cognitive science, requires the notion of the scientific project as worthwhile.[37]

In the pre-neo-Kantian view, concepts are in some sense 'real' and independent of the user. To Hegel the concept of the World Spirit was manifested in the Prussian state, which in turn gave us a glimpse of the World Spirit's essence. Neo-Kantianism rejects such essentialist thinking and 'intuitionism' and their opaque interpretative understanding. To view world history as the realization of reason is alien to the neo-Kantian nominalist. The difference is captured succinctly by Gilian Rose: 'In English a concept is taken to be that which a person possesses when he grasps the sense of a word. . . . In German *Begriff* may mean the referent of a predicate or what we in English would call a property, that is, a real attribute' (1976: 70). According to this doctrine, conceptual reality is a given; it is something to explore and through which to increase our insight.

'For the neo-Kantians, concepts cannot capture the essence of real entities, for there are no such essences to be captured' (Bergner 1981: 80). Neither the patient gathering of facts nor the revelation of some mysteriously hidden 'higher reality' can capture reality as such.

Weber is basically anti-Hegelian, and he contributes to the neo-Kantian-inspired nominalist turn to testable concepts as artefacts in the service of knowledge production. Weber's contribution to the conflux of contemporary controversies involved an elegant paradox in solving a problem of value-intrusion the historicists either did not see or did not manage to deal with, thus putting themselves at disadvantage, as compared to their positivist challengers.

Weber's elegant paradoxical twist was to use values as tools of selection and thus accomplish limited objectivity (intersubjectivity) in the defence against distorting uncontrolled value-intrusion; Weber's scientific value-relativism or 'value-aspect-choice' methodology leaves us with a predicament of polytheism or 'perspectivism'.

2
The Shaping of Weber's Conceptual Tools

Distinguishing the Natural from the Social Sciences

Wilhelm Roscher and Karl Knies, two of the most esteemed representatives of the older historical school, had been shaped by the mid-century intellectual climate that combined the legacies of romanticism and the Enlightenment.[1] They and other nineteenth-century historicists found the general progress of the natural sciences both attractive and frightening. They had even begun to make organic analogies, sometimes referring to history as a natural science. Generally speaking, they were not yet quite aware of the threat that natural science-inspired positivism might pose to their hegemony. In fact, they were so courageous – or naive – that they occasionally claimed ties with Darwinism. Impressed by the new Darwinian currents, they saw their own efforts as a continuation of Comte's research programme; and in support of an 'ecumenical' approach, they adapted a form of evolutionism that fitted their historical perspective and was in line with the naturalistic inclinations of the day, when book titles like *The Natural Science of Monarchies* were common.[2] 'A particularly hard blow to historicism was the growth of biological science, which apparently defined the concept of development along the lines of the traditional natural sciences. Here the very core of history seemed to fall into the hands of its positivist opponents' (Bruun 1972: 8). In a way, the natural sciences had achieved exactly what the historical school was to strive for later – *Wirklichkeitswissenschaft*, a science of empirical reality. The price of this naturalistic inclination of the older historical school was a weak defence against an enemy that had not yet come into view. The older historicists simply could not conceive that the progress of natural science would pose a threat to their own practice.

Weber was aware of these positivist tendencies within historicism, and the 'affair' with Darwinism was the first target of his criticism, when, after years of nervous enervation, he resumed a productive life with his methodological essays on Roscher and Knies, beginning with 'Roscher's "historische Methode"' ('Roscher's "historical method"'). In the essays there is already a clear dissonance between Weber and historicism; and it is here, at the very beginning of his explicit methodological production, that Weber begins to distance himself from other historicists, criticizing Roscher and Knies for their application of naive naturalism.[3]

Weber was against the programmatic idea of progress (as propagated by Enlightenment enthusiasts); at times he even characterized it as an intellectually romantic swindle.[4] He was critical of all 'naturalistic inclinations', and rejected all biological analogies, commenting, for example, on 'Roscher's metaphysical and organicist conception of causality' (*GAW*: 33 *et passim*). Weber scrutinized the inconsistencies in Roscher's methodological position, and before making more accessible his own position between abstract theory (Carl Menger's marginalism) and realist science (Schmoller's form of *Wirklichkeitswissenschaft*), he also distanced himself from the intuitionist approach of the more psychological kind.

A manifest part of the immediate background to Weber's early methodological polemics was the debate over the grounds for separating the human (historical, spiritual, cultural, social) sciences from the natural sciences, and the methodological consequences of various attitudes towards the positivist notion of the unity of science, in which natural science was regarded as the paradigm to adopt. According to Wilhelm Dilthey,[5] the natural sciences and the human sciences[6] refer to different objects (*wissenschaftliche Gegenstände*). He was inclined to stress the inadequacy of a nomothetic[7] understanding of human culture, which was too rich to be grasped in terms of empirical regularities. The central ambition in the Diltheyian tradition was to use so-called descriptive psychology to promote the scientific rigour of the interpretative method. Natural sciences deal with 'hard facts', such as physical objects. The spiritual or human sciences deal with the meaning of unique societal phenomena. Because of the nature of these objects, the spiritual sciences require *Verstehen* (understanding) – an empathetic, intuitionist (Hughes 1958), interpretative approach.

By contrast, for Heinrich Rickert (English translation 1986; orig. 1902),[8] the central distinction was between the respective methods. The natural sciences generalize, the cultural sciences individualize. In his view, different methods could be applied to the same object, depending on the purpose of the investigation.[9] Rickert thus reflected a 'softer' approach that allowed room for a certain overlap of the spheres of the natural and historical sciences. Competing approaches could even be seen as complementary: 'On the one hand, he [Rickert] attempted to provide historical and cultural studies with firm epistemological foundations, and throughout his life he maintained the firm conviction that this could be achieved. On the other hand, his examination of consciousness led him to the conclusion that all knowledge is radically subjective' (Iggers 1968: 134).

> The boundaries which the two schools wished to draw were therefore quite different, and it was possible for disputants to agree that there is a boundary while disagreeing whether the social sciences are to be distinguished from the natural because the former do, but the latter do not, seek to explain human thought and culture or because the former cannot, but the latter can, proffer well-tested explanations in terms of general laws. (Runciman 1972: 12)[10]

One is forced to choose: lose either the full specificity of the object or the ability fully to meet scientific criteria of proof.

A purely positivist stance in the *Methodenstreit* would have amounted to a total denunciation of traditional history-writing, and history would have had to retire from the scientific enterprise. But as long as historicism remained hegemonic, challenges to the scientific status of historical idiography would always ignite controversy.[11] Weber's complex, middle-of-the-road position[12] can be outlined as follows: he agreed with the anti-positivists that human society in its totality is inaccessible to naturalist analysis, and the application of strict laws as an exclusive approach is therefore problematic. Since human agents are part of the scientific object under scrutiny, a natural-science inspired search for laws would not get the researcher very far. However, Weber did not conclude that conceptual constructs and rational scientific procedure should be exclusively reserved for the natural sciences. Whatever the object under investigation, scientific criteria, in the strictest sense of the term, were always worth meeting; the more the better. Social science should not resign in favour of pure idiography, as diehard historicists suggested. The specificity of the social sciences – that is, the motives and values that guide human action – required special attention and measures because the existence of mutually interpreting and evaluating humans with often independent, incalculable and irrational wills, and varying and changing motives for intruding in the course of events, is a complicating factor.[13]

The demarcation debate and the growing attraction of unified science are the context of the controversy of methods between the Menger school and the younger historical school (Schmoller and his pupils).

From the perspective (post-Enlightenment) that we have termed a process of secularization, Menger could be seen as drawing upon the growing prestige of natural science, which combined theory construction with 'real' science and produced technological applications that revolutionized everyday life, such as Edison's electric bulb. This inevitably weakened the historicist claim that there was a fundamental contradiction between 'anaemic' abstract theory and 'real' science. The success of natural science continuously reinforced the authority of positivism; it could no longer be dismissed as merely anaemic. The marginalist position was also strengthened by the positivist notion of a science unified by the hypothetical-deductive method. From this strengthened position, the marginalists might well have sharpened their aspirations to claim a monopoly on behalf of pure theory. As H. H. Bruun writes, with a certain irony: 'Such a claim would be able to draw on the seemingly unshakeable prestige of the natural sciences, whereas Schmoller's 'historical induction' had methodological feet of clay in this respect' (1972: 83).[14]

Enter 'Values' and the Problem of Selection and Value-Intrusion

In studying cultural-historical products, what role is played by values – the cultural legacy of the actors who together form society? Values make for a crucial difference between the natural and the cultural/social sciences. Values present a challenge to objectivity; this must be understood on the methodological level as a problem of intersubjectivity. The more distinct the procedures for attaining intersubjectivity, the less the risk of being besieged by extrascientific elements, such as values. The established historicist method – that is, empiricist and inductivist *Wirklichkeitswissenschaft* – had great difficulty handling the value problem, in large part because of its unwillingness to make the problem explicit. Although values implicitly influenced the historicists' actual selection process, recognizing this would have threatened their alleged objectivity, which was based on positioning themselves above the turmoil of everyday politics, beyond mere value-freedom, in a supremely ethical realm.

The social dimension of understanding in Weber's early sociological texts tends to fall outside the realm of 'hard' science. In the spirit of Rickert, primacy is given to method, not object, to giving the nomothetic approach a try to see how well it does (such 'ecumenicism' is also characteristic of Weber himself). The intuitive, artistic, interpretive mode of analysis, having made its distinctive contribution, is free to satisfy scientific criteria such as intersubjectivity. For Dilthey, the road to intersubjectivity was built upon mutual and actual understanding and in this sense was less objective and reliable than scientific rigour would seem to require. But the naturalistic, 'scientific' approach could not catch what is really interesting about social life. To borrow an example from Weber: a scientist studying the works of Michelangelo as natural, and not cultural, products might provide us with much reliable and testable information, but in most cases that information would be irrelevant.

Although Weber never spoke directly of 'intersubjectivity', he did emphasize rational proof, *rationale Evidenz*, and thus distinguished himself from Dilthey and his school of empathetic interpretation. After all, if two practitioners pursuing empathetic understandings arrive at different interpretations, the problem of how to judge between them cannot be resolved. As an anti-positivist, Weber did not share Dilthey's limited ability to satisfy 'harder' criteria of scientific knowledge. In the case of rational interpretation, logical criteria, such as coherence, could be applied, and competing models could be purified and different top values (ultimate values) or preferences isolated. Although it would still be difficult to choose between alternative models of reality, it would at least be possible to agree on which models promoted a given purpose.

The criterion of intersubjectivity, though it allows for a sort of scientific proof, is by definition difficult to satisfy. Although Dilthey certainly did not neglect the problem, he allowed considerable leeway for subjectivity and the uncontrolled intrusion of values. In Rickert's thorough enquiry, the cooperation between naturalistic and historical approaches allowed for a degree of flexibility that optimized criteria of scientific proof on a case-by-case basis. This did not amount to an exclusive objectivity; in the individualizing historical approach, one must still select from reality. One way or another, the element of subjective evaluation remained an acute problem for social science.

The historicists could have stubbornly insisted on the status of history-writing as an art, thereby making themselves immune to methodological criticism. But questions about explanatory significance have to be addressed by the historian 'if history is to be raised above the level of a mere chronicle of notable events and personalities' (Weber, *GAW*: 266–7). Historical research after the Enlightenment simultaneously resisted Enlightenment rationalism and contributed to the secularization of historical research procedures. In order to develop as a scientific endeavour it would have to follow the path of science rather than art.

History-writing of the romantic national German variety had a potential credibility problem in meeting the demands of scientific legitimation, even though historicism was an attempt to do precisely that: pose questions about truth, critical evaluation and the rational use of sources. The result was a mixture of Enlightenment and romantic elements, truth and tales. Ranke, to cite the foremost example, was reticent on matters of method. In fact, in his impressive body of historical work, amounting to some fifty volumes, no more than roughly eighty pages (an appendix to his history of the German and Gothic peoples) explicitly discussed method.[15]

> Ranke 'divines' the past, and even the advancement of knowledge by an historian of lesser rank is poorly served if he does not possess this 'intuitive' gift. Where this is so, he remains a kind of lower-rung bureaucrat in the historical enterprise. But it is absolutely different with the really great advances in knowledge in mathematics and the natural sciences. They all arise intuitively in the intuitive flashes of imagination as hypotheses that are then 'verified' vis-à-vis the facts, i.e., their validity is tested in procedures involving the use of already empirical knowledge and they are 'formulated' in a logically correct way. The same is true in history: when we insist here on the dependence of knowledge of the 'essential' on the use of the concept of objective possibility, we assert nothing at all about the psychologically interesting question which does not, however, concern us here, namely, how does an historical hypothesis arise in the mind of the investigator? We are here concerned only with the question of the logical category under which the hypothesis is to be demonstrated as valid in case of doubt or dispute, for it is that which determines its logical 'structure'. (GAW: 278; Weber 1949: 176; see also p. 121 in the Runciman reader, E. Matthew's translation)

Bringing about idiographical Gestalt required an element of skilful art, in itself no obstacle to being scientific. However, both the generalizing as well as the individualizing approach had to select from raw reality in order to develop the genre of the science of reality.

The naive historicist might maintain that passionate contemplation of the material could bring it into order without any special criteria; it would organize itself, so to speak. In a way, this is a natural standpoint; it is the way much research functions, in fact, in the 'context of discovery' (to use the phrase made famous by Karl Popper).

Indeed, given the lack of explicit methodology, it is forced to operate this way. The conflict between nominalist conceptualization and its predecessors, such as Hegelian essentialism, however, becomes manifest at the point where the distinction between concept and reality is blurred, in the sense that there is no accountability for the establishment of concepts and central explanatory factors.

But even pure idiography requires selection. Identifying causal factors is not something cumulative science (in contrast to religion or ideology) can do by instinct or luck. The belief in the fortuitous discovery of causal relations backed by the authority of good craftsmanship was not persuasive, even within the historical school. Historicism's weakness lay in its neglect of the problem of selection: one rarely had to account for one's selection criteria within the idealist tradition of intuitionism. But if the criteria for selection were not accounted for, it could be assumed that they were still tacitly influencing the research process, in the form, for instance, of implicit value preferences. Even the most down-to-earth 'empiricist' variation of historicism could get lost in the vast chaos of endless and many-faceted facts. Schmoller himself never successfully accounted for any clear criteria for the selection of the 'real factors' that historicism saw as the cornerstones of explanation in its science of reality.

The dilemma here is that it is unrealistic to assume that all facts are unmediated; however, taken to its limit, the idiographic ambition would require precisely this – it would call for the object under scrutiny to be studied from every aspect, which is virtually impossible, since there are infinite aspects. Out of necessity one has to restrict one's study of the infinite reality of existence to one aspect at a time and to make this point of view explicit; one has to simplify, economize; that is, one has to make a value-aspect choice.

Weber does this under the guise of Heinrich Rickert and his views on *Gesichtspunkt*, i.e. that we approach reality from a perspective in order to grasp it without getting lost in the surplus of idiographic details.[16]

Rickert: Theoretical and Practical Value-Relation

It is true that Weber is not a card-carrying philosopher but depends on Rickert. But it is unclear to what extent he does depend on Rickert. Weber adopts the basics of Rickert's views on concept formation, although there are deviations, which we will return to. At this point it is enough to note that although Weber adheres to Dilthey's views on the specificity of the cultural/social sciences, it is nevertheless Rickert whom he develops for his purpose.[17]

> The fact that human knowledge of concrete reality in its entirety is impossible and, therefore, must be selective, must involve abstraction, poses for Rickert the problem of the 'objectivity' of scientific knowledge. For this situation creates the possibility that each scientist's knowledge is different from everybody else's, that everybody abstracts in a different way and thus arrives at a merely subjective, private picture of the world. (Burger 1976: 17)

Transparent tools are needed in order to avoid the extremes of exclusive intuition or empiricism. Because these tools are offered by competing models of reality, we face the risk of pursuing multiple discourses. Knowledge-formation would be better served by just one cumulative discourse.

The key to Rickert's position on *Wertbeziehung* (value-relation or value-orientation) is found in his distinction between theoretical and practical value-relation. It is not satisfactory to take any value as the point of departure for analysis, not even if it seems obvious that the value in question catches the aspect one is interested in. 'On the contrary . . . the historian may theoretically only relate his raw materials to values which have served as a basis for the practical value orientation (valuation, etc.) of persons living in the period under investigation' (Bruun 1972: 91). For Rickert, this created a sort of 'double historicity' because, in the case of historical material, there are two sets of value relations: first, those of the present, of the historian's audience – in some sense these determine the concerns of the historian; second, in an effort to understand the past, historians must collect data on the concepts and values of the past and make them part of their accounts – that is, values should be the points of departure not only for us but also for the historical actors in the period under scrutiny. It is a sort of two-step process. We have a stock of historical 'raw material', preserved sources, and a vantage point for our inquiry. If we approach a historical object from the vantage point of our cultural values we might find that it has already contributed to the selection of sources that were preserved or to the production of relevant sources. Actual historical evaluation is restricted by both our interest in and the availability of relevant sources.

The practical consequences of Rickert's view are demonstrated in Bruun's (1972) didactic discussion.[18] First, the possible selections are restricted by the object itself. For instance, if Magna Carta's relevance was political in its own day it should not be included in any history of the development of British art at the time. That is, the values taken as points of departure by the social scientist should coincide with (some) actual values in the period under study and be consonant with the historical object itself. However, Magna Carta may have influenced the development of art in medieval England, whether or not anyone noticed it at the time. Rickert would hardly have denied this. But in this case we would no longer be utilizing historical methods as they were understood by him: to qualify for such an art study as Rickertian history, at least some significant actor at the time would have to have seen Magna Carta as relevant to art. Rickert explicitly states that the values operating in objective concept-formation should be found in the historical raw material, which is thus assigned a sort of limiting veto on scientific discourse.

Second, Rickert required that the cultural values chosen as the social scientist's points of departure be shared by all those concerned today. If our contemporaries do not endorse our selection of cultural values, our analyses will be uninteresting accounts and simply not valid as history (Bruun 1972: 90). The limitation here is that Rickert's approach could easily become absurd if taken to the literal extreme: to follow Bruun's example, a family history would only be valid if everyone in the family agreed that the facts recorded were worth remembering – although who qualifies as 'everyone' in a given *Gemeinschaft* (community, the term made famous by Ferdinand Tönnies) in Rickert's usage is open to dispute.

We should here recall the danger of what Illka Heiskanen (1967) called 'multiple realities'. Everything is open to interpretation when there are many options as to what is family history.[19] If family members have different points of view, they might also have different family histories, and so competing truths. Thus, the general validity is endangered as soon as anyone in the *Gemeinschaft* (in this case the family) diverges from the consensus about what is worth knowing. The point was, after all, to restrict the choice of value-aspect to those values that represented both the lived experiences and the values of the actors in the period studied as well as those presently having a stake in the historical investigation of that period.

Rickert's double requirement of practical and theoretical value-relation, which was intended to assure the objectivity and relevance of historical study, makes it difficult to bring about valid history. Any dissenter could alter the validity of a political history by denying the significance of the history to his or her *Gemeinschaft*. It may have been in order to avoid such an absurdity that Rickert added the criterion of normatively general validity. However, although the introduction of a normative element might resolve a problem such as the 'historical veto' by any member of the *Gemeinschaft*, it creates other difficulties, such as the contradiction between the specific (time-bound) and the general. In stating that the values chosen should be both empirically *and normatively* generally valid (Rickert 1902: 626–7), Rickert's lingering belief in some eternal or super values becomes problematic in view of the 'pure' historicist position that values change with the times.[20] The problem for Rickert and those who shared his view was precisely that of proving the validity of any cultural value that is also proposed as normatively valid.[21] It was also a problem of how to discriminate between 'common' cultural values and eternal ones, which ought to be demonstrated in some more specific way than by referring to culture. After all, Goethe and Luther, whom Rickert saw as manifestations of 'valid values' of culture, were merely manifestations, not the creators, of those eternal, ultimate super-norms.[22]

Although the seemingly contradictory requirements of practical and theoretical value-relations are puzzling in themselves, allowing for conflicting but still sensible interpretations, Rickert's additional requirement of normative general validity for the empirical general values serving in the combined practical and theoretical *Wert-beziehung* is the most enigmatic. His refusal to grant reality status to values makes his plea for some objective values almost – even if not logically – oxymoronic, since the idea of objective metaphysics, the foundations of objectivity of values, transcendentally, appears as a task for practical philosophy rather than cognitive science.[23]

Weber: Scientific Value-Relativism

We need objective values to pursue an instrumental analysis – but cannot find them. Rickert is problematic since he is really 'the father of relativism', yet lapses back into objectivism. He thought we can find eternal values in history, a sort of eternal 'super-values'.

Weber did not share Rickert's 'objectivist' attitude; unconditionally valid 'super-values' were not an option for linking practical and theoretical value-relation and focusing upon a scientific object for instrumental action analysis. Since Weber's approach sought to accomplish causal adequacy, the choice of the significant value-aspect could not be arbitrary if progress in science was to be achieved. At least some important actors in society must adhere to the points of view chosen by the scientist, otherwise the analysis would not be significant and would represent empty and meaningless value axes. Although there is no need for any value allegiance on behalf of the practising scientist, some forces in society must have an interest in the applications of the recommendations resulting from the normative empirical theory – that is, the subject matter must be 'worth knowing' (to echo Popper).[24] Nor does the scientist have to generate any value preferences in order to bring about such analysis; she or he may simply adopt what the Swedish economist Gunnar Myrdal later called 'significant' or 'relevant' ultimate values, like economic rationality (the search for optimum return). Values as beliefs are not excluded; they are brought in and used as the vantage point from which the search for cognitive truth may proceed.[25]

Weber's 1917 essay, 'The Meaning of Ethical Neutrality', formulates his conception that there are value conflicts that cannot be resolved by rational means. Weber criticizes Schmoller and the founding generation of the German historical school: 'Forty years ago there existed among the scholars working in our discipline the widespread belief that of the various possible points of view in the domain of practical political preferences, ultimately only one was the correct one' (GAW: 492); 'Respect for our master [Schmoller] forbids me to pass over these points where I find myself unable to agree with him'.[26] The 'master', in short, was out of date on the topic of value-judgements in the practical realm.

Weber focused on the issue of how to promote unbiased knowledge undistorted by such things as party affiliations. By the second page, Weber speaks of the logical disjunction between the sphere of facts and the sphere of values and distinguishes the gulf between 'is' and 'ought'. Weber appears here as an engaged relativist with a strong sense of the proper relation between science and politics. His rhetorical technique is to point out distortions and misunderstandings of 'value judgements' and their place, rather than offering a 'proper procedure' and producing a positive programme. He stresses that the 'statesmanlike' way of compromise cannot solve the problem of objectivity, and that it is legitimate to deal with subjective valuations as the subject matter of science; he gives both sociology and marginal utility theory as examples of the scientific study of subjective valuations.[27] ' "Cultural values" are not identical with ethical imperatives, as Schmoller believes' (GAW: 504; Weber 1949: 515).

In my view, Weber's 'value-aspect-choice methodology', as a way of helping his fellow historicists out of their corner in the *Methodenstreit*, answers to a more general philosophical predicament, that of polytheism and anxiety of choice. We are not only free to choose but also forced to choose.

Weber's methodology was thus an expression in the scientific field of what I have called the traumatic dilemma of post-Enlightenment modernity expressed by Nietzsche and Kierkegaard (and later formulated in a more literary form by Sartre, Camus, and others). The individual must choose his or her ultimate values, 'decide which is

God ... and which is the devil' (Weber in 'Science as Vocation', *GAW*: 604).[28] According to Weber, since no ethical claim of value-validity is either demonstrable or refutable by means of science, absolute polytheism is the only appropriate metaphysic (*GAW*: 507). Weber's polytheistic conception of values is connected here to the process of gaining knowledge. The fruit of the tree of knowledge is the recognition that there is no escape from the existentialist dilemma of choice (*GAW*: 507–8; Weber 1949: 18). Humans choose their own fate; social scientists must live with competing value-hierarchies. Ultimate values are not delivered to us but are already there and already in conflict. Only once one chooses can one employ the means of instrumental analysis and scientific procedures. The shallowness of routine experience makes us less aware of the irreconcilable antagonisms between values. We do not face fateful choices daily, and we are often not even aware of having chosen; but this lack of awareness is the source of the error of thinking that practical and concrete policy directives and valuations can be derived from science.

Weber's account of what empirical science can do for us is succinctly expressed in the following passage:

> it may be asserted without the possibility of a doubt that as soon as one seeks to derive concrete directives from practical political (particularly economic and social political) evaluations, (1) the indispensable means, and (2) the inevitable repercussions, and (3) the thus conditioned competition of numerous possible evaluations in their practical consequences, are all that an empirical discipline can demonstrate with the means at its disposal. Philosophical disciplines can go further and lay bare the 'meaning' of evaluations, i.e., their ultimate meaningful structure and their meaningful consequences, in other words, they can indicate their 'place' within the totality of all the possible 'ultimate' valuations and delimit their spheres of meaningful validity. Even such simple questions as the extent to which an end should sanction unavoidable means, or the extent to which undesired repercussions should be taken into consideration, or how conflicts between several concretely conflicting ends are to be arbitrated, are entirely matters of choice and compromise. There is no (rational or empirical) scientific procedure of any kind whatsoever which can provide us with a decision here. The social sciences, which are strictly empirical sciences, are the least fitted to presume to save the individual the difficulty of making a choice, and they should therefore not create the impression that they can do so. (*GAW*: 508; Weber 1949: 18–19)[29]

Weber's instrumental creed is manifest here. Its core is the rationalization of value-hierarchies, isolating the normative element in order to avoid uncontrolled value-intrusion.[30] Although science

cannot act as an arbiter in conflicts over values, ultimate ends can
be subject to the sorts of evaluations that follow from a means–
ends analysis that takes secondary consequences into account;
that is to say, serve to reveal the implications and potential conflicts between value choices. We can also sense the existentialist
(Nietzschean–Kierkegaardian) dimension. The individual is alone
with his conscience and his choices. In this sense, then, Weber's polytheistic methodology is an expression of the human predicament in
the face of modernity:

> that old sober empiricist, John Stuart Mill, once said that, simply on
> the basis of experience, no one would ever arrive at the existence of
> *one* God – and, it seems to me, certainly not a God of goodness – but
> at polytheism. Indeed living in the 'world' (in the Christian sense of
> the word) [he] can only feel himself subject to the struggle between
> multiple sets of values, each of which, viewed separately, seems to
> impose an obligation on him. He has to choose which of these Gods
> he will and should serve and when he should serve, or when he should
> serve the one and when the other. (*GPS*: 145; Weber 1994: 78–9)[31]

For Weber there was no Archimedian point to which science could
anchor itself, and there were no core Aristotelian principles to solve
methodological issues.

Weber's so-called decisionism contains a paradox: to achieve
means–ends rationality and to live up to an ethics of responsibility,
that is an ethics of responsibility for the actual consequences of one's
actions, the researcher must himself/herself be dedicated to value
rationality in the sense that he or she must accept the necessity of
determining rationally the relations between the value commitments
that are pursued, and must also have a kind of ethics of conviction
that underlies the uncompromising search for truth.

Weber's scientific value-relativism,[32] with its sharp distinction
between 'is' and 'ought',[33] refuted modes of thought inspired by
natural law.[34] Instead, it recognized that the explanatory efforts of
science placed the burden of proof squarely on the shoulders of those
claiming that value statements contain empirical truth. In the scientific process, statements about reality had to be proffered in refutable,
if not verifiable, form.[35]

Value-relativism was not at all inconsistent with the methodological core intentions of historicism[36] – in fact, quite the opposite. Historicism denied the existence of any eternal norms and laws in order
to put phenomena into the context of time and culture, even though
many a historicist, innocent in matters of value-theory, had still
searched for eternal truths and values in history. This attitude might

seem self-defeating. Nevertheless, many philosophers, including Weber's philosophical mentor Rickert, manifested just such a tension-filled position through their belief in normatively generally valid cultural values. They were, then, guilty of an elision from 'ought' to 'is', a gulf that could only be bridged by postulating an ultimate goal-value. This is also the basic meaning of the concept of value-orientation, Rickert's legacy to Weber's methodology.

The value-relation Weber developed from Rickert, first in history and then in social science, made the cultural sciences independent of uncontrolled value-intrusion; at least it made that independence possible. Values, as such, have no place in scientific undertaking except as subject matter; in addition, they serve as the vantage points for instrumental goal-oriented action analysis.

The Limits of *Social* Science Concept Formation

With Dilthey, [Weber] accepted meanings and values as the basic subject matter of sociology. With Rickert, he viewed science as science, whether it deals with mental, social, or physical phenomena. In opposition to Dilthey, he did not believe that the isolation of the meanings of social events puts sociology in a different class from those disciplines which establish causal laws. In opposition to Rickert, he did not place science and history in opposite camps, leaving sociology the character of a purely formal science. Rather, Weber accepted the traditional situation of sociology as a scientific discipline, working with materials from history. He believed that a properly developed typological procedure was the primary device for increasing the methodological precision of sociology. (Martindale 1960: 381)

Dilthey's *Verstehen* (empathetic understanding) provides the typical language of and Rickert's *Wertbeziehung* (value-relation) provides the central tool for Weber in his efforts to solve the problems of the *Methodenstreit*, and adjacent controversies, touching upon the paradigmatic divisions of objectivity and meaning, the specificity of the cultural sciences, and the limits of scientific criteria for intersubjective concept-formation. Weber recognized sociology as a 'spiritual' venture dedicated to meaning, to the interpretation of events created by individuals producing, experiencing, and contesting the meanings of social life. Sociology was interesting to Rickert only as a label for the generalizing aspect of the cultural sciences, which he located in the border region between natural and cultural sciences. Weber, by contrast, considered sociology the nomothetic aspect of the cultural sciences,[37] and aimed to develop that border region in which the humanities and the natural sciences met and sociology emerged. Weber 's acceptance of values and meaning as indispensable to the social sciences should not suggest that he would neglect the standard criteria of science. Even though experimental methods are less suited to historical and social scientific research – data to verify natural scientific hypotheses can be secured, while supportive evidence in social science is largely circumstantial – these limits are necessary, since mere behaviourism could not catch all of the social reality we are interested in, and this social reality is not readily available to a science demanding rational evidence.

Weber furthered the secularization of social science theory to a degree that would not have been endorsed by Rickert, to whom the theoretical generalizations that Weber was prepared to accept were alien.[38] Nevertheless, the use of analytical constructs in the cultural sciences profited from Rickert's philosophy. If social scientific analysis were to account for discrete phenomena in an empirical reality, abstraction would be crucial, and only transparent, objective tools of analysis – like those advocated by Rickert – would raise history from an art to a science. In his demand that values be made explicit, Weber cleared the way for the analysis of the rational means–ends approach, and the manner in which Weber put values to work in the methodological realm simultaneously solved the problem of both intersubjectivity and objectivity. Values become the very criteria for objective selection, indicating both the possibility and limits of objectivity. The existence of evaluating actors is said to be specific to the human sciences, and Weber's teleological (purpose- or motive-oriented) approach is instrumental – *zweckrational* – in serving those actors' aims. The ideal-type (see below), Weber's own tool for analysing social acts through value-orientation, will turn out to be the instrument that finally dissolved the historicist methodological hegemony.

Postscript: Evaluating Rickert's Influence on Weber

Rickert's place in the history of the philosophy of the social sciences is difficult to estimate. He was an innovative scholar and made crucial contributions to the reorientation in German thought, but he was not a coherent system-builder. Rickert was a family friend of Weber and a younger colleague in Heidelberg. Some of the correspondence between them has been published in *MWG*, as parts of the first volumes of letters to appear (covering the years 1906–12). It is still to be decided what light it will shed on Rickert's influence, but it certainly documents a lasting and frequent exchange between the two scholars (and neighbours), addressing matters both mundane and scholarly. Despite Rickert's undeniable influence – indeed presence – in the early methodological essays, scholars continue to debate the precise nature and meaning of Rickert's influence on Weber, and the extent to which Weber transcends Rickert's influence (see, for example, Burger (1976), Tenbruck (1980, 1986, 1987), Oakes (1988), Turner (1990), and Nusser (1987)). It also remains to be seen to what extent Weber relied specifically on Rickert in the development of his methodology or whether he could have developed it independently and in another guise.[39]

Rickert certainly deserves credit as a founding father of much of modern social science. When an Anglo-Saxon scholar speaks of 'points of view', the roots are really in the pioneering work done in German history-writing and Rickert's *Wertbeziehung*. Weber took Rickert's concepts and used them innovatively. Any study of Weber's methodological breakthrough reveals a rediscovery of a partly lost intellectual connection, which is more viable than the historicist setting from which it stems. Although Weber poses as a 'loyal Rickertian', he had no philosophical ambitions of his own: 'You are mistaken about Rickert: even if he sometimes does use the phrase "generally recognized" values, he makes it clear that he refers to hypothetical points of departure from the point of view of the historian – not to the validity of values in any metaphycial sense' (*MWG* II/5, *Briefe 1906–1908*, letter to Gottl (later Gottl-Ottlilienfeld) of 28 March 1906, my translation). This passage shows that his defence of Rickert by no means indicates that Weber himself adhered to any idea about generally valid ultimate values.[40]

Although Rickert's theory of value is not best described as 'objectivism', Rickert does deny values any real existence; and despite his metaphysical belief in unconditionally normatively valid values, he pleads for the incommensurability of values – the very problem which value-relation is supposed to solve. After Weber's methodological elaboration of Rickert, the burden of proof increasingly falls on anyone attempting to plead 'normative validity' in any scientific sense.[41] Weber makes no claims to normative validity for any of the values that serve as his points of view. In his variation of value-historicism, the scientific community has a special responsibility to interpret the significant cultural values and their relevance to current analysis.[42]

Since the degree and nature of Weber's methodological dependence on Rickert remains controversial, it should be said that Weber transcends Rickert's philosophy of value, as well as his doctrine of conceptualization. Weber's scientific value-relativism is more fully-fledged than Rickert's lingering metaphysics. However, Rickert's centrality as a source for Weber's methodological endeavour is explicit. In the Roscher and Knies essay Weber tests the fruitfulness of Rickert's work for the methodology of historical research, and in an introductory footnote in the 'Objectivity' essay, Weber acknowledges Rickert's philosophy of science as a basis for his own work (*GAW*: 146, n. 1). Weber's central concepts in his early methodological essays are taken over from Rickert. This goes not only for value-relation but also for the 'historical individual', the construction of which is the task of the early ideal-type. Rickert was used by Weber as a toolbox for his methodological devices, although Rickert's ideas are left somewhat behind by the developments in modern social science.

From the Rickertian distinction in terms of method, social science appears as a problematic, not to say obscure, undertaking, standing on the borderline between the natural and the cultural or human sciences. In its early pioneering phase in Germany, social science was understood precisely as the generalizing aspect of the cultural sciences. It is in this domain that sociology slowly began to take root within the academy, leaving aside its first Enlightenment phase, the period of Comte and others. It is exactly here that Weber's value-aspect-choice methodology will cast some light on the problems of intersubjectivity _ and thus objectivity. Values are part of culture and thus both an object of as well as a threat to objective social science. This problem is less intrusive in the natural sciences, while it is manifest and always an issue in almost any social science approach.

I have no definite answer to the question of how much Rickert really meant to Weber, except that his influence is beyond doubt. But so is the independent character of Weber's elaboration of Rickert's *Wertbeziehung*. It is almost trivial to say that Weber's methodology has many roots besides neo-Kantianism: Simmel, Marx, Dilthey, Menger, Jellinek, Radbruch, and others come to mind. The point is that, through Rickert, Weber was influenced by the neo-Kantian view of concept formation, with its anti-Hegelian implications. Although Weber's allegiance to sociology can be questioned, no one seriously doubts that he was a nominalist in concept formation (in fact, he is vehemently criticized by his critics for this position, e.g. by Lukács). Moreover, although we have a whole range of different positions in evaluating Rickert's influence, no one questions Weber's 'commitments to neo-Kantian epistemology' (S. Turner 1990: 540).[43]

Neo-Kantian philosophy, in a longer perspective, could well be understood as part of a general reaction against naturalist or positivistic thought; at the same time it can be seen as a main source of the modernization and secularization of the philosophy of science. It contributed to a more 'relaxed' relationship between the naturalistic positivist and the humanistic interpretative approaches. However, opening the door to promoting *détente* would, in the long run, prove fatal to the historicist hegemony. Indeed Weber's contribution could be interpreted in this light, since his gentle break with all-embracing historicism meant precisely the end of that hegemony; the neo-Kantian doctrine of a distinction between historical and naturalistic analysis was a doctrine of peaceful coexistence. 'All these problems should be seen in the context of Weber's attacks on the scientific creed of his day: his fight against essentialism and conceptual realism and his defence of methodological individualism' (Lepsius 1977: 112).[44] In discussing Weber's methodology, Lepsius quotes a central passage from Weber's March 1920 letter to Robert Liefmann. Here the neo-Kantian legacy is overt, when Weber states that as a professional sociologist he feels obliged to end the lingering presence of 'collective concepts'. It is largely through Weber's mediation that neo-Kantianism had an impact on the standard positions of modern secularized methodology. Weber's critique of the 'reification of concepts' – in the Roscher and Knies essay that denounces the organic analogies of the older historical school – was indeed a neo-Kantian activity.[45]

Kant's legacy is subject to innumerable interpretations and seemingly endless controversies. It remains the case that Weber did develop his ideal-type methodology within the tradition we characterize as neo-Kantianism and very much in the space cleared by Rickert. Indeed, the notion of value-relation adopted from Rickert is the central element of the ideal-type procedure that will permit Weber to do what his fellow historicists could not: form lucid concepts and thus allow for intersubjectivity and rational proof.

3

An Analysis of Weber's Solution

Objectivity, Selection and Causal Significance

Weber's point in his famous 'Objectivity' essay of 1904 was that although values have a role in constructing or constituting problems and historical objects and in determining what, for us, is an acceptable solution to a historical problem, they commonly intervene in other ways, and these other ways are instances of scientific bias or the failure of objectivity.[1] In striving for a way out of the polarization emerging from the controversy over method, Weber asked what was to be understood by 'objectivity' when there were two competing and seemingly alternative schools to choose between in the study of political economy – historicism and marginalism:

> The genuineness of the problem [of objectivity] is apparent to anyone who is aware of the conflict about methods, 'fundamental concepts' and presuppositions, the incessant shift of 'viewpoints', and the continuous redefinition of 'concepts', and who sees that the theoretical and historical modes of analysis are still separated by an apparently unbridgeable gap. It constitutes, as a despairing Viennese examinee once sorrowfully complained, 'two sciences of economics'. What is the meaning of 'objectivity' in this context? The following discussion will be devoted to this question. (*GAW*: 160–1; Weber 1949: 63)

According to Weber, concepts and rules of the sort that are of concern to the sociologist are also of concern to the historian. In the case of historical material, however, there are two sets of value relations: those of the past and those of the current audience of the historian. Weber's reflections on this problem are self-consciously directed at the persistent influence of the historical school in German economics and the tension between history and theory, which was integral to its development and 'problematic even as it was 25 years ago' (Weber 1949: 115), i.e. roughly when the great debate over method broke out.

Weber does not suppose that this problem can be resolved by constructing a priori a method or methodological theory. Indeed, he is anxious to claim that methodology stands in the same relation to the activity of writing history as the 'knowledge of anatomy is the precondition for "correct" walking' (ibid.): 'in fact, whoever tried to walk by applying his knowledge of anatomy would be in danger of stumbling' (GAW: 217). The strict application of any instruction-like manual, whether for running railways or cooking, would be extraordinarily inefficient and probably ineffective. Historical methodology, like swimming and riding bicycles, is a matter of skill. The skilled historian writes history without reference to rules. But the skills of the historian may nevertheless be in need of codification, especially when there is a risk of the uncontrolled intrusion of value assumptions.

In his essay, 'Critical Studies in the Logic of the Cultural Sciences: A Critique of Eduard Meyer's Methodological Views' (1906), Weber examines the relation between history and sociology (that is to say theory), and tries to make peace between the two.[2] Meyer was an ancient and medieval historian for whom Weber had great respect, but who illustrated Weber's points about the flawed methodology of some historical approaches.[3] Like many nineteenth-century thinkers, Meyer had a narrow view of the possibilities of causal analysis. He wished to preserve a role in history for free will, a place for personalities and irrationalities that make history unpredictable – an issue found in all histories with theoretical ambitions at the time. Weber characterized this incalculability as a useful albeit problematic fiction: 'the characteristic of "incalculability", equally great but not greater than that of "blind forces of nature", is the privilege of the insane' (GAW: 226; Weber 1949: 124). Tsar Paul of Russia, who, as Weber concedes, appeared to be very strange and 'incalculable' at the end of his reign, is an example of incalculability that is hardly accessible to meaningful historical interpretation; the storms that broke up the Spanish Armada in 1588 are equally incalculable.

In commenting on Meyer, Weber says that the irrationalities of history are irrational only with respect to the ideal of rational action, not irrational in any absolute or metaphysical sense.

Action shares this kind of 'irrationality' with every natural event, and when the historian in the interpretation of historical interconnections speaks of the 'irrationality' of human action as a disturbing factor, he is comparing historical-empirical action not with the phenomena of nature but with the ideal of a purely rational, i.e., absolutely purposeful, action which is also absolutely oriented toward the adequate means. (*GAW*: 227; Weber 1949: 125)

Action of a more or less normal kind is neither blind nor incalculable. In a footnote that discusses Menger's 'theoretical schemata', which presuppose rational market behaviour of an ideal-typically pure kind, Weber says: 'Since all strictly teleologically (purposefully) occurring actions involve applications of empirical rules, which tell what the appropriate "means" to ends are, history would be nothing but the application of those rules' (*GAW*: 227; Weber 1949: 125).[4] Weber rejected the idea that one could deduce predictions about reality from the pure type of rational economic actor. Action, Weber says, cannot be interpreted in purely rational terms because of the various disturbances created by prejudices, errors in thinking (bad logic, for example), factual errors in the course of making instrumental choices, as well as the whole range of moods and other influences on actual actions (ibid.).

Weber looked instead to the causal historical significance of events (see Weber 1949: 121; *GAW*: 223):

> Causal analysis provides absolutely no value judgement and the value judgement is absolutely not a causal explanation. And for this very reason the valuation of an event – such as, for instance, the 'beauty' of a natural phenomenon – occurs in a sphere quite different from its causal explanation; for this reason concern on the part of history to judge of historical actions as responsible before the conscience of history before the judgement seat of any God or man and all other modes of introducing the philosophical problem of 'freedom' into the procedures of history would suspend its character as an empirical science just as much as the insertion of miracles into its causal sequences. (Weber 1949: 123)[5]

We pursue causal responsibility in history in the same way as we pursue legal liability, that is by taking into account not everything, but rather that which is pertinent to our interests. 'The possibility of selection from among the infinity of the determinants is conditioned, first, by the mode of our historical *interest*' (Weber 1949: 169). Selection (abstraction) is necessary because the determinants of events are infinite in number. However, selection is problematic: since there is an infinity of causal factors for any specific event, history cannot possibly claim to:

explain causally the concrete *reality* of an event in the totality of its individual qualities. To do the latter would not only actually be impossible, it would also be a task which is meaningless in principle. Rather history is exclusively concerned with the causal explanation of those 'elements' and 'aspects' of the events in question which are of 'general significance' and *hence* of historical *interest* from general standpoints, exclusively in the same way as the judge's deliberations take into account not the total individualized course of the events of the case but rather those components of the events which are pertinent for subsumption under the legal norms. (ibid.: 169–70; see *GAW*: 271–2 for original text)

Meyer stressed the enormous historical significance of the Battle of Marathon for the future of Hellenic culture and its survival. In contrast, the shots fired in Berlin in March 1848 had little historical significance, because the atmosphere was such that almost any small incident would have triggered the turmoil and riots that in fact occurred. Weber's problem, which Meyer did not sufficiently address, was to find a principle behind the difference historians correctly see in the significance of these two events. 'In order to penetrate to the real causal relationships, we construct unreal ones' (*GAW*: 287; Weber 1949: 185–6). Historians imagine a possible course of events and then compare the actual course of events to it. The differences point to the causal significance of the features of the actual course of events that needs to be assessed. But both history and social science can compare only a limited number of actual cases, which are ordinarily insufficient to distinguish the genuinely significant causes; thus, in order to make causal assessments, a kind of construction is necessary. We might assess the effects of the Battle of Marathon by constructing the counterfactual possibility of the battle having had the opposite outcome, that is, if the Persians had won. On the basis of events in other countries conquered by the Persians, we could construct a model of the effect on culture that was the normal consequence of Persian domination. We can then draw some conclusions, based on the differences between this hypothetical possibility and the actual course of events. The judgement, however, necessarily rests upon a rational scheme or imagined 'normal case'.

In his 1898 lectures, Weber characterized this activity of construction in a similar way:

To ascertain the most elementary life conditions of economically mature human subjects it [theory] proposes a *constructed* 'economic subject', in respect of which, by *contrast* with empirical man, it (a) *ignores* and treats as *non-existent* all those motives influencing empirical man which are *not* specifically *economic*, i.e. not specifically concerned with the fulfillment of material needs; (b) *assumes* as existent qualities that empirical man does not possess, or possesses only incompletely, i.e.

   (i)   complete *insight* into a given *situation* – economic omniscience;

  (ii)   unfailing choice of the *most appropriate means* for a given end – absolute economic rationality;

 (iii)   complete dedication of one's powers to the purpose of acquiring economic goods – 'untiring acquisitional drive'.

It thus postulates an *unrealistic* person, analogous to a mathematical ideal model.[6]

It is a case of a mental construct made for the purpose of knowledge formation by means of comparison with reality. Weber's strategy for assessing causes is really the same in history as in social science, and it is a very pragmatic strategy, primarily as a result of its inspiration in legal science. In the courtroom, decisions about causal adequacy have to be made continuously, and they are made without any pretence to having solved the nature of the ultimate character of the universe. 'Even this first step thus transforms the given "reality" into a "mental construct" in order to make it a historical fact. In Goethe's words, "theory" is involved in the "fact"' (Weber 1949: 173). The tension between isolation and generalization in the explanation of social action can only be resolved pragmatically, and the role of counterfactuals makes the resolution very difficult. Weber's attitude may in general be compared to that of the practising doctor or lawyer who operates under the necessity of making judgements, with the recognition that there is no solution to the problem of judgement either in the realm of idealization or in the realm of pure empirical fact.

Weber's own method was to begin with concrete behaviour that is intersubjectively accessible to the historian, and account for it through interpretative hypotheses that are culturally relative to the framework of the historian's culture. Under the best circumstances these hypotheses are not only causal but can be expressed in terms of probability. The causal character of the hypotheses provides the links to concrete behaviour that enable their relative validity to be assessed.

> Anyone can 'count on' the fact that the behaviour of other persons in their relationship to him will be of a certain sort. . . . This fact has a very high degree of probability. In other words, there is a certain probability that we can count on the unmolested use of a certain object.

Therefore we can – and we do – structure our affairs on the basis of
this probability. (Oakes 1977 [Weber 1907]: 128)[7]

People sometimes break the law, but we ordinarily count on their
obeying it and we do not and need not take into account the feelings
they might have about obeying the law. The normally expected course
of social interaction can be described without any reference to psychology. Deviations and anomalies might be accounted for psychologically, but the social pattern itself, as Weber conceives it, has a
kind of autonomy from psychology. In the same text, a few pages
earlier, Weber discusses what he describes as the general theory of the
law of skat, the card game. He makes a distinction between playing
the game correctly or incorrectly in order to make the point that the
rules of the game are themselves a 'causal factor' (ibid.: 119):

> The 'orientation' of action to an enacted order can also mean that one
> of the associates may consciously *deviate* from this subjectively com-
> prehended meaning. In a game of cards, someone who consciously and
> deliberately departs from the rules of the game, whose meaning he has
> subjectively understood, someone, that is, who cheats, nevertheless
> remains associated as a player, in contrast to the person who
> withdraws from further play. (*GAW*: 442–3; p. 161 in Edith Graber's
> translation)

A thief or murderer who hides her or his intentions adheres to an
expected pattern of behaviour even in the course of deviating from
the fundamental prohibition against theft and murder.

Weber makes explicit that this kind of teleological explanation –
one in which participants in a game have their behaviour explained
by reference to the aim of playing the game – has nothing to do with
values or feelings. The description of the game as game is a matter
of historical or empirical fact (Oakes 1977: 121). The 'game' is
described through a teleological conceptual construct, 'game'; it is
also an idealization: 'In other words, facts and processes that are
defined in this way and distinguished from the manifold of the empirically given constitute the point of departure for a causal investigation' (ibid.). The course that a specific game takes may differ as a
result of the amount of beer consumed by the players or their degree
of concentration, which influences the participants' ability to follow
'utilitarian' maxims in their actual play.

These passages are Weber's attempts to establish the fundamental
distinction between the rules and regulations, the conventions and
usages, that make up the ideal of conduct within a society and the
actual causally effective expectations that individuals in a society

have and upon which the causal force of collective facts entirely depends. One can scarcely overstate both the importance and the obscurity of this distinction. It may be comprehended most easily in terms of the difference between a top-down and a bottom-up approach.

According to Tönnies,[8] society, with its rules, imposes itself as a causal force on the individual, competing with the causes of individual action and overwhelming them. For example, in Tönnies's view the consciousness is really the causal voice of society. For Weber, society is the sum of the causal effects of individuals' expectations on their action: 'The decisive factor for the empirical "validity" of a rationally enacted order is therefore not that the actors continually orient their action to correspond with what they subjectively interpret the meaning of the order to be' (*GAW*: 443; p. 161 in Graber's translation).[9] Not the subjectively apprehended ideal but actual expectations determine the actual causal character of an order. The relevance of the ideal of instrumental rationality to a given order is culturally variable. In the case of value-rational fanatics motivated by an ethic of uncompromising duty (see *GAW*: 442), they would constitute a paradigm of normal behaviour in some societies and would produce different expectations on the part of members of that society.

The essay on Meyer, and especially the section dealing with objective possibility and adequate cause, is central to understanding Weber as a methodologist 'in context'.[10] It is not easy reading; for instance:

> Only by laying bare and solving *substantive problems* can sciences be established and their methods developed. On the other hand, purely epistemological and methodological reflections have never played the crucial role in such developments. Such discussions can become important for the enterprise of science only when, as a result of considerable shifts of the 'viewpoint' from which a datum becomes the object of analysis, the idea emerges that the new 'viewpoint' also requires a revision of the logical forms in which the 'enterprise' has heretofore operated, and when, accordingly, uncertainty about the 'nature' of one's own work arises. (*GAW*: 217–18)

The passage, however, is tantalizingly suggestive about the extent to which forms of historical analysis are themselves relative to history. As culture changes, the forms of science also change, as do the guiding values of the age which are points of departure. The transformation of cultural horizons contributes to an existential problem for science.[11]

Rational Understanding

The rational non-empathetic and anti-psychological (in both senses of that term)[12] character of Weber's *Verstehen* (interpretative understanding) is evident in most of his methodological essays.[13]

Weber's essay entitled 'Some Categories of Interpretive Sociology', published in *Logos* in 1913, begins with an affirmation of the necessity for *Verstehen,* verifiable, *rational* understanding: 'the "understanding" of the context must always be verified, as far as possible, with the usual method of causal attribution before any interpretation, however plausible, becomes a valid "intelligible explanation"' (*GAW*: 428; p. 151 in Graber's translation). Weber does concede that there is a 'specific qualitative "self-evidence"' that is a constituent of any 'understanding', but he makes this concession empty by noting: 'That an interpretation possesses this self-evidence in especially high measure still proves nothing in itself about its empirical validity' (ibid.).[14]

The essay is anti-psychological: 'Interpretative sociology, in keeping with all that has been said, is not part of a "psychology"' (*GAW*: 432; p. 154 in Graber's translation). In a section dedicated to the 'Relationship to Psychology', Weber explains how instrumentality (*Zweckrationalität*) serves as a kind of substitute for psychology, or rather for the role that psychological assumptions are sometimes given in interpretation. Weber's point is that even such domains as mystical contemplative religion may well be best understood in terms of instrumental rationality, and that these understandings may be most illuminating with respect to the causal character of the phenomena under study. Even in the context of mystical religion, people may attempt to achieve ends rationally. It may be that the ends are incomprehensible to us, but this does not mean that we cannot understand the choice of means made by the religious person. This suggests one way in which, for Weber, interpretation is bound to causal explanation: 'Sociology must reject the assumption that "understanding" [*Verstehen*] and causal "explanation" have *no* relationship to one another' (*GAW*: 436; p. 157 in Graber's translation).[15] 'Explanations of concrete behaviour in terms of its meaning are, even with the highest degree of self-evidence, only explanatory hypotheses for sociology. They therefore need to be empirically verified in essentially the same manner as does every hypothesis' (ibid.). The passage that appears between these quotations suggests that Weber's concern is with 'understandable relationships and particularly rationally oriented sequences of motivations' (ibid.).[16] The idea

Table 3.1   Interpretation and Evidence

Type of Verstehen	Type of evidence (proof)	
	Intuitive (Einfühlung)	Rational interpretative
Explanatory (erklärendes)	I	II
Immediate (aktuelles)	III	IV

that motivations are both understandable and 'links' in a chain is revealing, suggesting that the actual course of events supplies a kind of public or intersubjectively available set of facts that can be compared to an empathetic interpretation and serve to disqualify or exclude it.

The historical association of the notion of *Verstehen* with some sort of inner understanding or with acts of empathy compels us to deal directly with Weber's own conception. There is, as I have suggested, no psychologically empathetic aspect to Weber's notion; for Weber *Verstehen* is an act of *rational* interpretation.[17] Table 3.1 indicates the relationship Weber sees between types of evidence and types of understanding. Weber deals primarily with *rational* interpretative (and explanatory) understanding. Positions III and IV represent the kinds of understanding we normally do not question, such as why someone runs away from an approaching fire or chops wood for winter fuel. These are understandings in which the directly observable evidence is sufficient to establish an interpretation.[18] Such things as the mathematical relation $2 + 2 = 4$, or a car driver stopping before an approaching train, or a person avoiding touching a hot stove with bare hands are all in this general category of not requiring explanation beyond the immediately present fact. Positions I and II represent the sorts of thing that require more intellectual effort to understand. One role of critical science is to transfer subject matter from the realm of the immediately understandable to the realm of topics that can be given an explanatory understanding. Where frozen cultural patterns are beginning to thaw, for example, there may be opportunities to subject them to explanatory analysis. The nature of a ceremony and its significance may thus become apparent to us, whereas before it was simply unproblematic, be it a handshake, a wedding, or signing a contract. We might place in position I the sort of things Darwin spoke of, such as the universal recognition of emotions in faces – such as expressions of anger, disappointment or anguish – that is non-rational because it is part of our biology and biologically endowed capacities.

The kind of analysis and the cases of human action of explanatory interest to Weber are located in position II of table 3.1, rational interpretative (and explanatory) understanding. His concern is not with action whose meaning can be immediately apprehended, but with action the meaning of which is highly variable and which can be understood only by relating the action to its context through interpretation. Consider the example of the wood chopper. It may be that the person chopping wood is working out frustration after a family quarrel, that is to say, chopping wood therapeutically.[19] Anyone who has counted to ten before answering an aggravating question knows 'empathetically' what sorts of feelings such a wood chopper might have. But what about the more complex case in which chopping wood is part of some sort of plan or strategy;[20] for instance, the wood chopper might be a retired person in need of exercise. For Weber the fact that an interpretation of this sort cannot be derived directly from what can be observed and empathized with suggests that, for genuinely valid knowledge of individual subjective motives, some kind of procedure is required that involves assessing interpretative hypotheses as causes; ordinarily this would require comparisons with similar cases. In the case of actions like the wood chopper's, experimental psychology would tell us little, but past cases of wood chopping to which the present case could be compared would tell us a great deal.

The key passage in Weber is the classic opening from the introduction to 'Basic Concepts of Sociology' (those parts of *WuG* which are also included in *GAW*): 'Sociology . . . is a science which attempts the interpretative understanding of social action in order thereby to arrive at a causal explanation of its course and effects' (*GAW*: 542).[21] This might be understood in two ways, either (1) that through an act of understanding one has achieved explanation; or, the opposite, (2) that explanation has to pass through the stage of understanding, as an inalienable but not sufficient element in the process of explanation. Here, in the very cornerstone of his sociology, Weber manages to confuse posterity with a formulation resistant to unambiguous interpretation. It is clear, however, that we cannot ignore either understanding or explanation.

Weber's views on explanation were opaque and scattered throughout his works. In the 1904 essay, the most important one, we do not find a treatise on explanation, only a number of comments revealing Weber's ambiguous stand with regard to the relationship between rules and laws. Weber was at least attracted by what we might call the 'verificatory clout' of the natural sciences; although he maintained a Dilthey-based resistance to the unity of science, he nevertheless expressed an ambition to apply the criteria of science as far as the object of the cultural sciences allowed.

Weber's alternative of normative empirical theory, which presupposes a point of view, a value-aspect, as the point of departure for means–ends analysis, excludes the purely explanatory approach. Weber holds that instrumental teleological analysis (*Zweckrationalität*) is the mode of analysis we have to live with in the primitive social sciences. Weber as a neo-Kantian was able to drop the Hegelian and psychologizing ballast in the furtherance of a secular social science. Although his *Verstehen* is of the rational and not empathetic kind, it is less clear what he meant by explanation and what role he was prepared to ascribe to laws in social explanation. The answer to this requires a 'symptomal reading' or 'rational reconstruction' of a kind that threatens to transcend the intentions of the genuine classic under study.

Religion is of major historical importance. Indeed, the concept of the secularization of the social sciences indirectly refers to the immense, albeit decreasing, importance of religion throughout the history of the world. In the realm of culture, religion is crucial as the 'norm-sender' that provides the starting point for the analysis of action in instrumental terms. In a sense, then, the application of the methods of empathetic analysis and rational interpretation are themselves bound up with the problem of secularization. Weber, like Menger, stressed rational interpretative understanding, in contrast to empathetic understanding, and it is rational understanding that is particularly relevant to action in the modern world.

If we approach Weber with a concern to produce explanations rather than to evaluate his actual historical role in the intellectual process of development that he contributed to in his own time, we can ignore the context and Weber's purposes; we can create the 'Weber' we need and tell him what he should have said. But this threatens to distort the historical Weber. Weber had a somewhat different view of the purposes of explanation. He was concerned with creating testable explanations, not with ultimate explanatory truth in the sense of the natural sciences. These two distinct concerns, values and the criteria for selection of concepts and explanation, are closely related in Weber's work and in actual practice. But they have, as I have suggested, different historical trajectories and different relations to the present.

Weber's Anti-Psychologism

Weber's anti-psychologism was already apparent in his important essay on 'Marginal Utility Theory and the Fundamental Law of

Pychophysics' (originally published in *Archiv* 1908; pp. 384–99 in *GAW*).[22] His intentions in this essay were to demonstrate that economics did not depend on psychology, and to protect Menger from some of his overenthusiastic followers who had tried to make a 'theory' out of the model of marginal utility. Weber liked what the marginalists were doing – but not what they *believed* they were doing.[23] Weber wished to employ Menger's model but to reject the notion of the rational economic actor as a biological universal. Lujo Brentano[24] took the view that marginalist economics depended upon natural science-style ideas about psychological dispositions of the sort found in the so-called fundamental law of psychophysics.[25]

Weber, in contrast, saw 'economic theory as an enterprise working out the consequences of assumptions of economic rationality on the part of economic agents, precisely in purely analytical terms and again independently of any psychology whatsoever' (ibid.: 22, in the translator's introduction).

Weber distinguished between stimuli and needs and made the point that a subjective value-theory – like marginalism – starts with need, in contrast to psychology, which operates with stimuli, sensations, and so on.[26] Weber is clearly a long way from crude behaviourism or indeed any sort of psychological reductionism in the name of unified science. His enterprise instead attempts to preserve explanations in 'everyday terms' that are accessible to any member of the present culture, and within this general framework he wishes to appropriate the best of the methods of Menger's school. He is quite explicit in his rejection of any sort of psychologistic critique of marginalism or economic analysis: 'The rational theory of price formation not only has nothing to do with the concepts of experimental psychology. More generally it has nothing to do with any "psychology" of any kind which aspires to be a "science" going beyond everyday experience' (*GAW*: 396; p. 33 in Schneider's translation). For Weber, 'marginal utility theory and, more broadly, any subjective theory of value are not psychologically, but – if a methodological term be desired – "pragmatically" founded, that is on the use of the categories, "ends" and "means" ' (ibid.).

> And the general theorems which economic theory sets up are simply constructions that state what consequences the action of the individual man in its intertwining with the action of all others would have to produce, on the assumption that anyone were to shape his conduct toward his environment exclusively according to the principles of commercial bookkeeping – and, in this sense, 'rationally'. As we all know, the assumption does not hold – and the empirical course of these proceedings for the understanding of which the theory was formulated accordingly shows only an 'approximation' (varying considerably

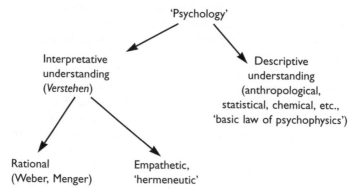

Figure 3.1   Double meaning of psychology

according to the particular case) to the theoretically constructed course of strictly rational action. Yet, the historical peculiarity of the capitalist epoch, and thereby also the significance of marginal utility theory (as of every economic theory of value) for the understanding of this epoch, rests on the circumstances that – while the economic history of some epochs of the past has not without reason been designated as 'history of non-economic conditions' – under today's conditions of existence the approximation of reality to the theoretical propositions of economics has been a constantly increasing one. It is an approximation to reality that has implicated the destiny of ever-wider layers of humanity. And it will hold more and more broadly, as far as our horizons allow us to see. (*GAW*: 395; pp. 32–3 in Schneider's translation)

Much of the confusion is caused by a double meaning of psychology, part hermeneutics and part descriptive behaviourism. Figure 3.1 might help to put Weber's anti-psychological – in both senses – ideal-type in its place. Weber's rational type is psychological only in so far as deviations from a rational means–end scheme have to be explained – and his tool of the ideal-type serves merely *rational* understanding and nothing more, basically because of the demands for intersubjectivity and objectivity. This does not exhaust the topic of the ideal-type.

The Ideal-Type

Weber's methodology is primarily about conceptualization and the problem of producing intersubjectively meaningful selections from vast and infinite reality. The tool with which he addresses this problem and reflects on its difficulties is the ideal-type. The ideal-type is drawn from culture and shaped by evaluative implications that are present in the cultural sources from which ideal-types must be constructed.[27]

In the 'Objectivity' essay Weber writes:

> The ideal-type is formed by the one-sided *accentuation* of one or more points of view and by the synthesis of a great many diffuse, discrete, more or less present and occasionally absent *concrete individual* phenomena, which are arranged according to those one-sidedly emphasized viewpoints into a unified *analytical* construct. In its conceptual purity, this mental construct cannot be found empirically anywhere in reality. It is a *Utopia*.[28] Historical research faces the task of determining, in each individual case, the extent to which this ideal-construct approximates to or diverges from reality (*GAW*: 191).
>
> What is the significance of such ideal-typical constructs for an *empirical* science, as we wish to constitute it? Before going any further, we should emphasize that the idea of an ethical *imperative*, of a 'model' of what 'ought' to exist, is to be carefully distinguished from the analytical construct, which is 'ideal' in the strictly logical sense of the term (ibid.: 192).
>
> An 'ideal-type' in our sense, to repeat once more, has no connection at all with *value-judgements*, and it has nothing to do with any type of perfection other than a purely *logical* one. (ibid.: 200)[29]

The special features of the ideal-type in its role of model (i.e. the characteristic notion of purification, stylization, accentuation, etc.) could be illustrated by Honoré de Balzac, a French novelist in the broad realistic tradition.[30] His caricatures of, for instance, *petit bourgeois* grocery merchants are droll, certainly exaggerated, yet still essentially true; the sort of portraits that are better than the original, as when a mimic successfully imitates a politician. Indeed, Balzac's ideal-type constructions of the *petit bourgeois* in France teach us more than any concrete person ever could.

According to Weber, the ideal-type is not itself a 'hypothesis' but offers guidance in the construction of hypotheses (*GAW*: 190; Weber 1949: 90). Some sort of theoretical function is thus ascribed to the ideal-type; its role is instrumental. Weber regarded the constructions of the Menger school as ideal-types: 'We have in abstract economic theory an illustration of those synthetic constructs which have been designated as "ideas" of historical phenomena. It offers us an ideal picture of events on the commodity market under conditions of a society organized on the principles of an exchange economy, free competition and rigorously rational conduct' (ibid.).

However, the instrumental heuristic functions in the theoretical process that the ideal-type is to fulfil were not endorsed by the historicists of Schmoller's school.

Weber's open criticism of Schmoller, and his implicit modification of Rickert, may be seen as important reasons for his characterization of the ideal-type as being *abstract, one-sided and unreal*; they also explain his emphasis on its *instrumental* function in scientific research. But thus defined, Weber's position is in fact identical with the moderate one taken up by Menger in the 'controversy over method': in Menger's view, the doctrines of theoretical economics were precisely characterized by their one-sidedness and abstraction; and he believed that no 'realistic', i.e., historical, science of economics could dispense with the help afforded by such abstract propositions. In fact therefore, Weber, in his discussion of the *nature* and general *function* of concepts, sides *with* the abstract school and *against* the historical one. (Bruun 1972: 209)

However, Weber was explicit concerning the limits of the influence of Menger's school, for instance when he declared that the theory of marginal utility also had its own marginal utility (*GAW*: 190).

Weber's way out of the *Methodenstreit* is, in context, a vindication of theoretical ambitions. As Göran Therborn notes:

Menger had distinguished between historical and theoretical science, which could deal with the same materials but from different points of view. He had also adumbrated Weber's ideal-typical discussion by making a distinction within 'theoretical research', separating out an 'empirical-reality'. The empirical-realist tendency worked with 'real types' (*Realtypen*) instead of generic concepts and strove for 'empirical' instead of universal laws. (1974: 224)

Weber manifested his critical attitude towards the historicists when he wrote:

Nothing, however, is more dangerous than the *confusion* of theory and history stemming from naturalistic prejudices. This confusion expresses itself firstly in the belief that the 'true' content and the essence of historical reality are portrayed in such theoretical constructs or secondly, in the use of these constructs as a procrustean bed into which history is to be forced or thirdly, in the hypostatization of such 'ideas' as real 'forces' and as a 'true' reality which operates behind the passage of events and which works itself out in history. (*GAW*: 195; Weber 1949: 94)

Essentialism and conceptual realism were both targets for Weber's irritation. Weber had to detach his own 'new' approach from both inductive and intuitionist historicism, from both Schmoller and Dilthey. When Schmoller paid lip-service to the law-seeking ambition in his debate with Menger he was certainly close to the confusion Weber rejects.

At the bottom line we find conflicting doctrines of concept-formation, the pre-neo-Kantian–Hegelian *vs* the nominalist. It did not seem to occur to the pre-neo-Kantians that clear distinctions between concept and reality as well as selective abstraction from reality with lucid criteria would really solve their dilemma. That became Weber's task. In this context, essentialism and conceptual realism occur as two only slightly different variants of pre-neo-Kantian innocence, both of which confuse reality with ideas.

Weber was well aware of the limits of the ideal-type. Its pragmatic function and character is one of its instrumental assets. The ideal-type 'serves as a harbour until one has learned to navigate safely in the vast sea of empirical facts. The coming of age of science in fact always implies the transcendence of the ideal-type, insofar as it was thought of as possessing empirical validity or as a *class concept* (*Gattungsbegriff*)' (GAW: 206; Weber 1949: 104). This intermediary role of the ideal-type in the research process should not be over-emphasized. The ideal-type is helpful in order to make us observant, aware of the peculiarities in the empirical reality we are about to explain. The rational-type has the potential to explain *rational* behaviour, to point out instances where the action of an actor has *not* been rational and remains to be explained. The ideal-type exposes phenomena and derivations of an elusive character. A positive formulation of the multifaceted ideal-type concept is not easily brought about, simply because it cannot exist as an exhaustive and all-inclusive interpretation. Weber himself even defined the concept in negative terms.[31]

Weber's basic distinction between real significance and motive (subjective significance) further indicated an effort to develop criteria of intersubjectivity (a term Weber did not use, but one that I retrospectively find useful), as well as the secularizing elements in the neo-Kantian and marginalist contributions to Weber's conceptualization. The ideal-type is supposed to help reveal the real significance, the meaning of an act, as distinct from the subjective meaning the actor himself might attach to it. In this way interpretative understanding could well serve the purpose of combining *erklärendes Verstehen* with *rationale Evidenz*. The ideal-type of the rational economic actor provides 'rules' with reference to which observed behaviour could be given meaning. Intuitive understanding of the empathetic type is in itself not enough and might in fact even be misleading (see, e.g., *GAW*: 432 and *passim*, or p. 189).

Understanding, in Weber's sense, rather means reference to a scheme, a 'blueprint', accounting for the possible rational interpretation of an act. The ideal-type of the rational economic actor is insensitive with regard to deviations. The 'true' reasons of an actor might not be identical with rational market behaviour, unless assumptions are made about the nature of human beings. They might also, of course, deviate from the subjective conceptions of the actor himself. We do not always act rationally, but often enough we try to act rationally, in order to provide realistic hypotheses about the reasons for real behaviour and social exchange that we can observe. Weber's methodology was primarily aimed at rational – 'testable' in the form of rational proof – understanding.

To start with, Weber was certainly more interested in individual than general explanation.[32] The rational ideal-type, however, appeared in a 'generalizing' guise, although allowing for the explanation of individual acts, which, after all, are the main object of social science. The rational model allowing for rational evidence falls 'in between' the extremes of the positivist *vs* anti-positivist continuum. Much is arbitrary in human activity, or notoriously irrational, or still apparently irrational, and each individual act will certainly not make sense if we utilize the model of rational economic actors, which, in addition, is not anthropologically generally valid. One might say that Weber's approach has a 'middle-range' generality, reflecting the culture-bound character of ideal-typical understanding. Cultural values provide the starting points for the type of constructed schemes needed for the explanation of acts. Maximizing individual utility is merely one alternative (of increasing relevance since the birth of modern capitalism half a millennium ago).

Alexander von Schelting (1934) was for long regarded as the foremost authority on Weber's ideal-type methodology and was evidently the main source for Parsons's interpretation (see pp. 53 and 106). His main distinction was between individualizing and generalizing types. The 'Protestant ethic' or 'early modern capitalism' are both examples of individualizing types, stylizing unique historical phenomena; 'bureaucracy' is a typical generalizing type, equally applicable to ancient Egypt as to imperial China. In one way, superficially, the two main variations of types could be said to correspond to Weber's slow and discrete development from history to sociology, since the ideal-type originated as a response to methodological problems within history. One reason for the difficulty in grasping the character of the ideal-type is that Weber himself did not intend it to be an unambiguous concept. His main concern was to grasp the cultural meaning of historical events in a structured way; at the same time he persistently declined to see any true essence in these ideal-types.[33]

Conclusion

Although the ideal-type does not fit into formalized theoretical structures, it remains an instrument for theory-construction, even when 'theory' refers to more complex systems of interrelated hypotheses. The grand schemes of Talcott Parsons (1937 and 1951; see chapter 4), Jeffrey Alexander (1983), Richard Münch (1988) and Wolfgang Schluchter (1989) go beyond Weber's intention, but these are over-ambitious extensions rather than interpretative errors. Any immanent or purely genetic analysis (in Quentin Skinner's use of these terms) of Weber's central methodological device needs to take account of the circumstantial argumentation if we are correctly to assess his part in the secularization of social science.[34] Projecting our own intentions onto Weber does not clarify or further our understanding of his role as a classic. Yet a purely immanent analysis, which shows up Weber adversely in relation to later methodological accomplishments, produces its own dissatisfactions. In the pure historic-genetic approach, moreover, we are doomed not to see the wood for the trees and might fail to catch Weber's significance.[35]

There is a gulf between the Diltheyian tradition of the sociology of everyday life,[36] as it is called today in its modern American variations, and modern secularized social science. Weber is much more compatible with the standard positions of modern methods of unified science. As a practitioner he developed sensible (for his time) strategies to balance the criteria of science with the requirements of the social objects of study, wisely not attempting to answer the old question of whether social science could attain the character of 'hard' science. In short, Weber cultivated the notion of unified scientific criteria, in line with the modern hypothetical-deductive method; but a consequence of the methodology he actually developed would seem to be a scepticism or pessimism with regard to the chances for a cumulative 'normal science' paradigm. Weber's value-aspect–choice methodology – or 'normative empirical theory' – with its anti-metaphysical conceptualization promotes cumulative cognitive *discourses* rather than one discourse, which are well attuned to the modernist predicament of normative polytheism and frustration.

And he himself gives rise to competing social action paradigms, instead of a unitarian tradition of his own.

There is in Weber a problematic connection between explanation and understanding of meaning, which makes him differ from both empathetic and naturalist approaches. To explain and to understand are two very enigmatically related purposes in Weberian (latent) causal doctrine. Weber differentiates between several interpretations of meaning. The understanding of meaning, however, is ascribed a role in the explanatory process. The route to explanation goes through the interpretation of meaning, but to what extent does motivational understanding of human action satisfy our expectations of a proper explanation? There is an opaque interconnection between the heuristic strategies of understanding and explanation, as well as objectivity and meaning.

Weber did not believe in orthodox causality, as usually defined in handbooks (i.e. a factor unequivocally produces a certain effect). For the social sciences he questioned the fertility of the sort of explanation within which singular phenomena are subsumed under a general law. On the other hand, Weber made it clear that his *verstehende Soziologie* should by no means be seen as just any 'psychology' (*GAW*: 432). The ideal-type above all deals with accountable *rational* meaning, merely approximating the actual meaning a social act might have for a specific individual, although it serves as an explanatory tool. In the choice between more meaning or more objectivity Weber's stand is clear, although a role for the irrationality of life persists in Weber's methodology through providing points of departure for rationalized means–end analyses.

The 1904 'Objectivity' essay gives us fair hints about what Weber did *not* endorse, but hardly provides us with a positive prescription for explanatory social science. As a practising social scientist, Weber adequately responded to the intellectual tensions of his day, which are to some extent – but not entirely – similar to those of our present day. That Weber chose to express himself in the form of essayistic reflections manifests this.[37] Weber's own and often quoted attitude, moreover, was very much in line with Alfred N. Whitehead's famous dictum that 'a science which hesitates to forget its founders is lost'. Instead we learn what fallacies he wanted the developing social science to avoid, as he was gradually confronted with the issues generated by the controversy over method and the crisis of historicism.

It is still intriguing to relate Weber to the alternatives of positivist nomothetic explanation and the more idiographical or even hermeneutical explanation, in the broad sense of that word.[38] We can at least conclude from an immanent reading of the sources that, according to Weber, general laws have some role to play in the process of establishing explanatory propositions. However, in Weber's view, the vigilant positivists were apt to exceed the proper limits of the rational economic actor metaphor in regarding it as a general law of nature. Instead, he said, it ought to be conceived of as an ideal-type. Weber was quite explicit in the 1904 essay both about his dependence on Menger, as well as the limits of the marginalist influence on his ideal-type.[39]

Rationality (calculability, *Zweckrationalität*) and accentuation (*Steigerung*) are two central features of Weber's ideal-type, and the rational economic actor metaphor serves as its prototype. There exists no ideal-type of the ideal-type;[40] it is found in several instances and in varying forms in Weber's work. The various applications of the ideal-type are one basis for differentiating the concept, from von Schelting onwards. Since von Schelting is Parsons's mentor (see p. 106), his interpretation of Weber's *Wissenschaftslehre* has become very influential; in fact, it is the most authoritative guide written in the twentieth century to the secrets of the elusive concept of the ideal-type. His distinction between individualizing and generalizing types corresponds to historical *vs* sociological types, reflecting the two dominant phases in Weber's intellectual development. There is a development in his preoccupations from cultural uniqueness to sociological theoretical constructions, from the historical individualizing type (modern capitalism) to generalized sociological types (bureaucracy).

The early historical, individualizing types were formulated by Weber before the typological procedure as such was made explicit, as in the idiographical studies on the economic history of antiquity. Moreover, they are often mentioned in this context since they actualize the parallels between Weber and Marx. In Weber's study of the social basis for the decline of the Roman market economy (1896), his manner of reasoning comes very close to that of historical materialism; it is still very Weberian, owing to the emphasis on the role of the market.[41]

Any attempt to interpret the ideal-type unambiguously will have to face anomalies. However, stressing the rational variant of the ideal-type makes the Weberian methodological project more comprehensible than other alternatives. If one purified ideal-type has to be selected, the rational one is congenial not only to our 'perennial' (retrospective) point of view but to the normative empirical theory of instrumental rationality.[42] My plea for the rational ideal-type as the one most consistent with Weber's place in the history of social science doctrine is seemingly further supported by the attempt to formulate a definition in an unequivocal manner.[43]

We are all working in the aftermath of Marx and Nietzsche, and our understanding of the world is definitely different from what it would have been before they were writing. I suggest that Weber's whole methodology is imprinted with the Nietzschean response to the predicament of modernity, the response to the post-Enlightenment necessity of existentialist choice. The resulting 'perspectivism' is built into Weber's instrumental analysis, the value-aspect–choice methodology of normative empirical theory.

The term 'sociology' is used rather restrictively by early German practitioners. Weber is, perhaps, a sociologist, but he was also a lawyer, an economist and a historian. In Göran Therborn's words: 'What happened is that Weber came to use the label of sociology for the views he had earlier, in his methodological essays, put forward as an economist and an historian' (1974: 211). I suggest that the ideal-type be seen as the unifying key concept not to Weber as a whole but to his methodology. My intention is not to use Weber as a toolbox for present-day purposes but to approach Weber as indicative of an important theme in the history of ideas – the long trend of secularization, in which instrumental means–end analysis is the core.

The ideal-type exemplifies Weber's liberation from the historicist milieu in which he was raised. This 'break' with historicism was gradual, as indicated by the original character of this conceptual tool as a vehicle for history; in retrospect, we use it as a tool for social science. It is not a dramatic parting; on the contrary it takes the form of building a bridge between historicism and the more modern ideals of science. Or perhaps it is even a release of something that is already inherent among historians. In helping the historicists to save themselves Weber, as the American saying goes, 'put the hay where the horse could get it' – or so it seems.

4

Three Paradigmatic
Conceptions of Weber

Introduction: A Brief Outline of Weber's Reception

The notion of a definitive Weberian paradigm is itself partly apocryphal, since theoretical as well as empiricist tendencies coexist
within the broad mainstream of social science. It is also partly
due to a search for the 'founding fathers' of a normal science paradigm within social science. However, to say that such a paradigm
is mere myth would also be an overstatement, since there is a
Weberian creed in the philosophy of social science that is found in
his, often misinterpreted, value-philosophy. Even disparate critiques
have recognized the centrality of the fact–value distinction. Both
value-objectivist, natural law adherents and the advocates of 'dialectical' social science wanted to transcend the self-imposed restrictions
on the proper scope of scientific reason that are stipulated by the
orthodox doctrine. Weber is seen as a 'benchmark' for a value-free,
objective, social, science.

Arnold Brecht, in his *Political Theory* (1959), is probably the
scholar who most energetically developed the notion of Weber as the
foremost proponent of so-called scientific value-relativism. This influential handbook on the history of social science doctrines reflects a
lifelong occupation with the development of basic social science
thought. A central section deals with Weber and the birth of the 'gulf
doctrine' (between fact and value, 'is' and 'ought'). An image of
Weber's role in the philosophy of value, similar to Gouldner's (1964),
although with a negative evaluation, is found in Leo Strauss's *Natural
Right and History* (1953), especially in the second chapter, devoted
to a critical review of Weber's philosophy of value from (what
I would suggest is) a basically pre-Enlightenment position. The

corresponding reaction from a different point of view, against the Weberian creed of science, is Gouldner's essay 'Anti-Minotaur: The Myth of a Value-Free Sociology' (1972). Strauss, who died in 1973, is widely regarded today as the greatest representative of the remnants of classical normativism, while Gouldner, until his untimely death, was the popular spokesman for a 'reflexive' (or 'dialectical') sociology. They both share the notion of Weber as a mainstream social scientist, with regard to his value-philosophical views on objectivity and values, which is also shared by mainstream social science itself, insofar as Brecht and Gunnar Myrdal could be seen as embodiments of this.

Weber's perspectivist or 'polytheist' methodology meant that an orderly hierarchy of stable norms was replaced by competing value systems, each of which had its own ultimate value standpoint. Modern political ideologies are all products of the Enlightenment, yet despite this common intellectual source their worldviews are in competition and irresolvable conflict – for instance, socialism and liberalism.[1]

Weber might be seen as a frustrated seeker taking refuge in the tentative solution of culture as the norm-sender replacing God's authority, as a representative of the secularization of social science obsessed with the proper scope of the scientific search for truth. However, this does not exclude other supplementary compasses; although scientific proof calls for certain procedures and actualizes certain problems (of testability, and so on), Weber's sceptical attitude seems offensive to those stubbornly clinging to the belief in 'total reason'.[2] Often the lingering belief in objective values is combined with a presupposition about the mission of science to serve various extrascientific goals, such as breaking through the bourgeois hegemony with which Weber's relativism is associated.

Although works by Brecht and others have been understood as attempts to canonize Weber as the founder of a value-free social science, the reception history demonstrates that the value-question produced very different Webers. These issues came to the fore in the 1964 German Sociological Conference in Heidelberg, where Ernst Topitsch was prominent in stressing the secularizing – antimetaphysical – elements in Weber's philosophy of science.

The Weberian paradigm with scientific value-relativism as its central core was stimulated by Topitsch's appearance at this centenary celebration of Weber's birth. The turmoil in Heidelberg – vehement controversies took place during the proceedings – came to public notice, and the presence of international scholars of repute further contributed to making the congress a major event in the history of Weberology and the fractured reception of Weber's work

(Stammer 1965). Topitsch's contribution appeared as an outspoken expression of mainstream scientific value-relativism,[3] separating the political from the methodological and countering much of the vulgar criticism of Weber. Scientific value-relativism appears to many as a standard position, although it is never uncontested, but is rather just one reaction to a perennial paradigmatic divide.[4]

For conservative natural law thinkers like Strauss the purely cognitive approach to social science is objectionable, because it conceals an unjustifiable commitment to relativism or even nihilism. In the later American debate, MacIntyre (1984) and Bloom (1987), wrestling with very Weberian problems, tried to return to Aristotle in their search for the Archimedian point that God no longer unequivocally provided, a problem-nexus we often associate with the names of Nietzsche and Kierkegaard. However, a flaw common to all these reactions against the anxiety the Enlightenment imposes upon us – the necessity of individual responsible choice between guidelines for the conduct of life – is that the burden of proof for a positive value-ontology is hardly resolved. Value-judgements or ultimate values have no cognitive truth-value – yet we are forced to choose.

What Topitsch exposed was the extent to which Weber acknowledged and refused to back away from the uncomfortable truths of this cognitive and existential insecurity. Forty years on, Weber's refusal to see the world through the rose-coloured spectacles of the Enlightenment (in one meaning) is given its due respect. But this has undoubtedly embarrassed the disciplinary ambitions of sociology as a value-free science – just as Weber himself embarrassed his colleagues who sought a sociology that could become a scientifically based social policy discipline.

Much of the debate in the late 1960s and early 1970s became mired in the dead end of the misconceived fact–value distinction and objectivity; Weber's special *modus vivendi* between reason and passion became a natural focal point. The obvious tension between the two souls in Weber's bosom, the political and the scientific, gives him genuine credibility as spokesperson for the creed of instrumental reason. On this central point, which, again, we could (with Brecht) call 'scientific value-relativism', Weber will never be doomed to obsolescence. His philosophy of value adds a dimension to his value-related methodology, a lasting expression of the post-Enlightenment agony of choice and responsibility. It is a fettering in the name of science of the indispensable irrational element.

Retrospective reconstructions of the Weberian paradigm have never been entirely convincing. Weber has always tended to be regarded as a strange advocate for a positivist value-neutrality. Here retrospectivism has exacted a heavy price on an adequate contextual understanding of Weber. Weber has been the site of the jousting of the giants of critical theory and the positivistic tendencies within social science. The huge debates from the mid-1960s onwards on values and objectivity in social science have proved to be something of a cul-de-sac. Weber's status as a classic has proved more of an impediment to furthering the progress of social science. Both critical theory and the proponents of a scientific social science share a responsibility for this regrettable outcome, and both sides are guilty of refusing to understand Weber in context. As Brecht rightly asserted, at the kernel of Weber's value-philosophy is a doctrine of value relatedness, which by no means unambiguously translates into a value-free science. In reality we have to choose our value-priorities, and while Weber's normative empirical theory might make these choices more rationalized and calculable, we are not absolved from fundamental choices between ultimate values. The complexities of Weber's value philosophy deserve better than either his demonization by critical theory for his defence of scientific criteria against uncontrolled value-intrusion or the attribution of inflexible and 'empiricist' value-freedom by the positivists. Weber's fact–value distinction is, as we have seen, combined with the notion of value-relation as a tool for (limited but intersubjective) objectivity.

The idea of objectivity is crucial for any vision of social science. Although Weber has become an icon for the doctrine of an objective social science, we often miss what is significant and interesting in his work: namely his preferred methods for attaining that objective. The history of Weber's reception has been strongly marked and determined by its own contextualist issues. Catching Weber's essence is like 'shooting at a moving target' (Dronberger 1971: vii), and what Zingerle (1974) has called the delayed Weber reception – that is, the recognition of the complexities and dilemmas of his position – has been taken up by the secondary literature (Scaff 1989; Weiss 1989; Whimster and Lash 1987).

Weber embodied both the scientific and the political problems his contemporaries had to face. He was certainly no free-floating intellectual; rather he was constantly being dragged into the central issues and debates by duty and by chance. In politics one might say that Weber had an unhappy love affair (see Eliaeson 2000b), a longing to be useful that was never quite fulfilled. Nevertheless it did bring him into touch with German nation-building and its changing environment, from the early contacts with Friedrich Naumann's social reform party, through the wartime policy articles in the *Frankfurter Zeitung*, to the reconstruction, or rather construction, of a constitutional Germany after the war.

During his own lifetime Weber was not as important as he later became. He was a learned man, sometimes even spoken of as the 'legend from Heidelberg', but he was still an outsider to the real academic establishment. Max Weber as both a loner and an *enfant terrible* was not the ideal-typical character to pioneer modern social research teamwork. He was not a man of compromise and diplomacy (see, for instance, Chapman 1993). His personality evidently lacked some of the qualities that also make a scholar a modern research director. Visiting the United States for a few months in 1904, Weber was by no means the most prominent German social scientist. Moreover, the conduct of his personal career after his recovery from a nervous breakdown to some extent had the character of 'inner exile', a withdrawal from full participation in academic life and an engagement in criticism of the German university system. After his untimely death, the Weber circle that formed around his widow Marianne in Heidelberg cultivated an almost hagiographic image of the dead master, as reflected in the great biography Marianne wrote of her husband (Marianne Weber 1950), as well as Karl Jaspers's (1932) lamentations over the lost possibility of Weber as a superman leading the Weimar Republic out of its disastrous difficulties.

Sociology was partly interrupted in Germany soon after Weber's death and especially during the Nazi period, a pause that enabled Talcott Parsons and other transatlantic travellers to introduce a partly transformed Weber into American sociology, cut off from the original context, while in Leipzig Hans Freyer (as the chairman of the German Sociological Association) cultivated an 'anti-sociology', being pessimistic about the role of the discipline (see for instance Käsler 1991; König 1987; Meja et al. 1987; Muller 1987; Üner 1992). The lack of a continuing Weber 'school' was also due to the circumstance that he was somewhat marginalized, a sort of outsider, albeit within the academic establishment: 'His works were not widely read. . . . However, his ideas left their mark on a small number of well-known men', as Guenther Roth writes (Bendix and Roth 1971: 43); 'Max Weber did not succeed in establishing a school of his own' (Mommsen 1974: 47), referring to Löwith and Runciman; 'There is no Weberian school, as there is a Marxist, a Comtian and even a Durkheimian school' (Freund 1968: 32).

'One of the interesting things about Max Weber . . . is that while he exerted great influence on social science he never became a fountainhead of a movement' (Rossides 1973: 183). Rather, he became the fountainhead of several. 'Many German university teachers vaunt the illustrious title of being a former student of Max Weber' (Freund 1968: 288). Karl Jaspers, Georg Lukács, Karl Loewenstein and Paul Honigsheim were all pupils of his, as were, in a broader sense, Leo Löwenthal and Robert Michels, to mention just a few.[5]

There is a debate over Weber's influence in the 1920s, between Schroeter (1980) and Factor and Turner (1982).[6] It is a delicate matter of evaluation. From a historicist point of view Weber appears as an important sociological scholar from the very beginning, as indicated, for instance, in Palyi's reader (1923). On the other hand, his role as a fully appreciated classic can, admittedly, only be understood in the light of the later development of social science. Jennifer Platt (1985) claims that the influence Weber is supposed to have exercised in America is really a retrospective construction, Cooley having earlier provided the same elements.

There is not much to be seen of Weber's international fame in the period between the world wars. In Germany, sociology was almost, but not quite, suppressed during the National Socialist dictatorship. Some activities went on, most notably in Leipzig, although the conditions for unbiased scientific endeavours were not the best, and scholars, such as Werner Sombart and Hans Freyer, had to 'accommodate' in order to be able to continue.[7]

Political passions inhibited German scholars from pursuing a purely scientific evaluation of Weber, whose writings especially on political issues were still living history – and remained so to some extent after 1989. At the same time the new Federal Republic needed a founding father and, in the search for a missing intellectual tradition, Weber had to suffice. It is not by chance that President Theodor Heuss (the Heuss brothers were pupils of Weber) wrote an introduction to the second edition of Weber's *Gesammelte politische Schriften* (*GPS*) in the late 1950s. Against this 'liberal' backdrop the young Mommsen's (1959) re-evaluation of nationalism and his systematic presentation of Weber's political thought led to howls of anguish and hurt feelings.[8]

After the peak of behaviourism, general interest in the classics was stimulated by the student revolt in the late 1960s – and the Weberian legacy was available for penetration and 'chronocentric' reinterpretation, in the form of 'paradigmatic hijackings' or rejections. The 68ers took great pains to reconsider the methodological bases of (in their opinion) a too restricted view of a 'bourgeois' science that was unable to come to grips with the real macroproblems of society: exploitation of man by man, imperialism, environmental waste, and so on.[9]

In the wake of Albert Salomon (1945) and others, Weber was alleged to be an anti-Marxist thinker, whose work grew out of a long and intense dialogue with the ghost of Marx, a stumbling-block to every attempt to overthrow 'bourgeois' science. Yet, after the downfall of communism in the East, Marx is 'out'. Weber remains, and his renaissance is thus prolonged.[10]

The crisis of science – in a way a continuation of Troeltsch's 'problems of historicism' (see p. 11) – is by no means a new topic. In Germany after the First World War there was a vivid debate that had many parallels to the discussions in the late 1960s, questioning the limits of reason and/or rationality. These repeated identity crises embody the general contradiction between the Enlightenment and romanticism; the victorious progress of the Enlightenment being interrupted by romantic revolts. In examining basic methodological problems that are still unresolved today, he condensed intellectual currents of his own day in a way that induced later scholars to utilize his thought as points of departure; and this at a time when sociology was about to become established as an academic discipline in Germany, outside the hegemony of historicism.

The powerful revival of interest in Weber occurred in part because functionalism was somewhat erroneously assigned to him.[11] Functionalism was popularly perceived as the rival to historical materialism, as offering a comprehensive general theory of society. This is clearly seen in textbooks like W. G. Runciman's *Social Science and Political Theory* and in Nicos Poulantzas's main theoretical work *Pouvoir politique et classes sociales* (*Political Power and Social Classes*) (1968). Although Parsons – as well as his Marxist-inspired critics – are to blame for the un-Weberian undertone of the early debate, functionalism provided the opportunity for Marxists to scrutinize societies as a whole in an environment hostile to Marxism, in the form of criticism of Parsons (see p. 64).

One evident reason for Weber's slowly growing popularity is that many recurrent topics – 'eternals' – are obviously associated with him: politics as a means instead of an end; the theme of rationalization (i.e. the pessimistic view that it is the West's special destiny to trigger an irreversible process), narrowing our personal freedom in becoming subjects of rational calculation; the theme of the expected 'end of ideology'; social classes defined in terms of status and attitudes, or in terms of relation to the forces of production; bureaucratization and the tendency to regard control of the means of administration as more important than the control of the means of production; and – not to be forgotten – the ongoing discussion about whether social science is a normative or empirical undertaking, often focused on the 'positivist' distinction in Weber between fact and value – that is, his doctrine of scientific value relativism, to use a later term for Weber's often misinterpreted position.

Weber's legacy remains to be divided among his principal heirs. He is still the victim of 'creative interpretations', both because of his great prestige as a scholar of remarkable scope and independence and because of his 'multidimensionality' (Alexander 1983). Differences of interpretation are also at the heart of the approaches of the inter-preters themselves, insofar as they draw on Weber's authority, which is the case for most of the present-day influential social science paradigms.

Weber is the most quoted classic after Karl Marx. However, Weber's writings have not been subjected to the same sort of exege-sis and do not have the same canonical status as do Marx's to some of his followers. Weber never founded a school, nor has there been a continuous tradition to facilitate his integration into later approaches. Indeed, even when Weber is built into their very foun-dations, as in the cases of Parsons and Schutz (1932), it tends to take the form of a 'had Weber only fully realized' claim to rectify and fulfil the intentions of the master. Weber is actually still very much alive in the methodological debate, since several contributions to it are evaluations of Weber's utility as an up-to-date guide for current social science procedure (Oakes 1987, 1988; Runciman 1972). In the Anglo-Saxon sphere there has been a lasting interest in Weber's methodology. In Germany the role of Weber's methodology for a *Gesamtdeutung* of his *œuvre* has been one of the controversial topics under scrutiny.[12] Various scholars aim to return the 'foreign', out-of-context Weber to his genuine intellectual realm, although no con-sensus has been established on how to accomplish this. Moreover, my suggestion that Weber 'won' the controversy over method on behalf of the 'theoretical' side is, in the German setting, more controversial than in the Anglo-Saxon countries. Furthermore, it is doubtful that the ensuing demise of the historicist hegemony was Weber's inten-tion. Just as Luther intended only to renew the Catholic Church, Weber wanted to contribute to the realignment of historicism, not to its end; as Tenbruck (1987) has hinted, the rational ideal-type was already immanent in Weber's 'Critique of Meyer' (1906) – or even immanent in Meyer himself.[13]

Ulrich Beck once remarked: 'Max Weber not only laid down the foundations for sociology, but he will also survive sociology' (*FAZ*, 19 Oct. 1988). Sociology has a retrospective reading of Weber built into its very identity, while contextual readings result rather in a stress on Weber as a historicist among historicists, renovating the methodology of historicism. Although sociology might be a correlate to the need for social technology and planning in a capitalist class society, Weber has a broader relevance for the destiny of Western culture and the predicament of modernity. Weber is himself a 'presentist', although we retrospectively have to interpret him in his historical context. He thought that his ideas would be superseded by the infinite progress of science.

Although contextualism promotes a better pursuit of intellectual history, it brings with it the risk of a contextual reductionism that violates the scientific core of primacy for the argument, inviting us to mistake origin for validity. Weber's work arose in a dialogue with his contemporaries over contemporary problems. 'Weber's methodology is a criticism of contemporary science' (Lepsius 1977: 112). He is more a mediator than a genuine classic. He still seems to address us today, especially now that we are back in a situation rather similar to the one before 1914. This calls for a balanced account.

We cannot fully regain Weber and his context – and if we could why should we? His lingering relevance depends upon 'contact' with perennial and crucial paradigmatic divides, such as value intrusion and objectivity; nevertheless the proper interpretation of his contribution calls for a recontextualization of his problem horizon and original sources of inspiration.

In the next section the paradigmatic bias of three prominent interpretations – and extensions – of Weber is demonstrated.

Talcott Parsons: Weber as a Macro-Sociologist

Background

Talcott Parsons has done more for the reception of Weber in America than anybody else. He is responsible for the tendency to identify Weber with sociology and to emphasize WuG (although on weak grounds) as Weber's main work (the first part of which Parsons translated together with A. M. Henderson), which became a canonical text in theoretical sociology.

The reception of Weber really got under way after the Second World War, with translations of his methodology (Shils and Finch 1949) and readers (Gerth and Mills 1948; orig. 1946, with the much used introduction, written mainly by Gerth). Although some intellectual immigrants (Sorokin and Schumpeter in particular) had brought Weber across the ocean in their luggage, it was Parsons's huge volume on Weber, the second volume (in the 1968 paperback edition, which is probably the most commonly used one) in his *The Structure of Social Action*, that was the dominant influence.[14] Even in the recent renaissance of interest in Weber, many studies aim at correcting or extending the image created by Parsons, who was so influential on the American scene for decades.

Parsons arrived in Heidelberg a few years after Weber's death. He had some first-hand knowledge of the European classics; his doctoral degree at the University of Heidelberg in the late 1920s focused on the genesis of modern capitalism, a topic that brought him in touch with Sombart, Marx and Weber (documented in Parsons 1970 and 1965).[15] Indeed, in his 'Introduction' to Weber's *The Theory of Social and Economic Organization* (1947: 6) he writes that, after an early contact with historical materialism, Weber 'soon recoiled from this, becoming convinced of the indispensability of an important role of "ideas" in the explanation of great historical processes'. This misinterpretation of Weber (and Marx), which tells us more about Parsons's own views than Weber's, is not representative of his Weber conception as a whole, but is rather a reflection of the ideological climate in which Parsons's macrosociology became almost a 'stand-in' for Marxism and criticizing his system became a surrogate for Marxist analysis. Parsons has become a natural and popular target for criticism (we need only note the attempts at 'de-Parsonizing Weber' – e.g., Cohen, Hazelrigg and Pope 1975). Although he is a more subtle and thorough scholar than his critics are apt to admit, Parsons is still partly responsible for the lingering American habit of reading Weber without regard to his relation to Marxism.[16]

Parsons's perspective is rooted in an American middle-class conception of stratification, and the structures and hierarchies of the old Europe are continuously watered down; the *Stände* (classes) of the old estates society become 'status groups', and *Herrschaft* (rule, power) becomes 'authority'. In the same vein, the irresolvable tensions between the different value-orders that are such a marked feature of Weber's methodology (*Wissenschaftslehre*) are resolved by Parsons into workable social scientific methods. The crude realities of Weber's sociology of domination are assimilated by Parsons to conform to the political and cultural affinities of mid-twentieth century America.[17]

But Parsons is no vulgar anti-materialist. He has, rather, an ambiguous role in inhibiting the theoretical integration of historical materialism into Western social science. There is an ideological background of anti-Marxism to be found in the 1930s (Gouldner 1970: 149–50), when depression facilitated the spread of Marxism and a turning to Europe for remedies and ideologically convenient alternatives. The ideological context is of course part of Parsons's

disposition towards system-maintenance and his often criticized har-
monizing tendency (emphasis on stability, revolutionary movements
seen as 'dysfunctional', etc.). Something genuinely Weberian is
lost when Weber's cultural value-relativism is built into a system of
value-integration.

Parsons cannot be reduced to a mere ideologist; he is too profound.
The ideological factor alone cannot explain his influence, and his
interpretations deserve serious contemplation. Although the sort of
flaws we find are similar in character to those of other paradigmatic
interpretations, the difference is that Parsons has been more successful and his image of Weber has carried the Weberian legacy for several
decades, through its integration into the foundations of sociology.
Moreover, the Parsonsian tradition is still viable, not only in the
United States, but also in Germany, where Wolfgang Schluchter,
Richard Münch, Niklas Luhmann – and to a surprising extent also
Habermas (see for instance Alexander 1983: 281) – have developed
their theories from Parsons.

Parsons's approach

Although Parsons contributed to the oversimplified dichotomy of
idealist *vs* materialist explanations of the origin of modern capitalism, it is to his own classic, *The Structure of Social Action*, that we
must look to gauge his decisive influence on Weberology. This book
reveals Parsons's own structural-functionalism, and Weber's writings
are appropriated as part of the foundations of this highly influential
tradition. 'Parsons's conceptual and theoretical effort to restore the
connection between the increasingly differentiated social-behavioural
sciences is unparalleled by any other contemporary. He created a
framework for the analysis of social organizational processes in the
broadest sense that places more different organizational processes
(psychological as well as cultural and social) on the same theoretical
map than any other existing scheme' (Martel 1979: 614).[18] Martel
continues: 'He has also broken through numerous philosophical and
disciplinary barriers, and has succeeded remarkably in forging a
bridge between science and history as well as between positivism and
idealism' (ibid.: 619). In the histories of American sociology, considerable space is always dedicated to Parsons's approach and his role
as a bridge-builder.[19]

In *The Structure of Social Action* Parsons formulates a synthesis
of four dominant European classics: Wilfredo Pareto, Max Weber,
Emile Durkheim and the economist Alfred Marshall. Parsons claims

a convergence of their theoretical frameworks, writing that 'in the works of the four principal writers here treated there has appeared the outline of what, *in all essentials*, is the *same* system of generalized social theory, the structural aspect of what has been called the voluntaristic theory of action' (1968: 719–20).

'The final chapter of *The Structure of Social Action* maps an approach for future work in line with the common directions that Parsons identified in his sources. . . . This approach derives directly from Weber's "action framework", which sought a grounding for the comparative analysis of large-scale institutions, conceptually anchored in individually motivated acts' (Martel 1979: 614). So far the intentions of Parsons and Weber are well attuned. However, Weber was sceptical of the functionalism of his own time, against which he had turned in his methodological essays, and the concept of a comprehensive 'system' was alien to him. This becomes an anomaly for Parsons in drawing on Weber for the development of his own conceptual scheme, and the construction of the structural functional paradigm involves Parsons in a degree of selectivity that amounts to violence upon the body of Weber's works.[20]

The fundamental elements in Parsons's general theory of action are his pattern variables for value-orientation and goal-attainment. Pattern variables form a value-orientation typology that could be understood as a formalization of Weber's cultural relativism. They are the origin of the mature social system; as Parsons writes: 'The most important thread of continuity lies, I think, in what came to be called the "pattern-variable" scheme' (1970: 842). Although there is a crucial link here, it appears in quite an un-Weberian guise when pattern variables are incorporated into the mature system approach. The attempt at incorporating Weber into a general theory of social action also means an adaptation of his concepts into a new – and, to Weber, rather alien – context.

Parsons's concentration on effectiveness is at the core of his approach, whether the goals are external or internal, and reflects the predominance Weber accorded to instrumental rationality (*Zweckrationalität*). In this we do have a genuine affinity between Weber and Parsons, and the role assigned to culture for normative orientation points very much in the same direction.[21]

Parsons's conception of Weber

The idea of social action as purposeful behaviour in terms of the self-understanding of the actors – as well as the actors' interpretation of other co-actors – is the basic point of departure for both Parsons and Weber. Yet in the very title of the Parsons–Henderson translation of part I of *WuG* as 'The Theory of Social and Economic Organization' there is a certain bias towards stressing the theoretical streak in Weber: 'theory' is not a headline likely to be endorsed by Weber himself. Weber writes that his ambition is to develop *Begriffsdefinitionen* (definitions of concepts), in the hope that 'sie in zweckmäßiger und etwas korrekter. . . . Ausdrucksweise formulieren, was jede empirische Soziologe tatsächlich meint' (It attempts only to formulate what all empirical sociologists really mean, *WuG*: 1). At the beginning of the second chapter Weber is even more explicit: 'Nachstehend soll keinerlei Wirtschaftstheorie betrieben werden, sondern es sollen lediglich einige weiterhin oft gebrauchte Begriffe definiert und gewisse allereinfachste soziologische Beziehungen innerhalb der Wirtschaft festgestellt werden.' ('What follows is not intended in any sense to be "economic theory". Rather, it consists only in an attempt to define certain concepts which are frequently used and to analyze certain of the simplest sociological relationships in the economic sphere', *WuG*: 31; *E & S*: 61; Weber 1947: 158.)[22] Parsons's title seems to promise more than the original ever intended. Weber's modest ambition was to clarify a procedure already in use in a way that might be instrumental for practitioners in the field and to outline some elementary sociological definitions. He explicitly states that theory is not a concern of his (see Erdelyi 1992 and in particular 1993).

Also Gisela Hinkle (1986) has scrutinized the art of misrepresentation by translation that Parsons stands for and even makes sociology – at least the powerful tradition of 'analytical positivism' – rest upon the foundation of an erroneous reading of Weber.

On the very first page in the Parsonsian version, Weber writes – in a different key: 'Sociology is a science which attempts the interpretative understanding of social action in order thereby to arrive at a causal explanation of its course and effects' (Weber 1947: 88; 'course and consequences' in Parsons 1968: 4). In Weber's case, 'causal' is a term that has to be filled in with content in order to gain meaning: the immediate associations are more far-reaching than Weber's text really allows.[23] Weber's views on causality are an 'iceberg', with much to be discovered beneath the surface.[24] Once more the importance of language is illustrated. Parsons as a translator must render such concepts as *Sinnzusammenhang* and *adäquate Verursachung* into comprehensive English, which is simply not possible. Mathematicians and musicians might have a common language, but not social scientists.

No one explored such a theoretical line in his interpretation of Weber as did Parsons. This is clear in *The Structure*, where we can read:

> Empirically his [Weber's] main attack was on Marxian historical materialism which, as has been shown, constituted, analytically considered, in essentials a version of the utilitarian position, placed in a historical context. Over against this he placed a theory of the role of value elements in the form of a combination of religious interests, e.g., value attitudes, in their relation to systems of metaphysical ideas. This was, however, placed in the context of a voluntaristic theory of action. (Parsons 1968: 715)

Although it is not incorrect to read Weber as a proponent of the normative action approach, this is more Parsons than Weber. Parsons's stress on the value-system is pronounced, both in his interpretation of Weber's so-called Calvinist thesis as well as in his methodological reading of Weber's ideal-type procedure. His version of Weberian social action theory reflects the belief in the causal adequacy of normative (often religiously oriented) action.

There *is* a stress on cultural values as selection criteria in Weber's value-oriented conceptualization. There is also a certain affinity on this point between Weber and Parsons's voluntaristic action theory and pattern variables for normative orientation. However, 'culture', which has a rather specific meaning when used by Weber, is given a more systematic twist in Parsons's extension. Even if Parsons's exposition of Weber has a broad handbook quality, it seems to focus upon Weber's methodology pure and simple, as well as its substantive application in the sociology of religion. But 'the admirable clarity in places' (Sica 1988: 131 n. 67) is combined with some less accurate elements, owing to a selective utilization of sources.

Parsons deals at length with Weber's methodological background, distinguishing between the 'idealist' and the 'positivist' as the dominant traditions in post-Enlightenment Germany. He emphasizes that Weber's main training as a scholar lay in the German historical school of jurisprudence and economics as they stood towards the end of the nineteenth century. Weber's thrust was to rebuild these foundations as a firmer basis for his historical-sociological investigations (Parsons 1936: 675 *et passim*).

Parsons distinguishes between two variations in the historicist branch – the 'intuitionists' and 'objectivists' – which from the 1880s on were important currents in the famous – and to Weber most important – controversy over method, between German historicism and Austrian marginalism, i.e. between history and theory. As Parsons sees it, both traditions are empiricist:

> Common ground for both is the denial that the sociocultural sciences can make use of 'general laws' of the logical character of those occupying unquestioned status in the natural sciences. The difference of the two schools is over what they consider to be the reasons for this alleged fact. Weber's quarrel with both is essentially over this issue. He still holds to the distinction of the natural and social sciences, but radically denies that it can rest on the exclusion from the latter of general explanatory concepts. (1968: 580–1)

Intuitionists and objectivists are united in their reluctance to search for theoretical laws. Although the atheoretical bias is the central feature of the German historicism that was then dominant, it is characteristic of Parsons's views that almost everybody qualifies as an empiricist.

In his review of von Schelting's (1934) classical study on Weber's ideal-type methodology, Parsons widened his perspective:

> The German 'historical' methodologies, going back as they did to an idealistic philosophical basis, created a deep gulf between the logic of the natural and the historical social sciences. The net effect of Weber's methodological work has been to go a long way toward bridging this gulf. The principal means of building the bridge has been the insistence, not only on the necessary role of general theoretical conceptualization, but on the abstractness of this theory in the case of both groups of sciences. So long as this is not realized, the obvious concrete differences between their subject matters tend to force the methodologist into maintaining an untenable logical distinction between the sciences. (Parsons 1936: 678)

'General explanatory concepts' and 'general theoretical conceptualization' appear frequently as key terms in Parsons's text, although they are somewhat flexibly applied. Moreover, Parsons draws on Weber in a way that makes him almost appear as a fellow spokesman for the unity-of-science ideal, which is indeed an oversimplification. Parsons even regards the positivists as empiricists, when he discusses them in terms of 'the fallacy of misplaced concreteness' and 'the reification of theoretical concepts'. This has to be understood as a manifestation of the epistemological tendency to identify theoretically deduced propositions with reality itself; it also reflects the Parsonsian tendency to ascribe explanatory power to general theory in its conceptual phase.

Parsons refers to the diehard position of the leading historicist (Schmoller) in the controversy over method. He seems well aware of the significance to Weber's method of this voluminous debate. Moreover, Parsons is evidently also well aware of the interdependence between Weber's ideal-type and subjectivist economics and marginalism, as expressed by Menger and others: 'Weber himself was fond of using the general concepts of orthodox economic theory as an example' and 'this example is taken from the field of the social sciences and involves *Verstehen*, which Weber regarded as essential to the ideal type' (Parsons 1968: 606). So far, Parsons is not an incorrect but still a misleading guide.

Parsons notes that Weber certainly 'repudiated the desire to set up a 'system' of scientific theory' but goes on to state his own ambition to stress those very elements in Weber which are in line with his own macrotheoretical approach. In Parsons's view, Weber is, so to speak, taken to task when he does not go far enough in 'a priori theorizing'. In a characteristic passage Parsons writes: 'Though he "hid his light under a bushel" its author [Weber] will unquestionably rank among the select few who have in a scientific sense been genuinely eminent theorists in the social field' (in Weber 1947: 7). Parsons's conception of Weber gradually emerges as biased by his own paradigm-building efforts, that is, his vested interest in a theoretical reading of Weber, oriented towards structural functionalism.

'Weber's essential starting point is an acceptance of the subjective point of view, combined with a critical attack on the "historical" position. His basic thesis in this connection is that generalized theoretical categories are as essential to the proof of causal relationships in the human and cultural field as they are in the natural sciences' (ibid.: 9). This formulation contains two overstatements. Weber was hardly attacking his fellow historicists, although he was critical of their position. By 'generalized theoretical categories', Parsons alludes to the schemes of proof provided by the model of rational economic actors, with the help of which real action could be compared in an intersubjective manner, thus allowing for some sort of 'testability'. The somewhat exaggerated characterization of those categories as 'generalized theoretical' is even more clear when he goes on to develop his views of 'the kind of generalized theoretical concepts to which he [Weber] paid the most attention, the "ideal type"' (ibid.: 10): 'Weber laid great emphasis in his earlier methodological work on the fact that proof of causal relationship in any scientific field involved reference, explicitly or implicitly, to the same logical scheme of proof' (ibid.: 11). Again we encounter the slight transformation of original intention through translation. Indeed Weber differs favourably from his colleagues in his attempts to promote *rationale Evidenz* in order to increase the validity of scientific proposals by using 'reality' as some sort of 'last instance' criterion. Yet, 'logical scheme of proof' has a more neo-positivist tone than is warranted by Weber. It is *not* an incorrect or erroneous translation; it only stretches the intention a bit far in retrospect. The 'logical scheme of proof' – correctly – is there, in the form of the rational type, but 'causal relationship in any scientific field' does not sound quite like Weber, whose ideal-type, after all, originated as a means to account for historical events.

Parsons understood the ideal-type from a genetic perspective, asserting that 'The most fruitful way to get at Weber's approach to the concept of ideal-type is to do so in terms of the polemical situation in which he was placed' (1968: 602). Parsons further characterizes the 'theoretically conceived pure type of subjective meaning' as follows: 'This pure type, which is generally known as the "ideal type", was the first and most obvious level of generalized abstract concept which Weber's analysis encountered, the concept which, while meeting the logical requirements of the scheme of proof, was closest to the concrete individual reality'; furthermore: 'there is no doubt [!] that the rational ideal type is an authentic generalized theoretical concept.' There is something in this, at least for that variant of the ideal-type that is modelled after 'rational economic actors' – and that type is the most significant one. Although I share Parsons's general line of interpretation, it still appears to me that he overestimates Weber's theoretical element in a 'symptomal reading'; that is, he becomes a victim of what Quentin Skinner characterized as the 'myth of doctrines': that in the era of conceptual realism and essentialism in which Weber wrote, even a rather modest act of 'transparent', lucid abstraction is a vindication of secular theory, 'theoretical generalization'. Weber represents only the first step in such a direction. Moreover, the rational type is only one of several variations. True, it is a possible vehicle – a heuristic tool – for theoretical propositions, designed to meet rational criteria of proof, and it is also a manifestation of general theory in the sense that it presupposes a special anthropology, a rational inclination in humans.

Although one cannot really blame Parsons, he does overstress those elements in Weber that support the construction of the Parsonsian system.[25] But when we turn back to Weber, the issue of 'testability' has to be seen as achieving the correct balance between *Verstehen* and *Erklären*, between the demands of the special status of cultural expression and the demands of scientific confirmation and evaluation. Within the hermeneutical tradition of Dilthey with its emphasis on empathy (an imbalance repeated in the succeeding school of the phenomenology of Schutz and his pupils; see p. 75ff) the place of evidence and intersubjectivity was for Weber unjustifiably excluded.

The ideal-type of rational action does not fully solve the problem of testability, but it does at least provide the possibility of intersubjectivity, since it has a logically calculable structure: instrumental means–ends rationality which both requires logical consistency and enables testability. This is all correctly observed by Parsons.[26] However, the tension between 'ideal-type' and 'theory', although obvious enough to us, is not registered by Parsons. There is an ambiguity in his interpretation: Parsons takes the ideal-type as a prototype for his own constructions, yet at the same time criticizes it for not being sufficient as the starting point for a 'generalized system'.[27] 'For this purpose [the generalizing approach], they must be arranged and classified in a definite order of relationship. Only then will they have highly generalized significance on either a theoretical or an empirical level' (Parsons 1948: 91). The more Parsons becomes a system theorist, the more Weber is excluded.

Parsons's concept of theory and explanation

In order to understand the paradigmatic specificity (bias) of Parsons's interpretation or rather extension of Weber, it is not enough simply to know the basics about Parsons and his scholarly ambitions. Parsons's understanding of the ideal-type must naturally also be understood against the background of his own way of understanding 'theory' and 'explanation'. In *The Structure*, Parsons touches upon this in an extensive footnote:

> there are two different possible meanings of the term 'theory' which are often confused. On the one hand, we speak of the total explanation of a given concrete phenomenon, a historical individual or class of them, as a 'theory', thus a 'theory of eclipses' or Weber's own 'theory of modern capitalism'. On the other hand, we may apply the term to systems of general concepts as such, thus the 'Newtonian physics' or the 'classical economics'. Weber points out quite correctly that a theory in the second sense cannot by *itself* explain a *single* empirical fact. It requires *data* which are always empirically unique, are part of a concrete historical individual, for any concrete explanation or prediction. (Parsons 1968: 598; compare also Parsons in Stammer 1965)

Parsons recognizes traditional historical and idiographical theory, where the purpose is to explain unique events by identifying and accounting for as many contributing factors as possible. However, and this is an alternative that Parsons prefers, theory might well also mean systems of general concepts, under which singular events are to be subsumed. However, he is clearly aware that nothing could be explained without data; indeed there would not be anything to be explained without them.[28]

Functionalism in its Parsonsian form tends to become more of a 'language' or common framework than an explanatory theory, which is at one with the tendency to identify theory with systems of general concepts. It would be more conventional, consequently more communicatively rational, to connect the concept of theory with the concepts of law and/or explanation. And sometimes it is even claimed that functionalism does not explain at all but only describes phenomena in terms of its own conceptual apparatus; thus, it is not only a language, it is an esoteric language.

The need to underpin further the macrotheoretical creed and its way of regarding causal relations as something abstract with a somewhat mediated relation to particular empirical facts might be negligible in Parsons's case. It is his most striking feature. In 1964 he delivered a lecture at Heidelberg on 'Causal Explanation and Generalized Theory', an address on Weber's theme of 'Value-freedom and Objectivity':

> Causal explanation, in turn, is simply not possible unless the particular facts are related, not merely in an historical sequence, but through analysis by means of a generalized theoretical scheme which is in the nature of the case abstract. Very bluntly, the conception of generalized *theory* as has been developed in the great tradition of the natural sciences is an essential component of *all* empirical science. This includes not merely definitions of generalized concepts, and classificatory schemes, but substantive propositions about the *relations* among abstractly defined variables. (Parsons, in Stammer 1965: 48; p. 35 in the English translation)

Parsons is here awfully close to blurring the basic distinction between theory and model, since the relations he speaks of could have numerical values (data) attached to them. Parsons here leaves room for interpretations of his system as characterized by a Platonic love of theory, which favours abstract models.

In sum, Parsons's studies in Germany in the 1920s generated sympathy for Weber as a source for challenging the dominance of behaviourism, the tradition of 'inductive' (in the 1920s a common term for useful social statistics) social research. But Parsons's ambition to develop his own alternative of structural functionalism results in a theoretical overinterpretation that appears to go beyond Weber's horizons, to become a Procrustean bed, less sensitive to Weber's own context and intentions.

Although there are some obvious affinities between Weberian 'action theory' (instrumental means–end analyses guided by 'top-values') and Parsons's pattern variables, these are exaggerated in Parsons's AGIL-system[29] and structural functionalism, in which the Weberian anguish of polytheism is lost. Parsons's interpretation is subverted into a paradigmatically biased and only partial retrieval. He saves Weber for the sociological enterprise in a way that obscures a genuine contextual interpretation of Weber's work between history and sociology. Parsons's attempt retrospectively to build Weber into the self-consciousness of the discipline of sociology can be criticized for 'extending' or 'extrapolating' Weber in his own direction by means of erroneous translations.[30]

Alfred Schutz: Weber as a 'Hermeneutic'

Influences and 'sea change'

Alfred Schutz[31] was forced to leave Vienna when Nazism and anti-Semitism became a threat to the Jewish population. He settled in New York in 1939, after a year in Paris, and became associated with the New School for Social Research, known as the 'university in exile' (especially its graduate faculty, which has been an important way-station for European intellectuals and their thought).[32] Many immigrants in the intellectual diaspora felt alienated and rootless in the United States. The attitude of the cultivated German bourgeoisie (*Bildungsbürgertum*) did not go down well with the Americans, who mistook it for arrogance.[33] Schutz, however, somehow came to terms with the predicament of intellectual migration and modern America, or at least New York. He retained his profession as a banker even after becoming affiliated with the New School, which was mainly organized as an evening school. In fact, his transfer to the New World was comparatively smooth, since he was able to keep his bourgeois job. Schutz was throughout his life primarily a private scholar, although from 1952 onwards he was a full professor at the New School until his untimely death in 1959.

In Vienna Schutz had enjoyed early contacts with Austrian marginalism, Ludwig von Mises being one of his teachers. The Vienna circle in philosophy was of course another major intellectual influence. He was also in touch with Hans Kelsen and through Kelsen's philosophy of law he also came into contact with Max Weber's methodology (Grathoff 1978: esp. p. 389). There is a strong natural affinity between Kelsen's legal philosophy and Weber's philosophy of value, both of which are basically anti-natural law. It must be kept in mind that Schutz strongly adheres to some of Weber's basic propositions about methodological individualism and the objectivity of social science – as well as the subject matter of sociology as the interpretation of interaction between humans. As a variation of Weberian *verstehende Soziologie*, however, Schutz's attempt ends where Parsons's starts.[34]

Schutz's early main theoretical work, *Der sinnhafte* [meaningful] *Aufbau der sozialen Welt. Eine Einleitung in die verstehende Soziologie* (1932; English translation 1967), should not only be read in relation to Dilthey, but as a paraphrase of Carnap's *Der logische* [logical] *Aufbau der Welt*. Schutz's polemical front is against positivism, which cannot catch our experienced social reality in either its nomothetic or empiricist mode. Since Weber remains a Diltheyian in the matter of how to argue for the specificity of the cultural sciences, he appears as a natural point of departure for an anti-positivist social action paradigm. However, Weber remains a 'positivist', in the sense that he simultaneously wished to satisfy as many unified-science criteria of proof as possible.

Schutz's work – like Weber's – has been to a large extent published posthumously with Berger and Luckmann serving as main guardians of his intellectual estate.[35] His position as both a banker and a scholar might have impeded his intellectual productivity, contributing to a certain unorthodoxy in his thought. As Grathoff (1978b: 389–90) points out, Schutz's work did not really emanate from the realm of academic institutions or seminars but kept its distance from the Vienna schools (for example, Lazarsfeld's empirical sociology). Schutz seems somewhat remote from empirical social research; he rather avoids it. He states that from early on his intellectual interest was in the philosophical bases of social science and that from the very beginning he was under Weber's spell, as he conceived of him. Schutz felt that although Weber had created the tools for concrete research, the main problem – the understanding of the subjective meanings of a social act to the agents themselves – still demanded a philosophical foundation.[36]

Phenomenology and intersubjectivity

In the search for these philosophical foundations of interpretative sociology Schutz was brought into contact with the works of Husserl, with whose work the term 'phenomenology' in its modern variant was originally associated.[37] Descartes posed the epistemological problem of solipsism, as later philosophy would label it: how does one know anything at all beyond one's own reflecting mind? Is any mutual understanding possible? Although the problem of intersubjectivity is Descartian in origin, it gained new significance in modern Weberian social science. Kant developed the problem of mind *vs* empirical reality, which raises the problem of the nature of concepts, essences or constructs. Weber's sociological synthesis of scientific criteria and the method of understanding was an attempt to purify social science of the intrusion of metaphysics, while seeking to interpret interaction between humans. Weber solved the epistemological problem of intersubjective concept-formation by way of a short cut that avoids the basic philosophical aspects. Schutz and Husserl, by contrast, wished to solve the problem through the notion of *Lebenswelt* (life-world), haunted by the problem of the stature of the conceptual scheme as reflecting genuine or imaginary mental structures.

Phenomenology, or descriptive psychology as it was characterized in its early European version, seeks to establish intersubjectively valid understanding between the ego ('me') and the Other. This fundamental epistemological problem offers several options. One 'primrose path' to a solution is to concentrate on the manifest expression ('behaviour') of social acts, not on the meaning aspect. If one regards understanding the meaning of action as an indispensable part of social science, a conflict arises between scientific evidence and true understanding. Another course would be to construct some schemes in terms of which acts could be rendered meaningful. In empathetic ways of understanding, alternatively, the actor might provide methods to account for the motives – conscious or not – guiding the subjective acts. In the case where the aim is to understand rather than explain, the choice is between *rationales* or *einfühlendes Verstehen* (rational or empathetic understanding), depending on the different sorts of proof that go with either undertaking. *Rationale Evidenz* (rational proof) offers a possible bridge between understanding and explanation. To Weber, rational motives could supply a cause of social action, even when we lack empathetic understanding ('We don't have to be Caesar in order to understand Caesar'; 'Logic of the Cultural Sciences' 1906). Rationality is simply presupposed, as in the case of modern marginalist economics, for the cultural relevance it might have.

Schutz does not get on this 'train', but rather remains on the platform, contemplating the philosophical bases and the options for establishing a mutual understanding transcending the Cartesian lone-

liness of the soul. Schutz tries to solve the intersubjectivity problem
by a quite different route. This is the central paradigmatic difference.
It is also the element in Weber that Schutz fatally misinterprets. The
task of phenomenology is to find the corresponding intersubjective
point of reference for the empathetic procedure; according to Husserl,
to find the way from firm intersubjectivity to the structures of the
life-world. Pure empathy must solve the intersubjectivity problem in
a way that is intersubjective. There seems to be an element of mutual
trust involved in the procedure. We might note that the same problem
goes for Austrian marginalism, if it is conceived of as a theory rather
than as a model with heuristic functions. Marginalist economic acts
could be and often were explained in psychological terms; they were
thus grounded in the individual's perception as opposed to the attribution of rationality that Weber insisted upon. Schutz's insistence on
'true' intersubjectivity has a different emphasis from Weber's concept
and could well incorporate the same elements as Weber's synthesis.

Schutz's importance is partly a result of his synthesis of central
continental elements and American pragmatist philosophy (William
James), which is displayed in his later American career. His main
problem is the perennial one of how to take the step from subjective
understanding of meaning to objective understanding of meaning.
This is, moreover, the basic problem of the phenomenological
approach as such, and is methodologically conceived of as the
problem of intersubjectivity.[38]

The intersubjectivity problem is the basic difficulty and obstacle to
phenomenological attempts at the scientific establishment of explanation. Schutz wrestled with it throughout most of his scholarly life.
Husserl had looked for a solution in *Lebenswelt* as a source of firm
reference, going back to Dilthey and other idealist philosophers in
the hermeneutic tradition. Later generations in the Anglo-Saxon
sphere speak of life structures and the 'sociology of everyday life',
which has been *à la mode* since the 1970s.[39] Their hope is that
reference to more elementary experiences of everyday life might
provide us with the Archimedian fixed point that saves us from solipsism and relativism.[40] To me this is a bold but not convincing attempt
to overcome a perennial paradigmatic divide.[41]

Modern phenomenology is often crudely conceived of as an anti-
behaviouristic, 'soft'-data approach. In a way that is true – but the
opposites here are very close. There is in fact a clearly atheoretical
vein in phenomenological research, the aim of which often appears
to be the exploration through experimental techniques of the 'least
common denominator' of transcultural understanding ('so that even
a Chinese would understand', to borrow Weber's dictum, from

one of his polemical methodological essays). 'Objective' meaning ought to be accessible to everybody – not specific to a culture. Phenomenologists face the risk of ending up with trivial everyday-life experiences as points of reference for the empathetic, interpretative understanding they strive for, such as our basic physiological functions, tiredness, hunger, and so on. In such cases not much progress is made, as compared with the naturalistic approach; phenomenology is after all striving for the transcendence of behaviourism, going for the 'inner' understanding of the subjective point of view. If true mutual understanding between ego and other is merely restricted to such things as the immediate mutual understanding of expressions like 'Excuse me. You are standing on my toes' – implying by this that the person addressed should cease standing on one's toes – the interpretative ambition is watered down. Any loud expression of being acutely hurt would fulfil the same function, and we would not be close to any meaningful cultural understanding.[42] The phenomenologists are obsessed with combining the subjective point of view of the actor with an intact intersubjectivity. Their basic epistemological problem is that the testability of naturalism in its various forms should correspond to a higher degree of cultural significance.[43]

Schutz's conception of Weber

Among Schutz's work, *Der sinnhafte Aufbau der sozialen Welt* from the early 1930s must be seen as the basic document; it reveals his sources, probably more explicitly than his followers today are quite happy about. Weber is the starting point for Schutz's discussion of the prospects of social action theory.[44] Weber is introduced in its first lines:

> The present study is based on an intensive concern of many years' duration with the theoretical [*wissenschaftstheoretische*] writings of Max Weber. During this time I became convinced that while Weber's approach was correct and that he had determined conclusively the proper starting point of the philosophy of the social sciences, nevertheless his analyses did not go deeply enough to lay the foundations on which alone many important problems of the human sciences could be solved. Above all, Weber's central concept of subjective meaning calls for thoroughgoing analysis. As Weber left this concept, it was little more than a heading for a number of important problems which he did not examine in detail, even though they were hardly foreign to him. (Schutz 1974: 9)

Weber's methodology was both the starting point and the vehicle for Schutz's own reflections. He never really challenged Weber's view that social science should be value-free and 'objective'. Schutz's programme maintains a 'scientistic' stance, as revealed for instance in his assertion that the social science method is 'a set of rules for scientific procedure equally valid for all empirical sciences whether they deal with objects of nature or with human affairs' (here quoted from Bernstein 1978: 137). It is a matter of interpretation and dispute, however, whether Schutz's criticism and elaboration of Weber makes sense – as an interpretation – and whether his approach to meet the requirements of scientific criteria through his *Soziologie des Alltags* is a viable alternative or a dead end.

The concept of action constitutes a problem of intersubjectivity which is not really manifest as long as we are satisfied with the study of behaviour. Schutz does not neglect this problem, although his approach to its solution appears scientifically obscure, giving primacy to empathy rather than proof. In the early passages of *Der sinnhafte Aufbau* we find a presentation of Weber's sociology of action. Schutz accounts for the common distinction between manifest and teleological *Verstehen*, or – in Weber's terminology – *aktuelles* and *erklärendes Verstehen*. According to Schutz, Weber's account of the distinction between real and self-conceived motives is unsatisfactory, obscured in the broad category of explanatory understanding. We cannot be sure that the alleged context of meaning is also truly valid to the actors themselves: 'Motivational understanding requires instead a certain amount of knowledge of the actor's past and future', that is, his biography (Schutz 1974: 37; translation from Giddens 1974: 36).[45]

Schutz wishes to supplement Weber with a distinction between 'in order to' and 'because' motives. The latter refer to the previous experience of the actor. The former require some sort of 'project', an image of the future, preconceived by the creative actor – 'I take my umbrella in order to avoid getting wet, because I know that I get wet from exposure to rain'. The time aspect is thus crucial to Schutz. Schutz's terminology is confusing, since his 'because' motives are easily associated with the restrictions of natural science imposed upon the teleological realm, whereas in his own conception it is really a distinction *within* that very realm; naturalistic factors rather being present merely as projections, via their effects on the experiences of the actors, reduced to *Sinnzusammenhang* (context of meaning).[46]

According to Schutz, Weber's two types of *Verstehen* should both be ranged within an objective context of meaning, that is, independent of the individual actor or observer. Schutz implies that Weber took a short cut through the field of problems in which Schutz himself was to remain all his life. This, however, is a misinterpretation of Weber, since it implies that Weber wanted to solve the intersubjectivity problem of empathetic understanding. In actuality Weber chose another route to intersubjectivity that claimed primacy over 'true' empathetic mutual understanding. Weber's alternative road to intersubjectivity via the rational variation of the ideal-type must have appeared to Schutz as a surrender to the naturalist approach of focusing on the behavioural instead of the meaning aspect of action; a naturalist approach that abstained in the name of science from full mutual understanding. To Weber it is rather the reverse: through the rational, purposive actor model the scope of secularized valid knowledge could be enhanced, since proof was made possible.

The basic flaw in Schutz's conception of Weber is that, in line with his own paradigmatic inclinations, he conceives of Weber as being more aligned with a psychological, 'hermeneutical', empathetic, interpretative (Diltheyian) understanding than is in fact the case. Circumstantial evidence of this is the fact that Schutz's Weberian legacy does not go down well with Schutz's own followers, who even display a certain uneasiness over seeing Weber hailed as a paradigmatic authority. It is obvious in retrospect that Weber never quite bothered to penetrate the problems that the phenomenologists are obsessed with. In a way this was clear to Schutz himself, although he still tried in a paradigmatic reading to mend and annex Weber, to conquer his image instead of defying it.[47]

In harmony with his phenomenological paradigm,

> Schutz proscribed the implicit causal analysis incorporated in Weber's ideal-typical concepts. For Schutz, ideal-types are typified meanings, called 'cook-book knowledge' or common sense, used by actors to interpret action. According to Schutz, the contextual problem of action, implementing goals or values, led Weber to idealize actors. Actors in Weberian theory are fictitious 'puppets', responding automatically to theoretical concerns not evident in the naive attitude of everyday. (Zaret 1980: 1192)

The ideal-types could well be regarded as an attempt to structure the *Lebenswelt* of everyday life – but according to the Schutzeans the *Lebenswelt* is very subjective, which creates the acute intersubjectivity problem that Schutz never really transcends in a lucid way. Weber has a more sensible and less sensitive solution, which to the Schutzeans probably seems like Alexander's solution to the Gordian knot.

In some Weberian methodological essays there is good 'ammunition' for interpretations consistent with Schutzean intentions. However, there are also good reasons to plead for the rational type, whose basic significance Weber himself heavily and continuously stressed. It is not by chance that when Weber does develop the common-sense 'cook-book knowledge' that he shares with Schutz, he uses the same example as Schutz: the marginalist model of the rational economic actor. It does not occur to Schutz – with his hermeneutical 'blinkers' – that actors are not *merely* 'fictitious puppets', but rather correctly and instrumentally so, since Weber's purpose is not really unique understanding but comparison in order to catch deviations (from means–end rationality).[48] Schutz is caught in an impossible dilemma: his goal is to achieve unique empathetic understanding, which may be possible; however, in the nature of things it is simply not intersubjectively transferable to an objective investigator, who is almost by definition an 'outsider', an intruder, from the point of view of alter and ego.

Even if Weber and Schutz have an obvious common interest in intersubjectivity, they travel only some of the way together. Weber's route is more seminal for the accomplishment of intersubjective cumulative knowledge, accessible 'even to the Chinese', but at the price of giving up the Icarian ambition of full understanding. Empathy might be indispensable to the practising psychoanalyst but it is simply not compatible with the firm point of reference needed in universally valid science. The utilitarian model of the calculating rational economic actor, by contrast, could provide us with the Archimedian point required to advance from primitive cook-book knowledge. Schutz is more inclined to dwell in epistemological matters (How is knowledge possible?), while Weber is more methodological (How do we confirm scientific knowledge?).

There are several passages in Weber's work where his antipsychologism and low propensity for *Einfühlung* (empathetic understanding) or *Nacherleben* (reliving) is clearly exposed, in favour of the 'fictitious puppets' of his rational ideal-types (as Weber speaks about interpretative schemes in the Roscher and Knies essay: p. 189 in Oakes's translation (Weber 1975)) and the way 'following a rule' and calculability is developed in 'Critique of Stammler' (p. 128 *et passim* in Oakes's translation (Weber 1977)).[49] However, Schutz seems to deviate more from Weber's typological and non-empathetic understanding than did his original mentor Husserl, whose position is not quite lucid, but can seemingly be given a taxonomical twist (for the purpose of classification).[50] Weber's appreciating remarks about Husserl have a certain affinity with his reverence for Schmoller.

Weber's rebuttal of the position that cultural knowledge is immediate and for that reason valid indicates that the Husserl–Schutz track to proof is not a viable alternative to the Menger-inspired evidence offered by the rational ideal-type that Weber develops.

The Schutz–Parsons divide

In the late 1930s Schutz was asked by a fellow countryman, Friedrich von Hayek, to review Parsons's *The Structure of Social Action* for *Economica*. This led to a very interesting exchange of letters between Schutz and Parsons over several years. The total paradigmatic clash in these crossing monologues is striking.

Schutz – then a newly arrived immigrant – wanted to debate with Parsons, whose book had impressed him deeply. Parsons felt himself attacked and responded somewhat aggressively. Like Weber, Parsons had no interest in philosophical matters; they were rather to be avoided if possible: 'at a great many points you are interested in certain ranges of philosophical problems for their own sake which, quite self-consciously and with specific methodological justification, I have not treated' (quoted from Grathoff 1978: xi).[51]

The so-called Schutz–Parsons divide is well documented in the correspondence published by Grathoff (1978b). Briefly, Parsons believes that he is already engaged in social science, in accordance with the classical ideal, while Schutz still contemplates the most fundamental dilemmas, with the possibility of a social science still an open question:

> The *Cartesian dilemma*, i.e., the problem of intersubjectivity, is still the stumbling block on the way toward a solution. (Grathoff 1978b: 129)
>
> While the *Weberian Suggestion* directed methodological interest in the foundation of the social sciences toward the texture of social action, Talcott Parsons and Alfred Schutz pursued this suggestion in different directions. (ibid.: 127–8)
>
> Both insist that every study of social action must begin with the individual actor himself. While Parsons takes account of the individual actor in terms of situational references within action systems, Schutz insists that a grasp of the concrete actor and his performances, of his interests and motives should become accessible through the study of the structure of relevance in everyday life. (ibid.: 129)

In fact, it is difficult to imagine a clearer illustration of the incommensurability of social science paradigms.

To a considerable extent the Schutz–Parsons divide is also the Schutz–Weber divide. For Parsons the starting point is Weber's ideal-type, a procedure that Parsons believed had to be developed in the direction of general systems theory. For Schutz, Weber's ideal-type is a vehicle for a critique of how social actors take the world for granted, an ambition that owes more to Husserl than to Weber. That both Schutz and Parsons should claim Weber as integral to their respective projects once again shows both the force and shortcomings of a paradigmatic (rather than a contextualist) reading.[52]

In sum, Weber's alleged social action paradigm could indeed be developed in many ways. Parsons and Schutz both used Weber's ideal-type of rational action as the point of departure for their paradigms. Parsons's elaboration of Weber in the direction of a general theory of action stretches Weber's theoretical ambitions beyond the limits of the conceptual scheme for rational understanding that we find in his methodology, in the form of the ideal-type of rational action. Schutz criticizes Weber for insufficiently differentiating the vital concept of *Verstehen*, while Weber's specific solution to the problem of inter-subjectivity – *rationale Evidenz* integrated into the interpretative ideal-type – is denounced. Weber is interpreted – and criticized – as a fellow follower of the Diltheyian tradition of empathetic under-standing, which is merely *one* influence of many on Weber's ideal-type concept. The instance of intersubjectivity, which Schutz looked for in the *Lebenswelt*, Weber found – although transformed – in Menger and the Austrian economists.

In a formal sense both Schutz and Parsons build 'theories of social action', but they fill that concept with different content and address different problems. It is tempting to describe their monologues as reflecting the difference between philosophy and science. However, Schutz argues for the need to differentiate Weber's crude notion of *Verstehen*. This reflects a misinterpretation of Weber's intentions. Weber's concern was rational understanding in the form of unam-biguously explaining the instrumentality of an act – or its deviance from such means–ends rationality; in this it possibly transcends the horizon of the actor as well as his or her context. There are two sorts of interpretative understanding: rational understanding, allowing for *rationale Evidenz* (intersubjective proof) and empathetic (*einfühlen-des, nacherlebendes*) understanding (*Verstehen*). In the case of the latter, intersubjective proof is more problematic. Weber's rational ideal-type is certainly cut out for the former, non-psychologizing and non-introspective, route to intersubjectivity and the cumulation of objective[53] knowledge about human social intentional behaviour, while Schutz here remains within the hermeneutic tradition. Weber is much more a positivist (adherent of unified science) than Schutz realizes. In fact, there are some striking parallels between Weber's position and that of Karl Popper.[54] The rational choice between competing theoretical interpretations of human acts requires criteria of proof. There must be possibilities of falsification in order to discriminate between valid interpretations and pure esoterics (which might be 'intersubjective' in an illusory sense). Weber's methodological individualism means that the observable act of man provides that instance of proof.[55]

Lazarsfeld and Oberschall: Weber as an Empirical Social Scientist

Background

Paul Lazarsfeld has been hailed by friends and foes as the leading social science methodologist in the United States, methodology in this case being understood as statistical survey techniques.[56] He was a pioneer in the development of survey research, and studies like *The People's Choice*, with their utilization of statistical techniques, have become standards in the genre of works on electoral behaviour. His background is rather complex, reflecting the changing winds of modern history. Early in his life he was a member of the Austrian socialist youth movement. As a student in Vienna he organized an interdisciplinary seminar together with Carnap and Voegelin. Originally a mathematician, Lazarsfeld became more and more interested in sociological applications and social psychology. In 1933 he published, together with Marie Jahoda (his first wife) and Hans Zeisel, the classic study on the unemployed in the small town of Marienthal (*Die Arbeitslosen von Marienthal: Ein soziographischer Versuch über die Wirkungen langdauernder Arbeitslosigkeit*).[57] This study on the effects of unemployment is regarded by some as the beginning of modern empirical social research. Considering his empiricist image, it is to be noted that throughout his life Lazarsfeld maintained a strong interest in social psychology.

During a journey to the United States in 1933 he decided to escape the rising tide of anti-Semitism in Europe. After an extension of his scholarship, he simply remained in the United States. The Bureau of Applied Social Research at Columbia University in New York became Lazarsfeld's intellectual home after his emigration.[58] In the United States Lazarsfeld got in touch with representatives of the Institut für Sozialforschung in Frankfurt, many of whose members had also been forced into diaspora, among them both Horkheimer, the original founder of the school, and Adorno. What they and Lazarsfeld had in common was an interest in empirical social psychology and how the individual is formed by the group. After the Second World War, however, Lazarsfeld denounced the anti-positivism of the later Frankfurt school. He noted that the critique of traditional positivism is never related to specific investigations but always to a 'generalized other'; nor did he share Adorno's worries about statistical techniques as a threat to the humanist aspect of sociology. He allowed himself a certain irony with regard to those who conceived of empirical research as trivial in comparison to 'the great aim of social theory to grasp society in its totality' (Lazarsfeld 1972: 174). Lazarsfeld simply did not accept the antagonism between theoretical and empirical efforts and found the later Frankfurt school less seminal in matters of concrete research.[59]

Lazarsfeld's interests are wide, ranging from psychology, to game theory, to mass communication. His stress is on application; basic methodological debate unrelated to concrete investigation is thus seen as less seminal. Lazarsfeld also advanced statistical techniques; typically he liked to deal with large sets of data, especially attitude surveys. He adhered to the unity of science, which connects him with the classical positivism of J. S. Mill, and he considered science to be predominantly teamwork. In this sense, Lazarsfeld is representative of modern behaviouralist empirical social research, with its need for diversified technical skills and specialization.

Lazarsfeld's conception of Weber was formed together with Anthony Oberschall, another – younger – European émigré born in Hungary. In 1965 they published 'Max Weber and Empirical Social Research', in the *American Sociological Review*. Lazarsfeld also wrote the foreword to Oberschall's book on *Empirical Social Research in Germany*, published in the same year. Lazarsfeld and Oberschall place great weight on Weber's alleged role in the advancement of empirical social research in its early phases in Germany. Weber cast as a survey pioneer may seem strange, but in fact there are several episodes in Weber's intellectual career to support this contention.

Weber was responsible for a series of inquiries that were concerned with the creation and assessment of 'reform' policies, in the Bismarckian tradition of paternalistic welfare policy or reforms designed to integrate the working classes into the German nation; his studies of the regions east of the Elbe in the 1890s, as well as his contributions to industrial sociology around 1908, are examples. He was a friend of Göhres, a priest who lived as a worker for a few months and wrote a book which was an early example of participant observation.[60]

These writings, which include some methodological comments, were not included in *GAW* and have not been translated into English, and have generally not been noticed. One reason for this is perhaps the common predilection among scholars to regard classics as either sources for the plundering of ideas or purely as objects of interpretative contemplation (as pointed out by Alexander 1987). It is certainly the case that these parts of Weber's *œuvre* are more outdated than the 'Objectivity' essay. Although Weber's empirical essays may be interesting from the point of view of the history of ideas, they are clearly technically inferior to later work in survey research. Weber would have expected this. He thought that science was constantly engaged in the business of surpassing itself. Although his lengthy discussions of problems in the design of questionnaires may seem primitive in retrospect, they are still a source of important evidence of Weber's diversity of interests, and the potential for the development of these interests in various directions. Both 'Columbia' sociology in the form of Lazarsfeld's surveys and 'Chicago' participant observation methodology, as I have suggested, are prefigured in these texts.

Weber also reveals himself as a participant-observer in his 1906 essay on the Protestant sects in which he clarifies his thesis about the influence of Calvinism by illustrative material from his experiences with his relatives in Mount Airy, North Carolina. Neither of the two essays on industrial sociology, 'Zur Psychophysik der industriellen Arbeit' (Regarding the Psycho-Physical Aspects of Industrial Work, 1908) and the essay called 'Auslese und Anpassung' (Selection and Adjustment, 1908) were included in Weber's *GAW*, though there are some indications that he wished at least the first paper had been included. They are both intriguing, and they both contain elements that are comparable to the 'Marginal Utility' essay. But here Weber appears almost as a founding father of 'scientific management'. He discusses, for example, the relation between return and effort (see for instance Eldridge 1971: 120) and comes very close to what would later be called 'ergonomics', especially with respect to fatigue and training.[61] The essay makes dull reading (perhaps this explains why it was not included), but it is important as an indication of Weber's own inclinations and combines interests that in retrospect we would be inclined to think of as in conflict.

In contrast to Parsons, Lazarsfeld and Oberschall were only too well aware of the prolonged historicist influence in German social thought, which they regarded as an obstacle to the breakthrough of empirical social research. 'Perhaps the most decisive consequence of the *Methodenstreit* for social research was that the concrete methodology and technology of research was left neglected in favour of abstract and philosophical arguments' (Oberschall 1965: 14). The gulf between philosophical and empirical undertakings nevertheless allowed the latter to develop in an independent, although neglected, manner.

> This was so because controversies such as the *Methodenstreit* were carried out on a philosophical plane completely removed and without reference to the more simple, basically fact-finding, social research activities that some of the protagonists in the debate were concurrently engaged in. Weber's solution to the problem of generalization from unique historical data by means of ideal types, which he conceived of as abstract limiting concepts not necessarily found in their total purity, but containing the essential features of real social phenomena (as was for example his notion of 'rational action'), did not prevent him from suggesting to Levenstein (see below) an inductive typological procedure for quantitative empirical data which had no relation to the notion of ideal types, and which was in fact quite similar to current procedure. (ibid.)

The founders of the first generation of historicist scholars were Roscher, Knies and Hildebrand. Gustav Schmoller, Lujo Brentano and Adolph Wagner, the second generation, founded the Verein für Sozialpolitik (Social Policy Association) in 1872. Schmoller thus represented the older generation in the Verein, but was the head of the younger historical school of political economy. The Verein was a 'mixed bag', in the sense that science and politics were equally vital concerns for its members, many of whom were characterized as 'Socialists of the chair'.[62] Oberschall (1965: 4) called it 'That unique association of reform minded men, part professional association, part pressure group'. Of the third generation, Weber, Tönnies, Sombart and Troeltsch are the better-known names, several of whom also contributed to the foundation of German sociology as an academic discipline.[63]

It might seem strange that although the fragile German empirical tradition was inhibited, not really starting to catch up with the United States until after the Second World War, there was nevertheless a long German tradition of socially concerned survey research. Oberschall believed this was partly a result of French inspiration, which otherwise rarely exercised any influence in Germany.[64] Social statistics and moral statistics had been on the agenda at least since 1848, 'the year of the people's will', as it was called. The working class was recognized as a new significant phenomenon with which the nation had to cope. In Prussia the government even encouraged these early investigations, while in France they were predominantly an activity for philanthropists and socialists.

The differences in attitude between France and the Prussian authorities had to do with the peculiarly mixed character of the Verein. Prussia, an early welfare state, was doing pioneer work in social insurance, as part of Bismarck's strategy to integrate his presumptive opponents – the workers – into the new nation. This ongoing and much-delayed German process of nation-building was of course a central phenomenon around which much of German affairs – scholarly as well as political – focused. It was also in line with basic state idealism, common to state officials and professors who were part of the Prussian *Beamtentum* (state bureaucracy), with its specific ethics and obligations. German academics thus had divided loyalties, serving both the sword and the pen. Moreover, this duality was reflected in their roles as representatives of the whole German nation, including all classes and regions. But while the *Beamtentum*, as well as the officer corps, had the *Junker* class in Prussia for its main recruiting base, the background of a university professor might vary considerably. In such a regionally fragmented country as Germany, professors were almost the only ones who did not identify themselves with any particular group interest. In the course of a normal career they would have moved from university to university and so to different towns and religious areas. They were, above all, Germans and not Bavarians, Austrians or *Junkers*, and felt it their calling to interpret and make manifest the general German culture.

The social compassion of the socialists of the chair makes them a strange hybrid between conservatism and socialism. In this case, social reform and the conservation of established society went hand in hand, the former being a device to achieve the latter, in a way akin to Bismarck's social conservatism.[65] This dual role was of course not unproblematic; it easily led to attitudes of both subservience and opposition, and brought with it the danger of obscuring the demarcation lines between science and politics.

In spite of the emphasis on archival studies and history within the German academic community, many investigations, and to a lesser extent surveys, were carried out. They were motivated by a wish for reform rather than an interest in accumulating knowledge about society.

Germany had the largest socialist party in Europe after 1890, the Social Democratic party. The cleavage between the working class and the rest of the society was quite pronounced and was referred to as the 'social question', and later as the 'working class question'. Bismarck's social policy and his social insurance legislation, which were based on the idea of paternalistic responsibility, did not succeed in the end in creating a genuine national community which included the industrial workers, but it was probably responsible for the less radical direction which the socialist movement took. (Oberschall 1965: 9)[66]

Six empirical episodes in Weber's career

Weber had no real central position in the Verein, as compared with, for example, Schmoller. Rather, Weber was an important dissident, more inclined to *Realpolitik* (a term he did not like, since at the time it had some 'Bismarckian' connotations) than social policy. This seems to be indicated for instance in his lengthy studies on rural workers on the estates east of the river Elbe. 'It cannot be denied, however, that despite the diversity of empirical work that was carried out in the period 1848–1914, a tradition of social research never became firmly established. Max Weber had tried to do so more than anyone else' (Oberschall 1965: 8).

In their joint 1965 article in the *American Sociological Review*, Lazarsfeld and Oberschall give an account of six episodes in Weber's intellectual biography.[67] They share Parsons's judgement that Weber 'hid his light under a bushel' – albeit another light. They do not claim that empirical quantitative techniques were Weber's main interest; from the vantage-point of their paradigm, however, they naturally focus on this element in Weber, so anticipating a later development in social science. The numerous debates on *Verstehen* and ideal-types do not bring Weber to mind as a predecessor of empirical social research; still, these elements, in the shape of a number of empirical studies that Weber undertook, are also to be found in the Weberian 'quarry'. His empirical efforts were in vain, in the sense that they tended to be forgotten, not developed. In this, Lazarsfeld and Oberschall illuminate and extend our knowledge of Weber's methodological scope.

1. In his substantial studies (which amount to 900 pages) on the conditions of the farm workers east of the Elbe,[68] carried out under the aegis of the Verein during the 1890s, Weber clarifies the conflicting interests of the new German nation, on the one hand, and those of the *Junkers*, on the other hand, whose economic decline was caused by the importation of cheap American grain. The *Junkers'* power had tended to grow, especially after the fall of Bismarck, since they were the power base of both bureaucracy and army, and as such were the main pillars of the new state. When Bismarck's strong lead-

ership suddenly ceased, the vacuum created had to be filled one way or another. Even if Bismarck was himself pre-eminently a *Junker*, and therefore had a vested interest, he nevertheless was a kind of unifying symbol of German national rebirth, and had enough political skill to keep the centrifugal forces under control. The conflict of interests between the need of the *Junkers* to survive their competition from American grain and the need of the nation to maintain a homogeneous population at its eastern border was sharpened. According to Weber, the import of cheap Polish labour onto the big eastern farm estates was dangerous, because it diminished the resistance to threats from tsarist Russia.[69]

At the Verein meeting in Berlin in 1893 Weber caused a mild sensation in transcending the traditional résumé by specifying the political consequences of his research; he saw the growing labour influx in the border regions in the East as damaging to the German race and national security.[70]

2. Soon after he began this research, Weber was consulted by the Evangelical Social Congress about the design of further research on the life conditions of the farm workers. The church's missionary work required more detailed knowledge about the lower-income strata as a target group. In modern terminology, Weber considered such matters as the selection of interviews and the analysis of open-ended questions. These contacts led to a close collaboration with Friedrich Naumann, Weber becoming his political adviser for a period.[71]

3. In 1908 Weber published his important – but still somewhat neglected – essay on 'Selection and Adjustment', a study in the field of industrial sociology. Weber was interested in the effects of modern large-scale industry on the lifestyle and personality of workers, as well as their response to varying salary arrangements. The investigation drew on already existing data and new observations, and on direct interviews with the scientific object under scrutiny, namely the industrial workers. Weber wrote a long methodological introduction to the survey. Oberschall (1965) utilized the term 'participant observation' to characterize one of the methods used in this investigation. On the whole it is interpreted in line with the development towards ever higher levels of technical awareness of social research.[72]

4. Weber's interest in industrial sociology was furthered in his studies of productivity among workers in the textile industry (the traditional Weber family business). His report 'Zur Psychophysik der industriellen Arbeit' ('Concerning the Psycho-Physical Aspects of Industrial Work') anticipates the later discussions between the schools of scientific management and human relations.[73] Among other problems, Weber was interested in the classic one of the relationship between piecework and productivity, a relation of importance to any

employer or employee. Weber found the costs of controlled experiments too high and consequently had to rely on the analysis of already existing data.

The study found that 'after a period of trial and error the workers find an optimum balance between effort and earning'; 'his data and discussion could be directly translated today into a mathematical learning model' (Lazarsfeld and Oberschall 1965: 189). Weber's contributions to industrial sociology were influenced to a certain extent by the psychophysical tendencies of the time, although by no means uncritically.

5. At roughly the same time, Weber also tried to stimulate (or provoke) Adolf Levenstein, a self-taught worker, to systematize and elaborate on investigations on the attitudes of his fellow workers. Levenstein received answers from 63 per cent of the workers he approached. The return might have been even higher, had not the socialist press compromised the investigation by denouncing it, afraid that the class enemy might abuse the results.[74] It was also a novel idea to ask the workers themselves about their own interpretation of their predicament. Previous research relied on reports from vicars, doctors, and so on; that is, people in touch with workers through their profession. This was of course a somewhat blunt and imprecise way of scanning the life conditions of the common people, in the primitive phases of social research.[75]

In general Weber's bibliography from 1908 to 1911 displays a vivid interest in the techniques of the *enquêtes* (surveys) of social psychology. Lazarsfeld and Oberschall suggest that there is a link between Weber's contacts with Levenstein, and the later development of electoral behaviour surveys.

6. Lazarsfeld and Oberschall account for Weber's effort to promote investigations of the German press. As a comparative historian, Weber pins down the problem as one of the relationship between media and power. Lazarsfeld and Oberschall suggest that some of his hints are close to modern content analysis. This was naturally an attractive topic to Lazarsfeld, who was interested in mass communication studies, especially theories about the effects of the messages from editorials in daily newspapers. It is, however, worth noting that these press investigations have also played a role in the later German *Gesamtdeutung* debate.[76]

Lazarsfeld's and Oberschall's conception of Weber

It is Lazarsfeld in particular who points out Weber's stress on probability in establishing explanations in social science: 'In all his work

Weber was explicitly concerned with quantitative techniques and with the notion that the meaning of social relationships can be expressed only in probabilistic terms' (Lazarsfeld and Oberschall 1965: 185, in 'Abstract'). This assertion is based not only on their 'Weber survey' but also on their interpretation of Weber's methodology as a whole. Although this completes the picture of Weber as an inductivist, it also has to be admitted that this empiricism is a basic trait in Weber's elusive views on social science explanation.

For Weber, *Verstehen* is characterized by the idea of probability, *Chancen*, to use his term. Utilizing the ideal-type of rational action we might understand why a person acts in a specific way, but we cannot be positively sure that he will always act in that rational way. The rational approach merely provides us with a point of reference. The departures from rational teleological acts are harder to explain while preserving intersubjectivity, but at least here we have a tool to identify cases where *ad hoc* explanations are called for. Most drivers stop at a red light. It makes sense, and we understand why they behave like that. Sometimes, however, drivers do not stop at a red light. There could be a number of reasons for this seemingly less sensible behaviour. The reason in every single case remains to be explained. The rational type – as an idealization of a rational act – thus serves as an 'Archimedian point' for the analysis, no matter that it is not in full accordance with the empirical reality. Moreover, it provides an alternative to more psychologically interpretative, empathetic, routes of (or even alternatives to) explanation. Although Weber sides with Dilthey on the specificity of the cultural object, he certainly would agree with Lazarsfeld and Oberschall that non-intersubjective methods of interpretation are to be avoided. Without any deeper analysis of the role Weber ascribes to probabilities in theoretical propositions, it is still possible to state that in stressing this element in Weber's view on causality Lazarsfeld and Oberschall bring Weber within their own paradigmatic allegiances. 'Lazarsfeld and Oberschall, from the behavioural end, saw this as a primitive attempt to operationalize dispositional concepts in the positivist manner' (Torrance 1974: 142).[77]

Other elements in Weber's methodology, less in line with their own approach, are neglected in the Lazarsfeld–Oberschall paradigm.

Max Weber did spectacular work in historical sociology, a field badly neglected in recent years. But he also wrote a few pages on what he thought he did, calling his procedure the construction of ideal-types. These self-declaratory statements contradict each other at many points; they have no [*sic*!] visible relation to the actual content of his studies, and they have led to endless and confused literature which is concerned mostly with terminology and, as far as I can see, has resulted in no new investigations. No one has explicated what he did in his actual studies, which has contributed to the difficulty in emulating his skill. (Lazarsfeld 1962: 464)

This telling passage is part of a discussion of Carl Hempel's views on 'constructive types', Howard Becker's (1934) more quantitatively useful variant of the ideal-type. Lazarsfeld here even regrets that Weber's own text is quoted by Hempel: 'What Max Weber said about ideal-types' is characterized as 'quotations, incidentally, which are only too well known to every social scientist who has tried to forget them when he wanted to know what Weber really did' (Lazarsfeld and Oberschall 1965: 165).

The merit of Lazarsfeld's and Oberschall's approach is to make us aware of features in Weber's sociology that had been previously overlooked. But in this they go somewhat too far. The above passage attempts to place Weber in intellectual custody and refuses to accept his central methodological concerns. Their approach is very much the reverse of that of Parsons. While Parsons pulls the ideal-type towards general conceptual schemes, Lazarsfeld and Oberschall operationalize the ideal-type through the procedure of establishing correlations at the empirical level. Although diametrically opposed in their reading, the respective paradigmatic concerns of both Parsons and Lazarsfeld and Oberschall shape their image of Weber's methodology.

Lazarsfeld and Oberschall express irritation with the barren methodological polemics that lead to 'no new investigations' and are thus irrelevant from the point of view of cumulative research. But they do recognize Weber's ambiguity on the combination of the motivational understanding of meaning with statistical covariation techniques. They connect it with ' "the action language" then current in German social science as a conceptual device, to be used deductively without reference to empirical research' (Lazarsfeld and Oberschall 1965: 185). They are here referring to the broad hermeneutical tradition – in all its variations: 'German humanists and social scientists in Weber's time tended to place a great emphasis on the notion of "human action". But the notion did not refer to the empirical study of action (*Handlung*). The idea was rather that the concept of "Handlung" could be used as a systematic frame of reference within which available procedures could be located' (ibid.: 196). 'The Germans who wrote in this tradition seem to have taken it for granted that some kind of "action language" is mandatory for a discussion of the human sciences' (ibid.: 197).[78] It is true that Weber must be understood in his German context, although Lazarsfeld overemphasizes this inhibition on Weber, who, one way or another, was still able to promote the secularization of historicist German social thought.

In their presentation of Weber, Lazarsfeld and Oberschall mention Gustav Radbruch as an influential example of action language. The concept of action was essential to Radbruch's theory of criminality and, as Lazarsfeld and Oberschall indignantly note, it 'has to be analyzed in the light of classificatory needs, and not as a result of empirical observations' (ibid.: 196). Casuistry to some extent grew historically out of (Roman) jurisprudence. It is true that hypothetical casuistry of the legalistic kind is an important part of Weber's scholarly background – and to this day the discussion goes on as to whether Weber was essentially a sociologist or a historicist law scholar. Clearly the legacy from jurisprudence has hitherto been relatively neglected; it is formative for Weber's methodology, and according to Lazarsfeld and Oberschall also part of what inhibited him from making a full breakthrough to empirical social research.[79]

Radbruch – who later became Attorney General in the Weimar Republic – had accounted for the historical doctrines (*Dogmengeschichte*) of the concept of action, in his *The Concept of Action in Criminal Law* (*Der Handlungsbegriff in seiner Bedeutung für das Strafrechtssystem*). It is by no means surprising that a law scholar pays such attention to the concept of action, since the sentencing of criminals is related to intentions as much as it is to the criminal act itself. There is no doubt that Radbruch had an impact on Weber, whose earliest scholarly experiences were in jurisprudence.[80] It is also clear that Weber's views on methodology and explanation were affected, although the extent to which Radbruch influenced Weber's view on social science explanation is still a matter of debate and interpretation.[81]

Weber's use of the concept of action does not primarily aim at producing empirical studies of social action, but rather (in *WuG* at least) at the development of an 'action scheme through which sociological concepts can be organized', to use Parsons's phraseology. Indeed it can be argued that this is the central purpose of *WuG*. Weber's systematic sociology was not really empirical in the modern sense of the word. The action language is an inhibiting or retarding factor, suppressing Weber's breakthrough to modern social research. This is in part a reflection of the previous neglect of Weber's empirical elements but also a reaction against the Parsonsian view of Weber. In their attempt to counter this tendency, Lazarsfeld and Oberschall hesitate to state that *Verstehen* is basically an empirical concept. Instead, they claim that *Verstehen* is an accidental encumbrance from idealist thought that Weber was never able to jettison:

> What was it in the German scene that frustrated him? Why was America receptive only to his historical writings and to the parts of his methodology that stood the test of time least well? (The confused but continuing discussion of 'ideal types' is probably the best and most regrettable example.) We have attempted elsewhere to explain the situation in Germany; for the United States, the explanation is probably simpler. When Parsons brought Weber to the attention of American sociologists, there was a widespread desire to develop social theory. Empirical social research was taken for granted; in its early and primitive forms there was enough, or perhaps even too much of it. (Lazarsfeld and Oberschall 1965: 198)[82]

The antagonism to Parsons is not exactly hidden; in fact Lazarsfeld and Oberschall try to counterbalance or neutralize the influence of 'the patron saint of large-scale theory builders': 'Talcott Parsons recalls that when he came to study in Heidelberg soon after Weber's death he was greatly influenced by Weber's historical and theoretical writings; but no one told him of the material we have summarized in the preceding pages' (ibid.: 164).[83]

There is, however, a strange affinity between the main perspectives of Parsons and Lazarsfeld and Oberschall, in the sense that both readings conceive of German historicism as the specific cultural factor that inhibited Weber's full breakthrough to modern secular social science. Their respective prescriptions for the ideal direction of the future development of social science indeed appear to be antagonistic: empirical substance *vs* macrotheory. Lazarsfeld's and Oberschall's contribution to the empirical sociology of knowledge, nevertheless, elucidates our understanding of Weber's pioneering work in three important fields of enquiry in modern empirical social research: industrial sociology, rural sociology and electoral studies. To Parsons, Weber appears to be a pioneer of general theory, of the kind proposed by Parsons himself.

Lazarsfeld and Oberschall conceive of Weber as primarily a pioneer in empirical social research, i.e. emphasis is laid on the techniques they represent by themselves.

Alfred Schutz takes Weber as his point of departure for developing his approach of empathic (*einfühlendes*) understanding, interpreting him accordingly as an incomplete authority for interpretative subjective analysis.

To Lukács, Weber appears, in the last instance, as an irrational and idealistic neo-Kantian, doomed to make superficial explanations of social phenomena, since he denied the reality of 'total reason' in his pessimistic view on the limitations of the scope of science and reason. 'Agnosticism' and 'relativism' are the shibboleths in this case, and 'analogies as explanation' are characteristic for a basically political Weber, who in effect is paving the way for imperialism and fascism.[84]

The ideal-type, Weber's central tool, designed to handle the problem of value-intrusion in the search for social science explanation, is conceived of in very varied ways.

5

Beyond Appropriation:
Weber Yesterday and Today

Preamble

In this final chapter we comment upon the 'state of the art' of Weberology in recent decades. What is dead or alive in Weber? What mistakes in interpretation have we learned to avoid from the paradigmatically flawed 'creative extensions' of Weber? What can we learn from Weber as a classic author in sociology?

The problem of value-incommensurability is a technical problem of how to deal with uncontrolled value-intrusion in social science, but also reappears as a more existentialist problem, about the search for guidelines for the proper conduct of life. The latter is a problem of modernity which is accentuated in post-modernity.

The importance of Troeltsch for the understanding of Weber's problem horizon ('polytheism') is noted. The importance of the late Tenbruck for the proper interpretation of Weber's legacy as a progressive mediator is emphasized.

Arnold Brecht (1959) and Gunnar Myrdal are both successful caretakers of Weber's methodological legacy. The technical solution to the rationalization of value-hierarchies for the pursuit of policy analyses reflects a general philosophical predicament in the post-Enlightenment era. The anxiety and necessity of choice is the core problem for Nietzsche, as well as for several scholars today.

The Weber Renaissance as a Living Legacy

Historically Weber has had several applications. He was, as we saw, a basic classic (authentic or not) for Parsons's structural functional-

ism, Schutz's phenomenology, and Lazarsfeld's and Oberschall's
survey techniques. He has had a decisive influence on Karl
Mannheim's sociology of knowledge (1936), Hans Morgenthau's
power realism (1948),[1] Norbert Elias's cultural evolutionism (1939),
Robert K. Merton's 'middle range theorizing' (1949), as well as
Edward Shils's studies on institutionalization (1951, 1982), and
Donald Levine's studies on Ethiopian rationality among the Amhara
people (1985). He has been the starting point for Anthony Giddens's
class analysis (1972), and Robert Bellah's studies on Japanese religious norms (1957) – not to mention H.-U. Wehler's history of
the Second Reich (1985).[2] In recent decades he has even been an
inspiration for Habermas's communicative action theory (Habermas
1984), and – perhaps less obviously – Francis Fukuyama's books.[3]
These are still only examples of Weber's influence, in addition to
his being the pioneer for the dominant scientific value relativism as
developed by Arnold Brecht (1959). Some of these efforts are indeed
a supplement to, rather than merely an application of, Weber. He had
no really elaborated, manifest notion of either nation or society, concepts he took for granted in his construction of ever more complex
societal structures from the basic unit of social action.

   The paradigmatically biased Weber was typical of the 1970s with
its post-1968 debate, in which Weber became a stumbling block for
young Marxians, which in many cases they never managed to get
over (like the present author). Those were the days when all texts in
social science, whatever they dealt with – be it regional policy in
western-central rural Sweden or imperialist oppression in developing
countries in the Third World – started with some 100 or more pages
on the basic concepts of historical materialism, and the spirit of
Thomas Kuhn inspired the revolutionary creed among young high-
flying optimists of a generation that felt science should deal with real
problems and widen the problem-horizon of behaviouralism and
'logical positivism', be it in the creed of Althusser or of Habermas.

   In what follows I shall comment on trends in Weberology in recent
decades, such as eclecticism, 'creative extensions', 'national styles',
attempts to find the ultimate interpretation, as well as increasing professionalization. These various strands point in various directions.
The *Gesamtdeutungen,* competing alternatives for all-inclusive 'keys',
continue the wishful search for a final thematically unified interpretation, and reflect the vested interests of the interpreters. They tend
to be creative extensions, just like the selective interpretations of the
paradigm-builders studied in chapter 4. Yet, increased professionalization, new translations and the rise of German Weber scholarship

has elevated Weberology to new levels, albeit with elements of 'recycling'.

The Weber industry still seems to be going strong, as reflected in articles, monographs, and the many thematic issues taken up in social science journals and readers on various aspects of his work. In the methodological field the secondary literature on Weber is 'very substantial', to use Runciman's understatement of a couple of decades ago, and bibliographies today list thousands of items.

The less reliable attempts at interpretative 'hijackings' are no longer possible, the neo-Parsonsians play down Weber's genuine (explicit) methodological writings, and the phenomenologists, with their vested interests, do not refer to Weber with the same high appreciation as Schutz did, whose intense wrestling with Weberian problems was not quite matched by his study of Weber's texts, to judge from the copies in his library kept today at the Social Science Archives at the University of Constance.[4]

Throughout the years we also find some eclectic uses of Weber of the kind actually aspiring to accomplish a normal science within social science. Early examples are R. K. Merton's study on *Science, Technology and Society in 17th Century England* and Edward Shils's work on academic ethics. C. Wright Mills might arguably also be included here.[5] More recently Anthony Giddens, Pierre Bourdieu, Ulrich Beck, and also to some extent Jürgen Habermas might be added to the list of happy eclectics.[6]

We started with the notion that 'There is just not "one" Max Weber', as Wolfgang Mommsen (1974: 1) put it, and demonstrated the paradigmatic flaws in three prominent 'creative' extensions of Weber's methodology that had a considerable steering effect on the handbook-Weber for student consumption, at least well into the 1970s. Indeed, Weber is traded on as a 'present day relevant theoretical classic in sociology', although the degree of his relevance, theory and status as a classic author are open to dispute and interpretation.

The elusive character of Weber's work is a source of frustration, but also contributes to his constitution as a controversial classic, which resists unambiguous interpretation. Thus there are many approaches. This is indicated in numerous instances, such as Lawrence A. Scaff's (1989: 3) observations about Weber's varying images as 'founder' of sociology, leader of the resistance against positivism (H. S. Hughes), proponent of *Machtpolitik* (Wolfgang Mommsen, Raymond Aron), defender of 'bourgeois' reason (Lukács, Marcuse), or spokesman for 'decisionism' and 'value nihilism'

(Habermas, Leo Strauss and Allan Bloom). We could add Jaspers's image of Weber as an existentialist philosopher, in his heroic pessimism a personification of the value-polytheist agony of our age: 'After Nietzsche, man had found, at any rate up to now, his last and definite personification in Max Weber' (here quoted from Mommsen 1989: 170; orig. ref. Jaspers 1946 (p. 88 in 2nd edn). This list does not exhaust the topic of varying images of Weber.

There is an obvious link between the Kierkegaardian–Nietzschean existentialist dilemma, the predicament of anxiety of choice in the post-Enlightenment era, Troeltsch's polytheist dilemma as an unresolved problem for historicist scholarship ('crisis of historicism'), Weber's central methodological agenda (value-aspect-choice as response to value-incommensurability), and today's talk about post-modern possibility and necessity of choice, a theme in Giddens, Bauman, as well as Isaiah Berlin.[7] Weber still appears to be relevant.

Moving beyond the situation of paradigmatically obscured competing images of Weber, we had in the continuing Weber renaissance a new trend, a search for the 'essential Weber', a Weberian 'programme', within or outside his methodology. This search for a thematic unity is exemplified by Tenbruck (for example, in 1975a, 1975b, 1987, 1989a, 1989b), Burger (1976), Oakes (1988), Hennis (1987) and the debates they have generated. The search for the ultimate key to the essential Weber might generate new knowledge even if it fails to achieve its goal.

The focus has shifted from political aspects of Weber's thought to the search for the unifying principle that would make the whole of Weber's work comprehensive and the problem of which material in the huge quarry of Weber's texts such an attempt should rely on. Friedrich H. Tenbruck in Tübingen has initiated most of the modern German *Gesamtdeutung* debate. Tenbruck provides one of the many links between Anglo-Saxon and German Weberology; he produced work on the interpretation of Weber (1959, 1975a, 1975b, 1977, 1986, 1987, 1989a, 1989b) until his death.

Wilhelm Hennis's *Gesamtdeutung* of Weber as a 'Greek' political philosopher adds to the same stack of diversity, as do Tenbruck's views on Weber as part of the historicist tradition of religiously founded cultural studies.[8] Weber is also represented as a 'Would-be Englishman' (Roth 1993), an anarchist fellow-traveller (Sam Whimster's ongoing research), and as a pioneer of economic sociology (Swedberg 1998).

The current biographical research by (for instance) Whimster might inform us about the essential Weber but does not add much to our knowledge about his positions as such, which must be based on his texts and seen in the context of his current contemporaries. Certainly Weber's troubled and inhibited sex-life, his relation to his mother, his encounters with bohemian anarchists (in Munich and Ascona), and his concerns in matters of family economy are formative ingredients of his biography. The biographical approach is much stimulated by Martin W. Green's work on *The von Richthofen Sisters* (1974), with its revelations about Weber and 'Lady X', as she (Else Jaffé) was called in Mitzman's (1970) account. However, although biography is often telling, it is no substitute for textual analyses.[9]

The reception history increasingly became a theme in its own right during the 1970s and 1980s,[10] since the Weber renaissance somewhat surprisingly went on, with ever new publications and an increased degree of professionalization and cohesiveness. Swedberg, for instance, does not claim to have found the ultimate key to Weber but restricts his ambition to finding the elements in Weber that are of relevance to a paradigm of economic sociology.

The contributions by distinguished scholars to Melchior Palyi's reader (*Erinnerungsgabe*) from the early 1920s attest to Weber's early reputation, significant but hardly overwhelming. The digestion of Weber requires a certain distance in time in order to distinguish between the unique and context-bound *vs* the universally relevant elements.[11] There was an incubation period during which Weber's legacy was victimized by 'special interests'; this has been given special attention earlier in this book. Weber's strategic location at the junction of several overlapping and interconnected crucial paradigmatic divides makes him difficult to neglect, particularly on matters of objectivity and value-intrusion. Leo Strauss's judgement is that 'No one since Max Weber has devoted a comparable amount of intelligence, assiduity, and almost fanatical devotion to the basic problem of the social sciences. Whatever may have been his errors, he is the greatest social scientist of our century' (quoted in Lassman and Velody 1989: 159). From relative anonymity to such recognition by the most un-Weberian of all thinkers is a reception history yet to be written. In this last chapter I reflect not only on the state of the art of Weberology, but upon my own interpretation as well. The essence I find in Weber's methodology should not be confused with my own extension of the same; Weber is a relativist[12] or polytheist, and I – not he – am a 'nihilist' (in the sense in which this term applies to Axel Hägerström; it is a term calling for qualification).[13]

We will return below to 'Max Weber's Swedish relatives': Axel Hägerström, the founder of programmatic 'nihilism' and Gunnar Myrdal, the great social engineer, especially in the 1930s and 1940s.

Myrdal offers one solution to the norm-sender problem, as a synthesis of Weber and Hägerström, whose value-philosophy he emphatically embraces. This extension of Weber is more 'Weberian' than the paradigmatically flawed interpretations by Schutz, Parsons, and Lazarsfeld and Oberschall; it is also more useful as a methodological manual for actual social research. Max Weber's qualification of *Wertfreiheit* to *Wertbeziehung* is methodologically codified by Myrdal in (for instance) *An American Dilemma* (1944).

Selective and 'Creative' Presentism

There is a shift in emphasis involving several simultaneous tendencies. The work of bringing Weber to America between the wars provided a certain structure for a scattered reception history, with a lot of 'ornamental' use of Weber *à la mode* to add the patina of classical scholarship to various endeavours in almost any field. Just as some authors liked to pose as Goethe, it was popular to pose as Weber. And, just as many scholars connecting with Machiavelli knew no more about their inspiration than the metaphors ('lions and foxes' etc.) they borrowed, many used 'Weber' as a somewhat opaque 'cover' for whatever they were doing.

The crude variable of 'national styles' (of interpretation) tinting our spectacles, as did the paradigms, is somewhat telling and has not yet played out its role; but it is gradually becoming less important, owing to the globalization of discourse and the ensuing increased cohesiveness and professionalization.[14]

The paradigmatic creative extensions have a continuing life, especially in the works of a number of neo-functionalists following in the wake of Parsons, such as Alexander (1983), Münch (1988) and Kalberg (1994). The strong vein of neo-functionalism on both sides of the Atlantic in recent attempts to extend Weber to modern usage is noteworthy (e.g. Schluchter 1989). In fact, 'neo-functionalism' is one of the most viable traditions today.[15]

Martin Albrow (1990), Bryan Turner (1992) and Fritz Ringer (1997) all display a similar presentist ambition, albeit with varying 'twists'.[16] I am sceptical of any author trying to address current burning issues through a return to Weber, and any title like 'Weber: Our Contemporary' makes me suspicious if it is not followed by a question mark. Although it is still a legitimate concern as to what is dead or alive in Weber's *œuvre*, we have to keep in mind that there is a potential conflict between interpretation and the utility of classic authors, and we need to recontextualize Weber in order to accomplish better interpretations of his 'project(s)'. Although Weber as a theorist of modernity still has considerable general relevance to us, he would presumably also have felt fairly alienated when encountering many topics of today. The 'chronological imperialism' that is promoted by the mechanisms of research fund-raising, teaching, as well as a certain creed among many scholars to prove their utility to society, are all distorting factors in our attempts to connect with the classic author on his own terms. And too many erroneous labels have already been anachronistically ascribed to Weber.[17]

The presentist interpretations mostly do not quite find what they are looking for in Weber's methodology and what they find is hard to square with their own concerns. They tend to look for the essential Weber in other instances of his work than his actual methodological writings, which remain relatively neglected.[18] Randall Collins (1986) is the ultimate in this regard, claiming that he does not really care about what Weber would have thought of Collins's *Weberian Sociological Theory*, as long as it is useful and 'in the spirit of Weber' (ibid.: 16).

Wilhelm Hennis, inspired by Eric(h) Voegelin (1952) and Larry Scaff (1973), also tries to appropriate a non-methodological Weber, retaining him for political philosophy.[19] In the 1980s several younger Weber scholars[20] found shelter for their undertakings in Hennis's seminar in Freiburg, and Scaff's sojourn in Freiburg has enriched Weberology on both sides of the Atlantic. In England Keith Tribe is approaching Weber much in the spirit of Hennis, meaning, for one thing, a stress on Weber's historicist legacy and his early production, when he was still under the spell of Schmoller. Weber's early production was for long relatively neglected in the English-language literature.[21] The main trends in the Weber renaissance over the last twenty years are growing professionalization and continuing 'creative extensions'.

That Weber has been hijacked and used as a vehicle for various schools in search of a prestigious founding father is itself no revelation: 'Working on the assumption that "as Weber goes, so goes sociology", leaders of different sociological perspectives have used Weber, over the decades, to legitimate their own specific theoretical ideas' (Alexander 1983: 1). Larry Scaff remarks in a similar vein that: 'Whoever controls the interpretation of Weber can entertain hopes of also governing scientific activity' (1989: 34). Already C. Wright Mills was well aware of Weber's 'clout'.[22] Weber was located at a strategic junction, touching upon several perennial paradigmatic divides, thus challenging posterity and provoking disputes over his proper interpretation.

Continuing Significance: Weber as Mediator

Weber's methodology grew out of most of the central traditions of his own time: historicism (in economics and jurisprudence), positivism, neo-Kantianism and economic marginalism. He combined elements from all these currents and touched upon the paradigmatic divisions of explanation and interpretation, unified science *vs* specificity of cultural science (the demarcation problem), intersubjective concept-formation, and solving the problem of value-intrusion and objectivity, in history and social science, and managed to build a bridge between positivism and historicism that still stands. There are, moreover, obvious parallels between the most crucial controversy in the background of Weber's methodological emergence – the *Methodenstreit* between history and theory – and the earlier antagonism between the tradition of idiography as contrasted with the positive study of society; this is repeated in the paradigmatic differences between theoretical social history (the Bielefeld school) and narrative tendencies, which thrive especially in France.[23]

This tension between history and theory appears to be the perennial main paradigmatic divide in social science, with its corollaries in the questions of objectivity and the specificity of social science. It repeats previous tensions between Ranke and Comte, as well as between Schmoller and Menger. Weber, as a representative of the second institutionalizing wave in the foundation of sociology, connects not only the Anglo-Saxon philosophy of science with continental cultural science, but also connects past and present. Weber is a mediator and bridge-builder; his role for the historicists may be best characterized as *maieutics*. He releases what is already inherent but the marginalist element taken from Menger appears as a 'leased' midwife's tool. This, moreover, becomes increasingly apparent in the texts we have emphasized (Weber 1904, 1906, 1908, 1913 and 1917).

That the more recent debates between the proponents of history (French narrative tendency) and theory (Kocka, Wehler) strongly parallel similar debates almost two centuries ago naturally promotes a certain pessimism with regard to the perennial discussion about social science as a real science or a pseudo-science, and how to meet or incorporate the challenge of unified science (positivism). This topic reconnects to the issue of the role of the classics – intellectual history as a preliminary stage to real science or an undertaking in its own right.

In Germany, with its specific legacy, the *Methodenstreit* between history and theory to some extent still goes on, and is the backdrop for several contributions of the last few decades, such as those of Hennis and Tenbruck (see also Swedberg 1998).

Increasing Professionalization and Cohesiveness

The gigantic *Max Weber Gesamtausgabe* helps to elucidate the image of Weber in all fields, making less noticed elements of his *œuvre* available and bringing them into focus. As long as the work goes on with the *MWG* there is, however, a sort of monopoly situation in which material (the letters, in particular) is not automatically available to the scientific community. The editors are most helpful but have to give their consent for material to be used and also have other concerns.[24] Some unpublished material might affect Weber's image, for instance with regard to his relation to Simmel, who is sometimes characterized as the big 'hidden influence' on Weber (see Levine 1981, 1989; Nedelmann 1988; Scaff 1988 and Szakolczai 1998.[25]

In the United Kingdom a new journal dedicated exclusively to *Max Weber Studies* is now being established; it grew out of the British Sociological Association's Max Weber Study Group, in the wake of the 1996 and 1999 conferences. These conferences have attracted scholars from several countries on both sides of the Atlantic and have resulted in edited volumes.[26] In the United States several colloquia have been arranged during the last couple of decades, and numerous monographs have been written (Antonio and Glassman 1985; Glassman and Swatos jr 1986; Murvar 1985).

Weber wasn't very consistent about his intentions and changed his mind over time; furthermore, much of the basic source material has simply been lost in the turmoil of war. To a considerable extent we have to rely on posthumously issued versions, without access to the original manuscripts, which of course can function as an excuse for intentional reconstruction. It is no surprise, then, that the full publication of Weber's letters to his editor is eagerly awaited.

The Mommsen and Osterhammel reader (1987, based on a 1984 symposium) embodies both the trend of growing professionalization, as well as the old differences of national styles in Weber interpretation, in Germany the methodological Weber being left largely for foreign consumption.

Bernard Pfister's (1928), Artur Mettler's (1934) and Dieter Henrich's (1952) books were exceptions to this trend in Germany but did not have too much follow-up in their home country; in contrast, von Schelting (1934) was echoed in Parsons's interpretation.[27] Yet, in the mid-1980s much German Weberology despite – and to some extend because of – the growing professionalization in the industry of Weber interpretation had a historicist bias, focusing on Weber's contemporaries. This laid the foundations for a reconstruction of his methodological endeavour, as well as for the search for a thematic unity in his work. Thus far there has been no successful 'closure' or a *Gesamtdeutung* that takes both into account. Both the key to unlock Weber as a whole and his methodology as such have been searched for in various instances of his *œuvre*.[28]

The Germans can't see the wood for all the interesting trees – all of which are well known to them – and the Anglo-Saxons see the wood, but have a blurry view of the individual trees. Weber's life and work and 'Weber and . . .' are typical German themes, while the Americans and the British are more prone to bold presentist applications.[29] Although German scholars often have digested the English-language research, the reverse is less true; some evidently important contributions, by for instance Peter-Ulrich Merz (on Weber and Rickert) and H. H. Nau (on Weber and Schmoller *vs* Menger), are still to be assimilated into cumulative discourse. Of course the 'relative autonomy' of the debates in various countries is gradually being overcome, and in recent English-language literature we find a number of detailed accounts of various aspects of Weber's scholarship.[30]

German Weberology has increased our knowledge of various aspects of Weber's scholarship. In part this is driven by the elusive goal of discovering the thematic unity within Weber's *œuvre* (Schluchter, Hennis, Tenbruck); it displays an idiographic mastery and tends towards a restoration of a German *Kultur* orientation. This is not all wrong; viz. Weber's stress on cultural values as points of view (ultimate or top-values), points of departure for instrumental analyses and rationalization of value-hierarchies. The contextual time horizon should transcend the proximate neo-Kantian influences and be taken back at least to the Enlightenment in its German guise. However, these scholars are prone to overlook the new elements Weber contributes to the German setting, with its traditional historicist hegemony and Hegelian idealist legacy. It might be true that Weber's ideal-type builds on Eduard Meyer and perhaps is to be found already in Meyer himself, just as Tenbruck suggested, but yet the inspirations from Menger and positivism are just as manifest in Weber's work. It remains to balance the account.

The Anglo-Saxons (American and British, etc.), on the other hand, have blind spots owing to their ignorance of the German language and German history; in many cases they are also unaware of the intellectual context of Weber's achievement. This promotes a strong tendency to pass verdicts on Weber or to interpret him from modern vantage points (which might simultaneously blur the interpretation and stimulate the preserved significance). The Anglo-Saxons in general are 'presentists' and more retrospectively inclined and motivated by utility; the Germans have difficulties in transcending the original German context, and risk neglecting Weber's role as a link between past and present. The main impression is after all that of a growing cumulativity and professionalization in modern Weberology.

The Dispute about the Centre of Gravity of Weber's Work and Methodology

From my perspective there are several good reasons to focus on Weber's methodological essays, since my interest is in the historical significance of Weber's contribution to social science doctrine. Weber represents a 'break' in the history of social science doctrine, although in a very tender, maybe even unintended, way as a mediator, as Kaesler says (1988a: 215). It is possible to see continuity and a break in the continuity at the same time in Weber's methodological endeavours. His methodological accomplishments in the borderland between history and sociology represent, in Mommsen's words, 'an uphill-struggle for a methodological reorientation of German historiography' (1989: 187), only slowly and hesitatingly received in Germany, with its particular historicist reaction against Enlightenment secularization as a typical *Sonderweg* trait. But to Weber himself this struggle might have merely been a gradual clarification – even to himself – of his own positions; he had to juggle with balls others had put into play.

Friedrich Tenbruck indicated to me (conversation in Tübingen, summer 1988, see also 1980: 79) that, today, he wouldn't quite endorse everything he wrote in the 1959 article on Weber's methodology, in which Weber's positivistic traits were somewhat exaggerated. Tenbruck launches a *Gesamtdeutung* of a sort, stressing the idealistic elements in Weber,[31] as a religious history of ideas in his long-time obsession with the major world religions (esp. in *GARS*); but in contrast to, for example, Hennis, he does not really believe one can find a single key to Weber's whole work.

From the mid-1970s onwards, Tenbruck, who was not a member of the editorial board of *MWG*, critically scrutinized the available editions of Weber's work, by Eduard Baumgarten,[32] Johannes Winckelmann, etc., utilizing the correspondence between Weber and his publisher (Siebeck-Mohr in Tübingen). Moreover, he initiated the healthy shift in emphasis from *WuG* to *GARS* in the search for Weber's 'research programme'. In the modern German *Gesamtdeutung* debate on Weber many scholars seem to share the ambition to find *the* – one and only – key to Weber's work, which would enable an unambiguous interpretation of Weber's contribution, although they of course differ about both the location of this intellectual Aladdin's lamp, and its meaning. This tendency results in readings of Weber as historian, anthropologist, economic historian (worldwide and/or Western), and, in the case of Tenbruck, historian of religious ideas – not to forget Weber as a sociologist. Weber of course remains a founder of sociology, although in a much less one-dimensional way than has been presented in the textbooks ever since Parsons.

Tenbruck's achievement in my view is to return Weber to his original context – and, strangely enough, simultaneously to build a bridge between the German and English discourse on Weber. Tenbruck answers well to recent 'culturalist' concerns in British Weber interpretation, such as Whimster (who translated what is probably Tenbruck's most central essay (1980) and Schroeder (1992). Tenbruck's main essays on Weber are now available in one volume (Tenbruck 1999).

Tenbruck (1987: 245) notes that in 1884 Meyer had already contemplated employing the term 'sociology' for what he tried to accomplish in his historical studies. The use of this French term is in itself not a big deal; only what it meant in relation to the problems historical research had to face is important. It is no doubt true that much secondary literature has taken a condescending tone in the description of backward historicism without lucid methodological procedure being replaced by modern science, but it is equally true that a development is taking place that advances cumulativity, that marginalism and neo-Kantianism promote testability and intersubjectivity and thus objectivity.

Tenbruck's 'anti-sociological' interpretation (he was himself a sociologist) is a bit paradoxical, when on the one hand he saves the rational element in historicism and on the other refers to Meyer's 'proto-sociologism', with its – as I interpret it – elements of rational proof. There is a historicist predicament as defined by Troeltsch and others, which still bothers us in post-modernity, that its characteristics are disorientation, moral deficit, etc. There is also a marginalist revolution. Weber mediates between a historicism in crisis and modern secularized social science, with its problems and prospects. Maybe we have to realize that radical 'breaks' are mostly retrospective reconstructions, further stimulated by the nature of academic discourse where the question often is 'continuity or break', which somehow already implies a presentist bias. In reality more evolutionary processes encouraged by some outer stimuli might release something inherent and dormant; and in this context Weber's role as mediator connects disparate currents in a way that 'points ahead' in the development that later resulted – as one of several options.

During the period of historicist hegemony, the academic environment did not look favourably upon sociology as an undertaking. Having been brought up in the historicist tradition, Weber was not eager to be seen as a sociologist – the controversy continues to this day whether he should be regarded predominantly as a sociologist, a historian, or a law scholar.[33]

In Weber's case, moreover, his overt appearance as a sociologist did not occur until several years after his early methodological essays. The transition is scarcely manifest in his work before 1913, although Wolfgang Mommsen sees that as the decisive year for Weber's move to sociology (see, for instance, Mommsen 1989: 127). Others see the transformation in 1909–10, when Weber participated in the academic institutionalization of sociology, in creating a national German professional organization. Others again deny that Weber was ever mainly a sociologist (although this is to some extent defined retrospectively). Burger (1987) says that Weber isn't much of a sociologist (see, for instance, his 'Postscript': pp. 209, 217 and 227, as well as p. xi in the 'Preface'), that he was more prone to reforming historiography, and that a reconstruction of Weber´s context shows that sociology was more of a necessary evil, a vehicle to overcome the resistance of historicist gatekeepers in the face of the positivist challenge. *Weber was more against metaphysics than for sociology.* Mommsen observes that the historical dimension is ever present in Weber´s work, even when it turns into formal sociology, and he shares H. Stuart Hughes's (1958) notion that Weber represented a conjuncture between history and the social sciences at a moment when the social sciences 'were turning a blind eye to the historical dimension of social change'. It would, however, be a mistake not to place

Weber's early methodological essays within the context of a nascent sociology.[34]

Does an Overarching Interpretation Matter?

There might be cause for a certain pessimism about the prospects for clarifying Weber's elusive image. From competing 'creative interpretations' of Weber's contribution to the scientific enterprise we have moved to less selective and more all-inclusive attempts at a *Gesamtdeutung*. 'Ultimate' interpretations claiming to have found the true meaning of Weber are themselves ambitions that fall back on pre-Weberian essentialism. German Weber scholars especially seem to be haunted by a strong inclination to achieve coherence. This flight from ambiguity might generate more profound interpretations, but it will not catch the key to Weber's work as a whole. There is no such key. The 'indecipherable hieroglyphic' remains out of view (Tenbruck 1989a: 77).

The various attempts to find some sort of unifying principle in Weber's work are chimeras. Even if we were fairly convinced about which extrascientific ultimate intentions Weber had or whatever 'secret love' we might find, it would still only serve as a sort of fallible vehicle for extrapolation in rendering his work more coherent than Weber did himself. Wolfgang Mommsen (1989) embodies the agony of the German debate, on the one hand acknowledging the evolutionary character of Weber's work, reflecting changing positions over time, yet still continuing to build two-dimensional models of social change in Weber's universal historical sociological conception. He thus remains a participant in the *Gesamtdeutung* debate we ought to transcend. The same predicament is reflected in Tenbruck (1986), as well as Schluchter's recent contributions (esp. 1996a and 1996b). They are haunted by a search for the lost foundations – or lost continuity – of German cultural science, in line with the spiritual manifestations of the German *Sonderweg*. Tenbruck is apt to stress the historicist elements in Weber, whom he does not really regard as a sociologist. Obsolete as it might be, this view still is evidently tuned in to a deep and viable streak in German social thought, since this basic historicist revival of sorts is something he shares with his domestic intellectual opponents.

Gerhard Wagner and Heinz Zipprian (1985), in criticizing Tenbruck, still regard historicism as a secular current, to be understood more as a part of than a reaction against the Enlightenment, as its self-reflection. And Wilhelm Hennis (1985) is not really inclined to see the problem of Enlightenment demystification shifting the burden and responsibility of choice from God to man. Weber's neo-Kantian methodology could also be seen as a reflection of this polytheistic dilemma, but Hennis prefers to ignore this aspect of Weber's methodology in favour of a unitarian refoundation of a firm human meaning. Hennis might cast light upon Weber's extrascientific concerns, but he abstains from dealing with the methodological consequences of Weber's 'nihilism', as Leo Strauss would put it; in this respect Strauss (and his followers, Hennis among them) represents a reaction to the modernity that Weber inhabited.

Many scholars (for instance Bloom 1987) have in various terms attacked 'relativism', and made the European classics, such as Max Weber's work with its Nietzschean echoes, responsible for a demise in public virtues. Although their diagnosis sounds reasonable they fail to come up with a remedy, instead turning to a revival of Renaissance republicanism as well as Aristotelian ethics (MacIntyre). Today's moral deficit might well be an unwelcome consequence of the radical anti-metaphysics of modern science. The predicament might be painful, but it is hard to escape.

All these voices in the debate nevertheless contribute to the clarification and expansion of Weber scholarship. Tenbruck has once and for all brought about a shift of emphasis from *WuG* to *GARS*. Wagner and Zipprian – and more recently H. H. Bruun – have revealed Weber's shortcomings – or more specifically Rickert's shortcomings as a mentor for Weber – in the light of modern epistemology. Hennis – as well as Scaff – brought our attention to long-neglected manuscripts in Weber's intellectual quarry.

Weber as a key figure in the history of social science doctrine is not diminished by any of this; quite the reverse. To read Weber's methodological texts involves an encounter with his context, even if no single modern social science approach could be successfully and reliably singled out as the true Weberian approach. The most promising 'candidate', the general notion of scientific value relativism, is, after all, a retrospective creation of Arnold Brecht (1959), although it is certainly less vulnerable to refutation than the attempts at what might be characterized as 'substantial methodological' paradigms. The wishful search for a thematic unity in a fragmented *œuvre* has – selectively assimilated – the positive effect of generating an ever more profound level of awareness of the complexity of Weber's roots and historical significance.

Weber shared the shortcomings, limitations and restricted horizons of his own day, with the difference that he had the synthesizing 'clout' to affect the course of social science. As the co-founder of a new discipline he had the opportunity to start anew. The stalemate of the *Methodenstreit* provided Weber with an attentive audience; its receptivity, however, depended upon his ability to dress in its guise and share its language and preconceptions. Weber responded adequately to the difficulties his generation of scholars had to face, which, because of Carl Menger's challenge to Gustav Schmoller in the *Methodenstreit* between history and theory, happened to be mainly methodological. Weber could not, despite his historicist background, easily find remedies within the historicist tradition to cure its own methodological shortcomings (see, for instance, Nau 1997).

Viewing Weber as a diplomat adjusting his message for optimal reception touches the heart of the methodological problem of intellectual history. Stressing the intentional element might result in prolepsis.[35] There is little point in treating Weber's texts as canonical, as a matter of exegesis, when what is needed is recontextualization, adjustment and correction, since we cannot be sure about intentions but merely know the effects. Treating the authority of the texts as cast in stone leads to the further danger of suggesting that the author himself misunderstood his own canonical text – this has been demonstrated in a few prominent cases, such as Parsons and Schutz. However, there are today so many scholars working on Weber's legacy that it is hardly possible to annex his scholarship and claim it for obscure purposes.

Tenbruck might be closer to the crucial core than he – or Weber – makes explicit, in the suggestion that we are stuck with a polytheist predicament; that the individual is exposed to unresolvable conflict (Tenbruck 1980: 77–8).

This is the point at which we have a conflux of methodology and general philosophy, two 'arenas' we should keep apart despite their interrelation. How to establish intersubjective propositions about a social reality of actions and motives is a project that differs from the human problem of how to find guidance for the conduct of our lives. The death of (the one) God because of the Enlightenment is the common source and in both cases it is a problem of value-incommensurability, although the conduct of life is a problem that calls for a tentative solution, precisely the 'Indian rope trick' science must avoid in order to improve.

Nietzsche, the Disenchantment Thesis and Methodology

The persistent interest in the interpretation of Weber's thought is, however, largely because of his relevance in the diagnosis of modernity (see for instance Bryan S. Turner 1992, esp. ch. 10; Charles Turner 1992; Schluchter 1996a) – disenchanted science failing to replace religion as the source of meaning, and throwing us into either the dilemma of (moral) choice or the lethargy of nihilism.[36] On a very general level one might agree with Hennis's basic thesis – as well as Parsons's (see for instance Schluchter's (1979) eulogy at the funeral of Parsons) – that Weber's central concern is the human predicament. However, this does not sufficiently clarify Weber's role for social science doctrine and is thus misleading for any scientific evaluation of Weber's paradigmatic contribution to social science methodology: how to find remedies to uncontrolled value-intrusion.

Weber's 'value-aspect-choice methodology' reflects the general philosophical predicament of modernity. Method can also be put into context and studied as an object in the history of ideas. This can be understood as an attempt to find orientation and to understand – and relativize – the predicament of the discipline (or tradition) within which one's work is to be pursued and assimilated, as a chain in the explanatory endeavour as a whole. That the social sciences today tend to lose their 'hard core' (Lakatos's (1970) term) and to be cannibalized by their empirical spin-offs (specialities) or economics (Udéhn 1996) is probably a symptom of premature closure in the name of the hypothetical-deductive method as the one and only correct method. The options are obviously more mixed, as already noted by Weber. There is no reason to denounce the unity of science and the possibility in principle of standard positions in the philosophy of social science, but it would be an illusion to mistake this option for reality.[37]

Modernity is conceived in different ways depending on how one evaluates the Enlightenment. The transformation brought about in the Western mind appears as a genuine turning point in the history of ideas, although the process is a gradual one. Humans replace God as the masters of their destiny (Alexander 1989: 74). For primitive humans God was ever-present in everyday life, while medieval humans tried to find out God's intentions and directives. 'Once God directed man, now man chooses his Gods' (ibid.: 79). Today's inner-worldly technical mastery of a secular society might rather bring us in conflict with the natural environment than with God. The problem of theodicy and meaning remains an issue despite the optimism about scientific progress reflected in the mixed ideological and cognitive scientific claims of liberals as well as Marxists.

There is a more humanistic, idealistic conception of modern post-Enlightenment, as reflected in, for instance, Jürgen Kocka and Detlev Peukert (1991), carrying on Condorcet's idea of progress into new applications, as in the case of Habermas's normative consensus through communicative competence. This cultural idealist progressivism has, in common with the American neo-Straussians,[38] the hope of a successful discourse in ethics, as a way to come to grips with the nihilist dilemma. As Horst Baier (1987) notes, the Europeans have been more apt to assimilate Nietzschean (Weberian) modernity, in accepting the tragic stalemate among ultimate values as an inescapable tragedy of all attempts at political ethics.[39] Weber's *Freiburger Antrittsrede* could be read as a Nietzschean argument for political modernization and 'education', something 'pre-Enlightenment' neo-Straussians, neo-Aristotelians (MacIntyre, Bloom), as well as (value-) philosophical Weberians, ought to be able to agree upon, albeit with very different verdicts.

The differences mentioned above among the lingering national styles associated with the name of Nietzsche have now been altered, for instance by a growing 'left-Nietzschean' interpretation (see Antonio 1995) as well as the differences between Schluchter on the one hand and, on the other hand, Hennis (in his *Göttinger Vortrag* [1985b]) and Baier, who hardly agree with each other on much else.[40] To Schluchter, Weber's rather frequent and evident allusions to Nietzsche do not fit his own reconstruction of Weber's ethics, which is clearly an extension of Weber's value-philosophy, making him less of a decisionist.[41]

The connections between Weber and Nietzsche are accounted for also in Szakolczai's book on Weber and Foucault (in which he piles up an impressive amount of supporting evidence for Nietzsche's importance to Weber, see Szakolczai 1998: esp. p. 112 *et passim)* and the discussion over the existence of such a link appears today as a moot point. Yet the meaning and consequences of such a link is a matter of interpretation and controversy (see for instance Runciman 2000). The 'death of God' and the 'nihilist' predicament might result in moral indifference, as well as in renewed Icarian flights or 'Indian rope tricks', or various attempts at 'leaps of faith'.[42]

Methodologically, the problem is simply that we need points of departure for instrumental means–end analyses, but have obvious problems in justifying or verifying such ultimate values or top-values. Provisional solutions include 'public welfare' or Enlightenment reason, or, as in Myrdal's case, a combination of the two, although some sort of (at least local) Socratic dialogue might be required in order to avoid a stalemate among the new competing gods which Weber envisioned – or end up in the pure decisionism which Schluchter fears and which we associate with Carl Schmitt.

'Nihilism' may be a misleading term, since the Russian original refers to indifference, which fits neither a characterization of Weber, nor its use in present-day value-philosophy. Moreover, the term is probably doomed to become misunderstood in the United States where the European classics have been under attack for promoting precisely this sort of 'nihilism' (Bloom 1987). 'Polytheism' or 'perspectivism'[43] might be better labels, if I were urged to pick one (despite my own warnings against labels, which in general tell more about the interpreter than about the classic under scrutiny). The term 'nihilism' refers here to the school of negative value-ontology developed from Axel Hägerström's 'emotive' theory of values (see p. 116).[44] It stands for a radicalization of the scientific value-relativism that grew out of the Weber–Rickert solution, which is of limited objectivity because of its explicit value-relatedness.

Weber distinguished among a number of what he called spheres of life. He mentions the economic, political, religious, intellectual, erotic and family spheres, and suggests that each of these has a corresponding set of values. Each sphere of life has considerable autonomy in its relation to the other spheres. Nietzsche would have ascribed a particular role to the aesthetic sphere, a place beyond good and evil. Because Nietzsche is so influential as an interpreter of modernity, it is tempting to relate Weber to him. Weber, I would argue, formulates a methodology that answers Nietzsche, as well as Kierkegaard and also the later existentialists, and is in accordance with them. However, this remark is no better than allowing us to replace Nietzsche with, for instance, Jaspers[45] – or Bauman, or Giddens, or, originally in the particular case of Weber, Troeltsch – all of whom deal with a new situation of choice, which is frustrating to any believer. What the existentialists formulate on the level of general philosophy, Weber formulates on the level of methodology. They agree that there is no Archimedian point in ethics other than the points of reference that we ourselves provide. We cannot escape the responsibility for our choices of valuative points of reference. Although Weber seldom mentions names, at times he is very clearly alluding to Nietzsche, for example when he uses the Nietzschean concept of the 'last man' (letzte Mensch).[46]

Although characterizing Weber as a 'nihilist' would be an overstatement, it is nevertheless less so than is often assumed. There is a relationship between the theodicy problem, nihilism and modernity as a predicament, and Weber's methodological work, which is clearly exposed in 'Einleitung' (1920), one of the key texts for understanding Weber.[47] In Weber's view science itself is meaningless, since it cannot teach us anything about how we are supposed to live our lives. Only 'big children in university chairs' hope science can be the way to 'true' art, existence, nature, happiness, and so on. We have to live with the anxiety of being responsible ourselves for the consequences of our actions, like Luther at Worms.[48]

For those who cannot bear the anxiety of modernity, Weber's recommendation is clear: one might just as well return to the church and pay the intellectual sacrifice (Lassman and Velody 1989: 29; GAW: 611). But if one can stand the anguish of scientific impotence in the field of normative orientations, Weber's 'value-aspect-choice' methodology is instrumental. It departs from two – basically neo-Kantian – insights: (1) reality offers an infinite plentitude; and (2) since nothing in reality itself provides its own interpretation, selection principles are indispensable.

'Philosophical Weberianism', that is, neo-Kantianism and anti-Hegelianism, methodologically refines the existentialist dilemma of choice and responsibility, what Baier (1985) refers to as 'the long shadow of the dead God' or 'der Schatten Nietzsches über Webers Wissenschaftslehre' (1987: 433). In the modern nihilist tradition (Axel Hägerström and various modes of legal realism) one cannot possibly ascribe any (eventual) cognitive value to 'moral force', 'good' or 'bad'.[49] It is striking that so many criticize Weber's alleged 'nihilism', or try to dismantle those tenets in his body of ideas. The nihilist interpretation may be the only viable extension, as the typical condition of post-Enlightenment modernity. Weber's scientific value-relativism, as a more radical non-cognitive form of value-ontology than Kelsen's legal positivism, is not an attractive position; it is simply difficult to escape. Value positions seem to rely on self-evidence, an act of revelation and faith not shared by modern social science, a realization that in its infancy caused Weber and his colleagues much agonizing.[50]

Even if it might hurt consensus-building within the political community, a privileged position for bourgeois natural law as a basis for natural rights is simply no longer philosophically tenable and credible, after the Enlightenment; and the modern combination of utilitarianism and natural law never ceases to astonish, since historically the rational calculus eroded natural law (Hobbes and Bentham). Value-nihilism might just as well promote a healthy sceptical tolerance, owing to an awareness of the undemonstrability of ultimate values.

This is in fact the way Axel Hägerström, one of Max Weber's 'Swedish relatives', thought of his own radical anti-metaphysics and value-nihilism.

Too many labels have already been ascribed to Weber retrospectively. His methodology is conceived of in very different ways. Weber situated himself at the heart of fundamental controversies in the social sciences. Within his context he provided a series of answers and solutions that still speak to us. The ideal-type resulted from the tensions within German historicism, which had come under such pressure from the seemingly superior claims of a unified-science ideal of positivism. Weber responded to the anguish of his colleagues with a position that mediated between both sides of the dispute. This mediation, in its turn, became a cornerstone in the construction of social science in its commonly accepted twentieth-century guise. As such, because of its mediating rather than systematic character, Weber's solution is built into the identity of the main and disparate paradigm of today's social science. Weber was not a 'card-carrying' philosopher, but a practising social scientist, and he aimed at scientific rigour within the constraints of the central problem – to find and develop non-arbitrary tools to represent scientifically the essential elements of an unstructured infinite reality. His way of developing an instrumental method within the limitations of the German *Sonderweg*, by means of commentaries on the works of contemporary colleagues, makes Weber less interesting as a guide to social science method, but more interesting because of his immense significance in the history of social science doctrine in one of its most formative periods. Above all he is an anti-Hegelian, favouring intersubjective concept formation designed to meet criteria of proof.

In the longer perspective, Weber responded to the crisis of the polytheism of ultimate values posed by Nietzsche and Kierkegaard (and Troeltsch). His solution was both loyal to the historicist tradition of which he was a part, and also made possible what I term 'normative empirical theory'; he became a key theorist of modernity. His achievement, then, was not a radically new departure but rather a breaking up and recombination of existing arguments. His critiques of historicism represent both breaches in and advances on that tradition that were crucial for the further development of modern secular social theory.

Appendix:
The Radical Solution? Gunnar Myrdal and the Diffusion of Value-Orientation/Relation

Max Weber had a great following in Sweden where there is ready soil for the radical anti-metaphysics inherent in his value-philosophy.[1] Gunnar Myrdal made a career on both sides of the Atlantic and early on in his career had fruitful contacts with the German intellectual realm also, like most Swedish scholars of his day.[2]

Gerhard (Jörd) Mackenroth was one of the closest friends of Gunnar Myrdal, whom he got to know in London in the late 1920s, and Myrdal visited the Deutsche Bücherei in Leipzig during his formative years. With an interruption during the period 1937–44, reflecting both a gulf[3] in their respective opinions about the German regime at the time, as well as the fact that contacts with foreigners were risky for a German during the Nazi era (Mackenroth was a Wehrmacht officer during the war, most of the time stationed in Alsace), they kept in touch throughout their lives. Mackenroth died prematurely of heart failure in 1955, when he was a full professor (*Lehrstuhlinhaber*) in sociology in Kiel. There are about 130 letters between Myrdal and Mackenroth in the ARAB (Archives of the Labour Movement) in Stockholm.[4] The Myrdals were also close friends of Dorothy and W. I. Thomas, as reflected in many letters.[5]

Mackenroth was fluent in Swedish and translated Myrdal's work on *The Political Element in the Development of Economic Theory* into German a couple of decades before it appeared in English. There is an intense dialogue in various intrinsic matters, touching upon basic concepts in political economy, value philosophy, political sociology and the nature of nationalism. At the time (1930) Myrdal was more of an 'Otto Neurath' than a 'Weber' and his task was to trace hidden values in economic doctrine. The material at ARAB suggests that Myrdal was familiar with Weber; but how familiar is somewhat unclear, although Myrdal seemingly applied Weber's 'value-aspect-choice' methodology in his later works.[6] There is more value-freedom than value-relation at this early stage of Myrdal's career. In fact, Myrdal in *The Political Element* refers to Weber as a source of inspiration for his early views on value-freedom. Later Myrdal in effect codified Weber's qualification of *Wertfreiheit* into *Wertbeziehung*, in the form of a useful methodological manual (1944). There is, however, no reference to Max Weber in this work.

In a letter of 22 October 1932 Myrdal writes to Mackenroth: 'I have received and kept the work on Max Weber and have found some of it intellectually profitable. I am grateful if you also in the future would keep me *à jour* with what is printed in Germany' (my translation, letter kept at ARAB, in the Myrdal *Nachlass*). Myrdal does not say which work on Weber. It seems, though, that Mackenroth kept him updated. This does not exclude the possibility that Myrdal on his own came to positions close to those in Weber's methodological work.

Myrdal's main target around 1930 is utilitarian marginalist economics. This is perhaps easy to misunderstand, considering Bentham's variation of utilitarianism combined with anti-natural law philosophy, which is much in line with the 'secularized' Weber–Rickert position on value-orientation. What Myrdal is criticizing is lingering natural law elements in economic doctrine.[7]

Gunnar Myrdal also discussed value-philosophy with Alf Ross (a Danish law scholar who took his PhD degree in Uppsala), who was to become a prominent exponent of so-called Scandinavian legal realism. Myrdal was also a friend of Karl Mannheim, who promoted the English translation of *The Political Element*.[8]

The main philosophical source of inspiration for both Myrdal and Ross was the radical anti-metaphysics of Axel Hägerström, professor in practical philosophy in Uppsala and, so to speak, 'world famous in Sweden'.[9] He writes in his inaugural lecture of 1911, 'On the Truth of Moral Propositions', that: 'Science has only to indicate what is true, while it is nonsense to regard the idea of obligation as true', and further, 'moral philosophy as a science is purely and simply a science of actual moral evaluations in their historical development, based on a psychological analysis and conducted by a critical philosophical investigation of the ideas which are operative therein. . . . Moral science may not be a teaching *in* morals, but only a teaching *about* morality.'[10]

To Hägerström values are not only hard to prove as valid, they are neither false nor true, or, in a tougher interpretation which might be closer to the mature Hägerström, 'values are always false' and have just as much cognitive (scientific) truth value as interjections, such as 'Whoops', 'Damn', 'Shit', etc. – or as a sneeze or a cough.

This radical doctrine of negative value ontology combined with non-cognitivistic value-sentence theory was labelled 'nihilism' by its critics, which was soon accepted by the adherents as the proper name, although it became better known abroad as 'Scandinavian legal realism'. It is sometimes also called the 'emotive' theory of value. The affinity between Max Weber's 'scientific value-relativism', Axel Hägerström's nihilism, Edvard Westermarck's anthropological relativism and Hans Kelsen's legal positivism is obvious and it is noteworthy that they almost simultaneously developed similar ideas informed by radical anti-metaphysics.[11]

Most of Hägerström's apostles were law scholars, such as Carl Olivecrona, whose *Law as Fact* has been translated into many languages. They argued that laws have no morally binding obligation but are like traffic rules – or, in a more 'Nietzschean' formulation, fences for the domestic cattle. Might precedes right.

The echo of Nietzsche is manifest both in Weber, for instance in the twin lectures, and also in Hägerström. In both Weber and Hägerström we find formulations that seemingly allude to Nietzsche on the Last Man, slave morality, etc.[12]

It is unclear to what extent Hägerström knew of Weber; probably he was aware of Weber, although he was more influenced by Austrian philosophers, such as Meinong. But there was no exchange. Hägerström also influenced Myrdal, as is made *very* explicit in Myrdal's *Nachlass*. Myrdal was very probably influenced by Max Weber as well, despite some minor technical differences. Myrdal's own 'political commissar'-solution to the norm-sender problem is in fact an extension of Weber–Rickert on value-relation, independent of the extent to which Myrdal was himself familiar with Weber's example. The values promoted by large organizations, such as big trade unions and the leading labour party, served Myrdal as guidelines for instrumental policy analyses, securing social significance and relevance.[13]

The precise nature of Myrdal's relation to Weber remains a matter of interpretation. In an article from 1933 he criticized Weber, but a 'Weber' interpreted more in the Rickertian vein, with lingering natural law elements, including transcendental systems of value that (perhaps) could provide the 'Archimedian' points that enable a rational choice between incommensurable competing ultimate values. However, Myrdal's criticism aims at improving the Weberian position, making it less vulnerable to natural law abuse, or natural law-suffused interpretation and/or criticism.

We need *Wertobjektive* to be employed as top-values for the purpose of instrumental means–end analyses but cannot reach them without a sort of 'Indian rope trick'. Rickert's solution of eternal suprahistorical values generated much interpretative pain for later scholars, such as Wagner and Zipprian, Burger, Oakes and H. H. Bruun, as we have seen in previous chapters. Weber's way out is to select cultural values, such as the autonomy of man as a cultural being, without claiming any scientific truth value to his ultimate-value points of departure, although it remains unclear if they perhaps could be true or false. Such knowledge is merely beyond the reach of present-day intersubjective science. Myrdal's way out is to make the jump to value premises subjective and explicit, in order to prevent uncontrolled value-intrusion in the rationalization of value-hierarchies. Whether this position means that objectivity and value-freedom in social research are possible or impossible looks like an ever recurring play with words, especially in the wake of 1968; it is a restricted objectivity accomplished through the isolation of the value-element, which is anchored in politics rather than culture.

An important difference (although without methodological consequences) is that Myrdal's anti-metaphysics is more radical, in the vein of Hägerström. However, value-nihilism does not exclude a compassionate engagement in politics. Myrdal was a world-improver, much in favour of social reforms of various kinds and later also concerned with underdevelopment and development in the Third World, etc. The consequences of his Hägerströmian nihilism for the truth value of civil rights and human rights is by no means incompatible with his role in the promotion of civil rights and racial equality.

The way Myrdal lists his value points of departure in *An American Dilemma* (1944) is very probably the most important and most consistent application of the methodological device of Weber–Rickert, although Myrdal conceived of this as an invention of his own. In any case it is true that he further developed the Weber–Rickert method of objectivity and value-freedom, by the use of explicit values, for the purpose and needs of piecemeal social engineering. A whole chapter is dedicated to a thorough account of all value premises that guide the investigation (in this case an 'operationalization' of the American creed, taken from the US constitution). This reflects a development in Myrdal. He no longer advocates the 'Viennese' creed of value-freedom, but explicit top-values or ultimate values enabling intersubjectivity (and objectivity), and he thus avoids uncontrolled value-intrusion.[14] It is, moreover, in effect an extension of the Weber–Rickert stand on *Wertbeziehung*.

Myrdal is clearly an extension and radicalization of Weber, whose ideas were, admittedly, not immediately operative on a technical methodological level, 'solving' the norm-sender problem in a way that answers to the needs of the era of social engineering and welfare reforms. It is a shift, from history and culture, to sociology, in a period when intellectuals overlapped with the political power in society.[15]

Myrdal had so-called 'larger than life' qualities; he was also an egocentric megalomaniac who mostly quoted himself, well aware of his own importance. This is justified in his case, since he had a genius's talent for expressing the core of very difficult methodological problems in a few clear words. His admiration and reverence for Hägerström is very explicit; it is *very* ostentatious. Here are a few, almost touching, examples: Myrdal writes to the admired master and asks for his portrait, which is to be 'not too small', expressing worries that his honoured master perhaps would find this humble request too sentimental.[16] According to Myrdal's daughter Sissela (Bok), Myrdal also took the trouble to browse in antiquarian bookstores to find Hägerström's main works, which were to be a present to her upon the occasion of her PhD thesis. This is a somewhat different image of Myrdal as a thoughtful and caring father, compared to the image in the autobiographical fictions by his son Jan – and to some extent also in the books by his daughters.[17] Late in life Myrdal, in his personal copy of a biography of Hägerström, makes marginal notes precisely where the radical anti-metaphysical elements are emphasized in the text.[18]

However, Myrdal admitted that he never really scrutinized Hägerström's main work, the two dense volumes (in German) on *The Concept of Obligation in Roman Law*. Very few have. At the same time, there are formulations in Myrdal's works on value-relatedness and bias that sound very much like Rickert–Weber. Myrdal's relation to Hägerström and Weber calls for more research. That he contributes to the same project is beyond doubt. This common project might be labelled 'The Long Line of Secularization'.[19]

Methodological Appendix

Recontextualizing Weber at the Crossroads

In his methodological writings Weber is notoriously elusive, but some themes do persist. My approach rejects the idea that Weber's thought falls into radically distinct stages or is characterized by dramatic shifts of emphasis.[1] Moreover, I do not view Weber primarily as a founder of the discipline of sociology, which much of the secondary literature does. Indeed, the way Weber was presented to scholars in the period after the Second World War, for example by Parsons, was precisely as one of the pillars of modern sociological thought. Weber's 'methodology' was treated in some respects as a scheme for the conduct of social research in the same way as Durkheim's rules of sociological method. Weber does not live up to the expectations implicit in these characterizations.

Weber, as a founder, is commonly thought to possess some sort of distinctive theory that can be compared to those of Marx and Durkheim. In fact he has no such theory; he is not at heart a theoretician.[2] Weber sometimes does use the word 'theory', as when he speaks of the 'Theory of the religious rejections of the world and their directions' ('Theorie der Stufen und Richtungen religiöser Weltablehnung') in the 'Zwischenbetrachtung' in *GARS*. Weber's 'theoretical statement', *Economy and Society* (*Wirtschaft und Gesellschaft*), is more a storeroom of tools and concepts, each of which can be used in isolation from the others and in conjunction with intellectual purposes radically different from Weber's own. If a classic thinker is an innovator, as for example Hobbes was in the English tradition of political thought, or Herder, Kant and Fichte were in the German philosophical tradition, or Friedrich

(Frederick) List was in connection to the historical school of economics, it is difficult to see why Weber should be awarded this title.[3] The thinkers of Weber's generation were more typically synthesizers; indeed, synthesis was part of the task of German nation-building.

Weber's identity as a 'sociologist' is a complex and somewhat delicate topic.[4] Weber did not see himself in the way that he came to be seen retrospectively, as one of the pillars of the new discipline of sociology. To be sure, Weber was involved with sociologists. He was a co-founder of the German Sociological Society in 1909–10. He and his brother Alfred attended its meetings, and the contract for the last professorship he held, in Munich, lists sociology as one of his disciplinary concerns.[5] And as Schluchter reminds us, Weber from 1913 onwards speaks of *Economy and Society* as his 'sociology'.[6] But the focus of his methodological essays is the practice of historians. Weber laid the foundations for the furtherance of 'testable' procedures in 'social science', that is, lucid conceptualizations that could meet criteria of rational proof, originally within theoretically ambitious history. Weber sought an 'explanatory' rather than a merely descriptive or idiographic history, although his views on explanation are opaque and not theoretical in the unified-science sense. In a sense, indeed, Weber's development recapitulates the development of social science itself, beginning in theology and passing through stages of jurisprudence, history and economics, coming in the end to sociology. There are, however, few radical breaks in this development. It is illustrative that Weber opposed Schmoller, the leading figure of the German historical school, but nevertheless took Schmoller's explanatory concerns in the history of economics to be not only valid but as providing the core explanatory concern of his own social science, namely the problem of understanding the historical origin of capitalism and the consequences of Western modernity.

Weber was not himself occupied with the project of founding sociology: this became an allegiance fairly late in life, increasingly on the agenda after he wrote his best methodological essays (between 1903 and 1907). What conclusions should be drawn from this fact is still a matter of dispute in modern Weberology. Weber was not preoccupied with the methodological underpinning of our identity crisis, which he could not have been aware of. He was, however, responding to the identity crisis of the historical school (Troeltsch), facing the challenge of positivism in the guise of Austrian theoretical (marginalist) economics. There are parallels, both with the days of Ranke and Comte as well as with present-day tensions between theoretical social history (Kocka, Wehler) and narrative tendencies (building for instance on the archives from the French courts of inquisition), since the relationship between theory and history was never resolved. History *vs* theory was the main paradigmatic division in social science and history two centuries ago, as well as today. One might say that just as Weber, brought up as a law scholar and historian, is no methodologist at heart, neither is he a sociologist, although he gave important methodological impulses to modern sociology, in which he came to serve as a 'founding father' to a number of 'adopted' – or self-adopted – children. For an interpretation of his views on explanation and value-intrusion these questions about the proper retrospective label do not necessarily have to be resolved, the philosophy of science being much the same for historical and theoretical explanation, as we have also considered.

I do not suggest that we should disregard later developments in order to achieve a better understanding of Weber on his own terms. On the contrary, I would say that the retrospective concerns ('intellectual investments' in Weber as a paradigmatic guru for a diversity of social science paradigms) and Weber's actual influence might explain some peculiarities in the reception history of Weber's methodology. Why is his legacy so difficult to establish? We don't have the same sort of confrontations over the proper interpretation of, say, Tocqueville, who might be considered almost equally relevant today, while Weber seems to generate endless debates and ever more reinterpretations. There are answers to this.

Weber's apostles, like Schutz and Parsons, do not co-ordinate their efforts in the same direction but try to create entire paradigms out of a rich but fragmented and opaque *œuvre*. Because Weber is coloured by the paradigmatic ambitions of his various interpreters there appears to be more than one Weber. This calls for a better contextual understanding of his methodology, although there are some reasons to remain pessimistic about the chances of coming to *one* uncontested all-inclusive interpretation.

I am not suggesting that it is illegitimate to use the classics unhistorically as a toolbox or as discourse partners, treating them as contemporaries, only that it creates – certainly in the case of Max Weber – confusion in the case of virulent competing interpretations. I am not claiming that a more contextual/historicist reading is the way to the full understanding of Weber. At worst it might even blind us to the innovative or mediating elements in his methodological work that are well attuned to the important overcoming of pre-neo-Kantian

('Hegelian') metaphysics; that is, in seeing him as a more loyal historicist than he really turned out to be. It is difficult to overlook the fact that we approach Weber from a level of a discourse that actually resulted from one of several options, although we might disagree or hesitate as to whether it is to be understood as a renovated historicism or a new sociology. We have a problem of interpretation created precisely by presentist ignorance of the genuine context, the understanding of which would at least make us less vulnerable to the risk of premature theoretical overinterpretation. Theory (in social science) develops in a dialogue with the classics.

As a historian with a scope we can hardly imagine any longer, Weber turns 'sociological' but does not really deal much with 'society'. Instead he develops varieties of 'social action', which moreover is the link between his methodological and substantive writings. When he turns 'theoretical' it is more casuistry than theory.[7] Utility versus the interpretation of the classics is a crucial topic and Weber a very illustrative case. If by a classic we mean a creative originality that has been left to us in a perfect and finished form, then Weber does not fit this label. He saw himself as a 'sociologist' only reluctantly and hesitantly. He made no claim to be a sociological system-builder, yet some of the most distinguished figures in twentieth-century social science have sought to fashion a classical sociology from his legacy. One explanation for the coexistence of the disparate yet paradigmatical readings of Weber is the imputation of classical authority to an *œuvre* that lacks some crucial attributes of the classical and allows for paradigmatic 'hijackings'.

Synthesis, originality, solutions, combativeness are all to be found in Weber's work. But to say that these combine to achieve a classical form is to claim too much. Subsequent interpreters have been emboldened to recreate Weber as a classical sociologist, and his very reluctance to constitute his work as a unified whole has had the paradoxical consequence of more 'classical' interpretation being reconstructed from the various parts of his *œuvre*.

Weber's methodology is like handling a bar of wet soap. Moreover, catching the essential Weber is not the remedy for original misrepresentations, biased by paradigm-building ambitions. A more contextual reading is called for when we have several 'Webers' cut off from the original situation. A critical scrutiny of the competing interpretations might contribute to a better understanding of the formative factors in sociological discourse. Part of that work has been done in this book.

Having realized that my notion of secularization as a relevant long-term trend does not match the commandments of orthodox contextualism, I have tried here to apply what I call a retrospectivist ('Whiggish') contextualism.

Approaching the Classics

There are three main approaches to the classics: (1) the textualist (immanent analysis); (2) the retrospective (presentism); and (3) the contextualist (historicism).

In a pure immanent analysis we attempt to wipe away everything that has been written after the 'classic text' and then we seek to recapture the text in an unprejudiced reading. However, the resulting sequences of influences and traditions might in itself indicate something about the classic texts and, moreover, we most probably have some reason outside the original context that is motivating our return to the classics in the first place. The recent renaissance of the classics must in itself be put into context. To avoid misrepresentation any immanent reading should be supplemented by contextual sensitivity, since the meanings of concepts vary over time. Otherwise the immanent textualist approach becomes in effect a retrospective reading, in which we tend to treat the meanings of concepts as static.

Elements of immanent analysis are always indispensable; in order to interpret a text it is a reasonable start to know its content. Immanence helps us to a *von oben* perspective, implying transcontextual standards of comparison outside the limited horizons of the classics as well as outside ourselves. This is hardly satisfying, except for the more restricted purpose of bringing about critical editions of texts. There is supposedly some – retrospectively defined – point of view for our approaching the classic; a point of departure not likely to be the fruit of virgin birth. Various structuralist attempts to accomplish timeless criteria of textual comparison might be of great value but, as the case of Weber shows, contextualism must be added for such a context-bound thinker, as is already implied in our critical discussion of textualism.

The second way of approaching the classics is explicitly retrospective. Its main aim is the utility of the classics for today's needs. Our prime interest might be building social system theory or inquiring into the philosophical foundations of an interpretative sociology rather than the 'correct' interpretation of the texts of the classics we approach. We use the ideas of the classics, for example, in order to create better conflict sociology, or political sociology, or 'middle-range theories'. This approach is a matter of retrieval rather than a genuine interest in the classics in their own right.

If we read the classic from a retrospectively defined perspective, in order to learn something about our own society, we expose ourselves to the dangers of 'premature closure'. We simply find what we want to find and immediately fall into the traps of methodological fallacies and myths, against which the Cambridge historian and political scientist Quentin Skinner has repeatedly warned since the mid-1960s. There is also a danger of being too eager to conceive of the classics as consonant with one's own ideas, responding to today's problems rather than to those contemporaneous with the classic. This is indeed a recurring problem in the case of Weber, who is repeatedly interpreted as an up-to-date guide to our present perspective. Variations on this include attempts at paradigmatic posthumous annexation, or attempts to use the authority of the classic as a surrogate for one's own arguments. The alleged utility of the text tends to deform its proper interpretation, although there is in principle no obstacle to using the classics as a junkyard, where bits and pieces of arguments may be retrieved.

Problems occur in the case of competing interpretations, so obscuring our true understanding of the classic. Wolfgang Mommsen (1959) showed that attempts to recruit Weber as a founding father of modern parliamentary democracy were at variance with Weber's own more complex nationalist political thought. Similarly, any attempt to recruit Weber for a 'value-free' sociology (as friend or foe), *Verstehen* sociology or structural functionalism will likewise be at variance with Weber's original formulations. Retrospective interpretations have a tendency to become 'creative'. The author was not concerned with our problems. The task of intellectual history thus is to reveal the tracks of vested interest in the interpretations already at hand. Parsons, for instance, does not launch a 'false' interpretation so much as one that is selective and flawed, carrying the original source beyond the intentions of its author.

A third way to approach the classics is to regard them as acts in a particular context. Although we can learn much from Hobbes's contract theory about the respective sovereignty of individuals and the state, a contextual reading of Hobbes would rather show it as a response to Cromwell and the English Civil War in the seventeenth century. Although I have strong sympathies with this approach, it does carry with it a certain anti-innovative bias. On this approach Machiavelli would emerge more as a late medieval thinker than as a pioneer of secular political science. It might after all be the case that the author of a classic created something new, the full implications of which he did not himself realize. Moreover, it is not possible fully to escape the limitations of one's own language community, with its specific contextually determined conventions and allusions.

That we approach the classics in order to gain a better understanding of our own society is by no means wrong, but adventurous, inviting us to do retrospectively determined violence to the classics, at the cost of a full understanding of their thought. One might argue that inherent in the concept of a 'classic' is a communication between past and present, where the author speaks to us over the centuries but posterity decides upon the status of the work by ascribing certain qualities to it and interpreting it as a classic.

There is no clear choice among these three approaches. Skinner's orthodox programme for the proper pursuit of intellectual history does not come as a rigid doctrine but rather contributes to a better understanding of the classics in their context, and so avoids the fallacies of theoretical overinterpretations. The case of Max Weber is a good example of Skinner's view. However, pure contextualism tends to sterility, somehow reducing itself merely to an undertaking of historiographical interest, a speciality for the cognoscenti. There is a certain paradoxical affinity between the extremes of unified science and pure contextualism; both reduce the classics to *l'art pour l'art* historiography.

My belief is that we cannot act as an arbiter in the conflict between presentism and historicism, to use the terminology of the Anglo-Saxon debate; rather we have to strive for an optimal balance between these pure types. Most works in the field are mixtures of varying proportions. The search for roots and developmental discourse appear as perfectly acceptable starting points, insofar as they do not obscure our knowledge of the genuine thought of the classics. In order to be able to use the classics it is helpful to know what they actually tried to express. In this respect Skinner has promoted a better, less innocent approach to the classics.

There is an inscription on a bell in S. Petri in Lübeck. It reads: *Qui struit in triviis, multos habet ille Magistros.* This could be rendered as, 'Who builds at the crossroads has many masters'. In Weber's case it is equally true that if you build at the crossroads, you have many followers.

Notes

Introduction

1 Although I have made an attempt to do so; see my contribution to the Schroeder (1998) reader.

2 Collected in the English translation (1971) of Stammer (1965). The English version is somewhat abbreviated.

3 The relation of his methodological writings to his substantive writings, has remained an open issue and the consistency between them is much debated. It is a dividing line in modern German debates; see for instance Prewo (1979), Henrich (1952), and various contributions by Friedrich Tenbruck and Thomas Burger (preface to 2nd edn of his book on Weber's ideal-type conceptualization).

4 It could perhaps be argued that Weber showed signs of being a *repressed* believer, not wishing to appear too religious because of his mother's exaggerated religiosity. It could be argued that Weber remained a 'privately' religious person. His problem horizon is defined by Ernst Troeltsch's work on *The Problems of Historicism* (see ch. 1, n. 25). Troeltsch's theology deals with the loss of meaning (the theodicy problem) which is captured in the metaphor of the 'iron cage' and which calls for values but throws us into polytheism or 'perspectivism', the necessity of choice. In a letter to Tönnies, Weber combines a searching attitude in matters of personal conviction and the scientific and anti-metaphysical creed (Weber, 19 February 1909 in *MWG* II/6: 63 *et passim*). Weber here makes a very clear demarcation between faith and science, yet indicates that on the personal level he is neither anti-religious nor areligious, even if he is religiously unmusical (ibid.: 65).

5 With aspirations to omnipotence on the part of his interpreters: those who control Weber's reception, control social science activity. See Methodological Appendix for a more elaborate view on Quentin Skinner's methodological tools for the proper pursuit of intellectual

history, avoiding the Scylla and Charybdis of chronocentric presentism and pure contextualism.

6   According to the ancient myth, Procrustes had only one bed; anyone too tall or too short was either cut down to size or stretched out to fit. Attempts at approaching Weber as a contemporary give one reason to be sceptical, perhaps sensing artificial attempts to have Weber address our issues rather than his own. Rather we have to try to recontextualize in order to understand. This might be difficult since the original context appears as remote and alien – so perhaps a bridge between past and present is the best we can hope for.

7   I do not elaborate on the long perspective but it is a tacit dimension in my identification of Weber's 'central problem', in terms of post-Enlightenment 'polytheism'.

8   Values and evaluating actors define the specificity of the object in the cultural sciences and the danger of uncontrolled value intrusion is the main flaw of idiographic historicism. Weber's elaboration of Rickert's *Gesichtspunkt* into his ideal-type ('value-aspect-choice methodology') solves – for the practical reason of means–end rational investigation – the problem of value-intrusion and value-incommensurability, values offering points of departure for selection and instrumental analyses.

I The Contexts

1   Joseph Schumpeter himself could not name even a half dozen who were not. See Schumpeter (1954: 781 *et passim*, esp. pp. 818–19). The distinct German character of historicism and its hegemony are also well rendered by Iggers (1968). See also Kluback (1956, esp. pp. 20–51) and Cassirer (1950, esp. p. 217 *et passim*). A more detailed account of its roots is found in Meinecke (1936). See also Schulze (1974), Merquior (1980, esp. p. 140 *et passim*), Topolski (1976), Szacki (1979a), and Oexle (1986) for more diversified examinations.

Ranke is often mentioned as the historicist *par excellence*, although Herder coined the term and Fichte also must be seen as an early historicist. Later, for instance, Droysen and Theodor Mommsen and in the twentieth century Meinecke should be mentioned. Historicism is by no means unique to Germany and is typical of all nation-building. It became very strong and hegemonic in Germany, partly because of delayed nation-building, compared to France and the United Kingdom. Many esp. mid-nineteenth century thinkers were at the same time both historicists and positivists (e.g. Marx) and historicists had positivistic ambitions (e.g. Roscher and Knies), in a sort of innocent flirtation, before the days of confrontation.

2   The first sentence of Munich historian Thomas Nipperdey's standard historical account states that everything started with Napoleon. There is a telling story about Goethe, bowing his head in respect for the French invading army, whom he evidently regarded as visitors providing the

opportunity for cultural exchange. He welcomed the intruders to his home town in a way that would qualify today as treason in most nation states. It is hard to believe that the stimulation of nationalism was once a difficult task in Germany, when the last century has been a history of containment. It can only be understood by bearing in mind that the fragmentation arising from the elected German-Roman Kaiser, a rather powerless representative and embodiment of the old Roman dream of a universal monarchy, and the Thirty Years War dramatically inhibited German development.

3   Fichte with his 'Speech to the German Nation' (1807) is another prominent example.

4   Now of course this state idealism in the era of early nation-building mostly refers to the Prussian state and Prussian virtues, since Germany consisted of many states, many of them with their own foreign policy. It is for instance easy to forget that Bavaria and Prussia were at war with each other as late as 1866. And some of Kurt Eisner's activities, such as his correspondence with US President Woodrow Wilson, as the first *Ministerpräsident* of the Bavarian republic in 1919 might well have been aiming at independent statehood.

5   'Freddy' List already had this tendency (see 'Short Biographies').

6   It might be illuminating to compare Karl Popper's (1957) somewhat eccentric (not totally erroneous, albeit confusing) attempt to link 'historicism' with the search for deterministic laws in history. For a critical evaluation of Popper's unconventional use of the concept of historicism, see Passmore and White (1974). Hegel and Marx, in effect the whole Enlightenment idea of progress, are targets for Popper's criticism; my criticism merely concerns his terminology.

7   The basic sources for the central debate are Schmoller (1883) and Menger (1883, 1884). See also Louis Schneider's 'Introduction' (1963) to his own translation of Menger's *Untersuchungen über die Methode der Sozialwissenschaften und der Politischen Oekonomie insbesondere* (1883). There are several good accounts of the *Methodenstreit* between Schmoller and Menger: for instance, Kaufmann (1936; the later English version is abridged on this topic), Mises (1929), Oakes (1977), Pfister (1928), Nau (1997), Swedberg (1998, esp. Appendix) and Bostaph (1978).

    I have been especially influenced by Bruun (1972) and Therborn (1974) in conceiving of the *Methodenstreit* as an essential part of Weber's methodological context. For the relationship between Weber and the controversy over method, see also Holton and Turner (1989) and Bittman (1986).

8   The Austrian intellectuals' receptiveness to new ideas might be explained by their being alienated from the cause of the nation; a high percentage of these intellectuals were Jews, already marginalized by the standards of the establishment.

9   Indeed, much of Weber's endeavour must be seen in that light. The title of his first chair at Freiburg was *Volkswirtschaftslehre*, the German term

for historical economics, which stemmed from the tradition of Friedrich
List (1856), the pioneer of German political economy. List thought that
Adam Smith's theories did not tell the whole story and had developed
his own approach in a fascinating career on both sides of the Atlantic.
List had noticed that the expansion of the principles of British utilitar-
ianism and liberty (free trade) was sometimes assisted by gunboats.
Volkswirtschaftslehre also rejected abstract theory.

10   Sombart's *Händler und Helden* (1915) is a prominent example. Admiration turned into hatred.

11   It is naturally confusing when central concepts change their connotation over time. Although positivism always means anti-metaphysics
and unified science – and, in one way or another, also law-building
ambitions – its attitude towards 'theory' changes significantly over time.
It is confusing that in the history of ideas, positivism's original meaning
is dominant, while in the current epistemological debate, the more
recently coined meaning prevails. Hence 'positivism' is a contextually
defined term. The shift in emphasis is less difficult to explain than one
might think: all explanations include some notion that cannot be
reduced to an elementary statement.

12   On the whole, the Weberian secondary literature adheres to the 'older'
and more theoretical understanding. See Giddens (1977), especially his
chapter on 'Positivism and its Critics'.

13   According to hypothetical deductive procedure, neither path is necessarily inappropriate.

14   Of course an aspect of *Begriffsgeschichte* (history of the transformation
of concepts) is also involved. The concept of the state, for instance,
definitely has another meaning after the formation of national states by
means of taxation, wars, central administrations and national Bible
translations, during the sixteenth and seventeenth centuries, as compared to the days of Machiavelli, not to speak of Plato.

15   A concept in need of qualification. The German cultural realm is much
broader than the borders of the German state, also including for instance
parts of northern Italy. A *Basler Bürger*, such as Jacob Burckhardt, is a
participant in German cultural life, but very few German-speaking Swiss
would like the idea of becoming part of Germany. The same is true of the
Austrians, after the Second World War, despite the fact that the main cultural divide is marked by the rivers Main and Donau, the *Weisswurst-* or
Masskrug-line, coinciding with the old Roman frontier. In most dictio-
naries this is also the divide, between 'South German and Austrian' and
North German terminology. That the 'German-speaking world' has a
number of limiting cases is also manifest in the careers of Mannheim and
Lukács, both Hungarians.

16   It might be suspected that, because of its hostile attitude towards
theoretical abstraction, the historicist position implicitly employs
assumptions about what is worth knowing when it comes to identifying central causal factors in social reality. What, then, should be the
actual tool for selection, in order to avoid the obfuscation of politics,

prejudice, or other blurring factors? We will return to this point below, in connection with Rickert.

17 Schumpeter at one point even suggested that the conflict could be reduced to the difference between gathering facts and analysing them (a view that implies an inductivist philosophy of science). See also Bergner (1981).

18 Menger had good reason to feel vindicated by these developments. The threat he felt from the historicists was similar to that posed today by economics to the humanities: 'The historians have stepped upon the territory of our science like foreign conquerors, in order to force upon us their language and their customs, their terminology and their methods, and to fight intolerably every branch of enquiry which does not correspond with their special method' ('Preface' to Irrthümer des Historismus [1884]).

19 I suggest that the debate never quite ended, to judge from the reactions to Weber's methodology from Tenbruck, Hennis, Wagner and Zipprian, and others. Even aspects of the positivist controversy between Karl Popper and Theodor Adorno can be understood as its continuation; see Adorno et al. (1969). Also, see Steinvorth (1978).

20 'Rightly conceived, the historical method is no rival of the abstract method rightly conceived', as the British political theorist Walter Bagehot once remarked. The clash between the two schools could also be considered in light of the extent to which the marginalist revolution indicated a genuine paradigmatic revolution. See Hayek (1978), Laudan (1986) and Kruse (1990).

21 The state typically is ascribed a much greater role in the European context than it is in America; the legitimacy societies ascribe to the state or individual citizens is reflected in the social science each developed.

22 We become soulless specialists, a well-known theme in Weber's study of the Protestant ethic (Weber 1905).

23 Scaff (1989: 130), points out the great generational role of Lebensphilosophie, as indicated by Thomas Mann's comments in Reflections of a Nonpolitical Man (1918: 58). Lebensphilosophie appears, however, as another 'Indian rope-trick' in the search for guidance in life, while Lebenswelt as an instance where one might look for transcultural intersubjectivity is taken up by Schutz. As far as the validity of norms is concerned, intersubjectivity is not in sight. Whether it is impossible in principle is a topic on which the neo-Kantians (e.g. Weber) and later anti-metaphysical scholars like Myrdal and Hägerström differ.

The wishful longing for firm norms which still lingers in the United States and Germany (not to mention the Islamic world), represents a natural attempt to escape from the sinister 'Nietzschean' predicament of existential anguish. The loss of firm moral authority and guidelines for conduct has created a modern hardship stemming from the strain placed on individuals by being responsible for making their own choices between competing norms. Although competing value-hierarchies are subject to increasing rationalization and secularization, ultimate choices take place in the irrational existentialist sphere. The growth of instrumental reason goes together with a limitation on its proper application.

24 To judge from recent works by Alasdair MacIntyre (1984) and Allan Bloom (1987), this predicament of existential anxiety and moral relativism continues to be controversial. The issue is understood not only in terms of ontological (ontology = the nature of reality) doctrines determining the proper scope of secular science, but also as a cultural crisis calling for remedies to re-establish ethical 'truth'. During the nineteenth century, the dominant traditions were unable to separate science and ideology; both Marxism and liberal political economy defined themselves as the way it is *and* as the way it ought to be. '*Secularization* is the wonderful mechanism by which religion becomes nonreligion. Marxism is secularized Christianity; so is democracy; so is utopianism; so are human rights' (Bloom 1987: 211). Weber's interventions in the various stages of so-called *Werturteilsstreit* (controversy over value judgements) are well documented in esp. Nau (1996).

25 Troeltsch's *Der Historismus und seine Probleme* appeared in the early 1920s but had been 'in the oven' for a while – and it is very likely the case that he defined Weber's agenda in a way which also influenced Weber. They saw each other on an everyday basis, as neighbours in Heidelberg.

26 This is the root of Leo Strauss's (1953) disgust with historicism, since he saw these consequences and refused to accept them. In the United States, this basically pre-Enlightenment, objectivist, natural law tradition is still in existence, with parallels in Freiburg and Munich. Works by Robert Eden (1986) and Wilhelm Hennis (1987) must be understood with Strauss in mind, for a tendency to conceive of Nietzschean elements on a normative rather than a cognitive level.

27 On the crucial topic of neo-Kantian nominalism as a remedy against Hegelian essentialism and conceptual realism, see for instance Dahrendorf (1987: 574) with its strong statement that Weber's methodology is far from one-dimensional, but 'above all non-Hegelian'. The same point is made by Bjarne Jacobsen (1998). It is also documented in Weber's famous statement that there are two ways to proceed: Hegel's way or our way (documented in Bruun 1972: 39n, letter to von Eulenburg of 11 May 1908).

28 In the United Kingdom, David Hume and John Stuart Mill had already achieved what the German social scientists had to fight for. This, in a sort of dialectical paradox, also meant that the generation of founding fathers of German sociology, such as Weber, Tönnies, Simmel, and others, would have to elucidate basic problems of the philosophy of science much more thoroughly in order to consolidate their 'breakthrough'.

29 There is a great deal of literature on the Back-to-Kant movement; Willey (1978; esp. p. 161 *et passim*) and Iggers (1968) have been particularly important to my argument. There is also a much more recent German

literature: Ollig (1986), and others. See also Segady (1987). See further n. 36 below.

30 Magic is the predecessor of secular science, as we learn from early anthropological functionalists like Malinowski and Radcliffe-Brown. Moreover, science also often appears to be magical.

31 This description of neo-Kantianism brings to mind the theory-prone, trial-and-error model of Karl Popper, which uses falsification instead of verification to promote the cumulativity of science.

32 Indeed, the traditional criticism of neo-Kantian epistemology views it as the first step down the primrose path to empiricism, even solipsism (in which we are alone and know nothing for certain about the world outside our own mind): observational data tend to become a barrier between reality and the researcher, impeding the subjective mind's search for testable knowledge. Sometimes the critique is modified and claims a 'formal' streak in neo-Kantian epistemology, particularly in concept formation, with its programmatic distinction between the real object and the object of science created out of unknown reality and serving as the 'model'.

33 For instance, Rudolf Kjellén held that the state was an organism, not metaphorically but really. The same pre-neo-Kantian conceptual realism reappeared in the Marxist discussion in Denmark and Germany on the proper interpretation of Marx's reproduction schemes in the second volume of *Das Kapital*, which were evidently not conceived of as models valid *ceteris paribus*, but understood as statements of empirical theory.

34 This belief in our ability to deduce all the way to a 'pure' reality parallels some dogmatic stands in the debate over the correct interpretation of the reproduction schemes in Volume II of *Das Kapital*, where Marx constructed models of the economy from Quesnay's *Tableaux d'économique*. Most Marxists are still 'pre-neo-Kantian' – i.e., anti-nominalist – in their ignorance of the methodological accomplishments that have come after Marx. The German (and Danish) *kapitallogische Schule* seemingly adheres to this pre-neo-Kantian dead weight of dialectical materialism, mistaking Marxian models for current and relevant theoretical propositions, judging from Danish (Schantz) and German (Altvater) texts in the 1970s.

35 The demarcation is not really between positivism and historicism, but rather between neo-Kantian nominalism and the older attitudes of conceptual realism and essentialist thinking, in both cases claiming non-observable and non-intersubjective – but rather revealed – insights, about the 'true' nature of phenomena. The debate has deep roots in German epistemological thinking and parallels even in the Middle Ages, when the debate on 'universalism' was at its height.

36 See, in German, Köhnke (1986), Merz (1990), Schnädelbach (1983) and others. Schnädelbach (1983) is probably the most popular introduction to German philosophy.

37 Today much of the debate between 'neopositivism' and various forms of critical theory, as it is called, could be resolved by realizing that the

two camps are engaged in different projects. For example, the human project and communicative vision of Jürgen Habermas, being based on another understanding of the meaning of Enlightenment, is, in a pre-neo-Kantian fashion, strangely congenial to the German *Sonderweg*. My aim in these reflections is not to argue for a specific form of methodology or a specific conception of the Enlightenment, but to place the Back-to-Kant movement in a long-term context (tradition) as an off-spring of the Enlightenment tree of knowledge. This is manifest, for instance, in contributions by Peukert (1989) and Kocka and Peukert (1991). See also Steinvorth (1982), where the same predicament is reflected in the way the paradigmatic front lines are defined.

2 The Shaping of Weber's Conceptual Tools

1   In the middle of the nineteenth century, examples of prominent and successful syntheses can be found between ideas of progress, inspired by the Enlightenment and the natural sciences, and various forms of romantic idealism. Thomas Buckle in England is a good example of such a synthesis. It is unclear whether even Darwin is primarily a historian or a natural scientist. The same could be said of Hegel and Marx. The phenomenon is typical of its time.

2   Roscher and Knies were by no means unique in their acceptance of naturalism. Marx – it is said – wanted to dedicate *Das Kapital* to Darwin, since he thought his own book was a corresponding accomplishment in the field of political economy. There are many examples of this fatal flirtation between 'the two cultures', Buckle's (1857) and Guizot's (1826) respective histories of the English and French civilizations being only two.

3   It is no accident that these alternatives were also those against which Weber would turn in his even more central essay on objectivity in social science and social policy ('Die "Objektivität" sozialwissenschaftlicher und sozialpolitischer Erkenntnis'), in *Archiv* (1904). In that essay he would discuss, although opaquely, his own alternative of the ideal-type and causal explanation, which has served as a basic source for social science methodology ever since its publication. We will return to this in chapter 3. Weber touches in the Roscher and Knies essays on a wide range of contemporary topics within the realm of social science philosophy. The somewhat encyclopaedic and tortured prose, part of which was written as he recovered from depressive illness, spanned three contributions over three years (1903–6) in *Schmollers Jahrbuch*.

4   Evolutionism and organic analogies often go hand in hand. In particular, elements of Wilhelm Wundt's theories – such as his *Völkerpsychologie* (psychology of nationalities) – were anathema to Weber. Wundt's notion of the growth of psychic energy also incorporated several of the elements in social science against which Weber warned

and embodied precisely those metaphysical notions he transcended. Weber's relationship to Wundt remains to be explained, and is a project beyond the scope of this book. However, since sociology grows out of psychology, it is important to be aware of Weber's clear deviation from Wundt.

5 Dilthey, half a generation older than Weber and Rickert and with personal roots in romanticism, embodied German anti-positivism. He had absorbed Herder's romantic humanism and regarded history as essentially a matter of biography. According to the German-American historian Georg Iggers (1968: 140), Dilthey nevertheless conceived of history as a whole, as a process rather than idiographical events. Dilthey's production is voluminous; the most relevant document in this context is *Introduction to the Moral Sciences* (*Die Einleitung in die Geisteswissenschaften*) (1883). See also Windelband's *Präludien* (1903).

6 Terminology typically varies here, depending on standpoint and inclination: where Dilthey speaks of *Geisteswissenschaften* (originally merely a translation of J. S. Mill's 'moral sciences'), Rickert prefers *Kulturwissenschaften*. These variations reflect different ways of conceiving of the ideal relationship between the natural sciences and their methodological alternatives.

7 '[I]n the vocabulary which we owe to Wilhelm Windelband, the historical sciences are not nomothetic but idiographic' (Runciman 1972: 12). These terms refer to law-building activities, on the one hand, and interpretative and descriptive activities, on the other, striving for *Gesetz* or *Gestalt*, respectively. The same phenomenon can be studied from both its idiographic and nomothetic aspects; in principle everything can be studied either historically or naturalistically. Windelband's famous inaugural lecture as new Rector at the university in Strasburg in 1894 was generally received as a declaration of war against the advancing forces of positivism, and launched the often – and still – used dichotomy of idiographic *vs* nomothetic sciences. The speech was not particularly sophisticated; ceremonial contexts rarely offer opportunities for innovative stimulation. However, Windelband had a large audience, and he appeared at the right moment. Many scholars were provoked to articulate their own opinion on the topic of the status of cultural or historical science *vs* natural science.

8 Above all in *The Limits of Concept Formation in Natural Science* (*Die Grenzen der naturwissenschaftlichen Begriffsbildung* (1902)). Although this appeared in 1902, the more readily available 1913 edition is more frequently quoted. Parts have appeared in English, in Guy Oakes's translation. Oakes's obsession with the inconsistencies in Rickert's philosophy of value is reflected in numerous essays over the years, culminating in his 1988 book. According to Oakes, Rickert's incoherence would damage Weber's contributions. I do not agree. There are many subtle differences between Weber and Rickert, as well as slight lapses into 'backdoor normativism' in Weber's own text, as Bruun (1972) has

discussed. Bruun (2001) has recently returned to the Rickert–Weber relationship, building upon partly apocryphal sources.

9   In the English-language literature, Rickert is frequently discussed in terms of 'science' *vs* 'history'. This is misleading, since it implies that Rickert did not regard history as a science. He did. His ambition was to constitute history as a science, even if in a sense other than the natural sciences. The different connotations of the English term 'science', in comparison to the German *Wissenschaft*, is a classical and difficult problem of translation; for instance, no German historicist would hesitate over the status of history as a science, a status the English sense of the term seems to preclude.

10 It is commonplace to compare the positions of Dilthey and Rickert, although they were really never in direct confrontation with each other. These juxtapositions, also common practice in the case of Marx *vs* Weber and Ranke *vs* Comte, are not without methodological problems and call for a balance between the contextual and the immanent in the pursuit of intellectual history.

11 In retrospect, the historicists seem too 'sensitive'; after all, no matter what the outcome of the debates, almost no one would have called for the abolition of traditional idiography. There is always a place for the historical muse (Clio) – fettered or not – and the art of historiography has indeed survived.

12 Some qualification for characterizing Weber's position as 'middle-of-the-road' is appropriate: of course Weber had an independent position of his own, based on the practice of current research and tran-scending the stalemate in the debate between sides claiming intrinsic values.

13 Sociology, in this context, is to be seen as a later concept.

14 My exposition of Weber and the *Methodenstreit* is influenced by a long period of digesting Bruun's pioneering work.

15 Of course, I simplify in characterizing Ranke as a crude inductivist. In his concept-formation strategy, he – no more than, for instance, Marx – could not be expected to become a neo-Kantian before neo-Kantianism.

16 The extent to which Weber depends on Rickert or uses him more as a matter of convenience is much discussed and a matter of controversy, as Homann (1990), Stephen Turner (1990), etc. show.

17 It will be profitable for our purposes to dwell a bit longer on the logical nature of value-analysis. The attempt has been made in all seriousness to understand or to 'refute' H. Rickert's very clearly developed idea that the construction of the 'historical individual' is conditioned by 'value-relation' (*Wertbeziehung*) as asserting that this relation to values is identical with a subsumption under general concepts such as the 'state', 'religion', 'art', etc., and similar concepts, which are assuredly, it is said, the 'values' in question; the fact that history brings its object into relation with these values and thereby attains specific 'viewpoints' is then equivalent – this is what is added – to the separate treatment of the

'chemical', 'physical', etc., 'aspects' of events in the sphere of the natural sciences. (*GAW*: 251–2)

18   In the following presentation I am indebted to Bruun's (1972) work.
19   Lawrence Durrell's *The Alexandria Quartet* is one example of multiple conceptions of the same reality.
20   We have only to read Norbert Elias's great analyses of the civilizing process, which are not wholly un-Weberian, to realize this. For a criticism of Bruun's analysis, see Oakes (1988: 177–8, n. 32). Although it might be true that Bruun does not always make a clear distinction in his terminology between 'value' and 'value-aspect', it remains a certain sophism in Oakes's criticism, if the deduction from 'is' to 'ought' – or the reverse – is founded on normative postulates. 'As the above account of Rickert's argument shows, his solution to the problem of values is the polar antithesis of the position that Bruun ascribes to him. Rickert derives values from facts. He attempts to demonstrate the nonempirical validity of empirical cultural values by showing that they approximate objective or unconditionally valid values' (ibid.). Oakes's may be correct, but his analysis remains rhetorical and marred by the lingering objectivism implicit in a phrase like the 'nonempirical validity of empirical cultural values'. Oakes evidently adheres to the notion of objective values in some transcendental sense.
21   The plagued and formalistic paradoxes about truth as an eternal value of unconditional validity, as a basis for any cognitive claim, appear almost juvenile in light of, for instance, Weber's 'twin lectures' that address the paradox of a value-rational ethic of conviction and an ethic of responsibility. Weber was prepared to face the methodological consequences of polytheism, while Rickert could not keep himself from arguing and hoping for some firm Archimedian point of moral imperatives. Oakes discusses at length the problem of the unconditional validity of values in Rickert (Oakes 1988: 102 *et passim*, esp. p. 106 *et passim*). Rickert's attempt to destroy 'the glass house of relativism' – a strange formulation from someone arguing for the incommensurability of values – is simply not convincing, even in light of Oakes's sympathetic reading. I cannot see any way out of the predicament that the incommensurability of ultimate values leaves us stuck in that glasshouse, a concept that is so offensive to many.
22   Bruun's question remains: When God is dead, who is the norm-sender? – or are we forced to choose ourselves? The 'norm-sender' problem can be seen as escalating after the Enlightenment. This is a genuine paradigmatic division, one not always obvious to those facing it. Oakes, for example, still speaks without irony of notions like 'unconditional validity of values' (1988: 178, n. 32). On the other side of the divide, Bruun (1972: 94, n. 48) discusses Weber's failure to criticize Rickert's understanding of the cultural norm-sender as that which should be a crucial concern for all members of society. Bruun points out that 'Weber's defence is an indication of his own solution to this problem, a solution which – at least unconsciously – carries him quite far away from

Rickert' (ibid.). I would characterize this as a rationalization. This is a matter of rather delicate judgement in interpretation. I am inclined to agree with Bruun.

23 One should bear in mind that, after all, Rickert is a philosopher whom Weber used as a resource in the pursuit of an anti-metaphysical social science. In the early 1920s, when Rickert criticized some aspect of Weber's work, Jaspers told him that Rickert himself would be forgotten if it weren't for his appearance in Weber's footnotes. The relationship between the two philosophers never quite recovered from this encounter. Much in line with Jaspers's judgement, Rickert is of lasting interest to the extent that he is of use to Weber in the early construction of abstract sociological concepts.

24 We might further note that the tension between Weber and Rickert concerning theoretical and practical value-relevance somehow tends to be dissolved in present- or future-oriented applications, since practical value-relation here merely provides the basis for tentative propositions about theoretical value-relation; for instance, the practical need for profit in profit-based enterprise as reflecting individualist rationalist cultural values, i.e. utilitarianism.

25 This combination of political as well as scientific passion, as Golo Mann (1971) – and, indeed, many others – has pointed out, is autobiographical for Weber (see also Portis 1986, esp. p. 145 *et passim*). We should keep in mind the degree to which social reality was politicized a century ago, when so much happened in such a short time. Citizens in the modern Western welfare state are no longer willing to die for their country or their party; rather, their concern is with their return from the distributive system of collective goods and the mortgage on their house. Politics tends to lose primacy and become a function of the welfare system; the heat and passion of 1848 Berlin or 1934 Vienna are no longer likely to occur, except as lingering phenomena in areas with underdeveloped political cultures, like parts of the Balkan peninsula.

26 Shils–Finch translation, p. 12. See also *MWG* II/5: 595: 'You have reserved more of a place for historical thinking in our science than in any other nation, in a time of dry economic rationality' (my translation). It is easy to find quotations from Weber in which he expresses his esteem of Schmoller. It is also easy to find passages where he is critical. We can find quotations where he is very appreciative of Menger, as well as critical passages. Weber's position between marginalism and historicism remains to some extent elusive.

27 'Another almost inconceiveable misunderstanding which constantly recurs is that the propositions which I propose imply that empirical science cannot treat "subjective" evaluations as the subject matter of its analysis – although sociology and the whole theory of marginal utility in economics depend on the contrary assumption' (*GAW*: 500; Weber 1949: 11).

28 In German: 'welches *für ihn* der Gott und welches der Teufel ist'. The norm-sender problem is scientifically irresolvable, although we

cannot tell what science might achieve in the future. The combination of anti-metaphysics and scientific rationality binds us to a negative value-ontology, leaving to practical philosophy and deontic logic what were once integrated parts of science. There are still questions we have to answer one way or another, alas without scientific authority as yet. We have better theories, but no unequivocal answers, in the long tradition from Socrates to Habermas. Only the violation of the borderline between metaphysics and testable propositions is illegitimate. On this point we are not beyond Weber.

29   The incommensurability of ultimate values is here explicit, as well as the rationalization of means–ends hierarchies that are typical of Weber's demystification and secularization of social thought.

30   This is where Gunnar Myrdal develops Weber and Rickert on value-relation. See for instance Eliaeson (2000d).

31   'Zwischen zwei Gesetzen' from 1916 ('Between Two Laws', in *PW*) is a greatly under-utilized key text in Weber interpretation. The reference to Mill is of interest, since the essay was published during the war, when German scholars were less likely to quote British scholars. It is translated in the 1994 Cambridge selection from *GPS*.

32   Arnold Brecht (1959). This is perhaps the most influential work contributing to the diffusion of scientific value-relativism.

33   On the philosophical aspect of the 'is' *vs* 'ought' problem, see for instance Hudson (1969).

34   The basic anti-natural law character of Weber's work should be stressed, since it is not immediately obvious from his sociology of law, which is characterized by a detailed historical exposition of one segment of society, where rationalization promoted calculable modern capitalism (available in English in Rheinstein's translation; Weber 1954). Weber's anti-natural law position is hardly an issue; however, see Brugger (1980) and Midgley (1983). Weber's sociology of law is his best documented text. It is probably still underestimated as a clue to his views on modernity and rationalization. It is not reader-friendly, and presupposes a lot of historical education. Important recent works on Weber's sociology of law are Rehbinder and Tieck (1987) and Breuer and Treiber (1984).

35   Scientific value-relativism, conceived of as a combination of a negative value-ontology and a non-cognitivist value-statement theory, means that value statements are neither *scientifically* meaningful nor correct or incorrect.

36   Even though historicist scholars like Schmoller happened to come under attack from Weber.

37   See, for instance, his letter to Rickert of 3 November 1907 (p. 414 in *MWG*, II/5).

38   According to Plessner, on the occasion of a Weber centennial in The Netherlands (here quoted after Wertheim (1971: 79, in Swedish edition), anecdotally, Rickert is held to have said about Weber: 'jetzt fängt der Kerl schon wieder an zu generalisieren' ('Then the guy begins to generalize again': my translation).

39   This problem has recently been especially scrutinized by Stephen Turner (1990) and Wagner and Zipprian (1985). *IJPCS* 1990 features a symposium on 'Weber and Rickert: Concept Formation in Social Science'; see contributions by Homann, Turner, and Wagner and Zipprian for revealing and varying views on this specific topic.

40   My own reading of Weber is influenced by the 'nihilist' doctrine of Scandinavian legal realism, in which any idea of transcendental values appears as metaphysics. This is for instance the background of Gunnar Myrdal's criticism of Weber, although methodologically their positions are pretty similar. My reading is certainly encouraged by this passage, in contrast to the interpretations of Hennis and Oakes.

41   The notion of objective values in a merely logical rather than cognitivist sense is evidently the key to understanding of Oakes's otherwise – at least to me – incomprehensible argumentation.

42   For a different interpretation, see Sahay (1971: 70) on Rickert's 'suprahistorical values'.

43   The controversies are more subtle today than in Lukács's day; Wagner and Zipprian demonstrate that the Rickertian elements fail to assist Weber's methodology and that the value-relatedness he gains from Rickert does not add much to what was already at least implicit in what he derived from the jurists, especially Jhering, as S. P. Turner (1990) argues. Turner and Factor (1994) elaborate in detail these influences from law scholars before neo-Kantianism and especially before Rickertian neo-Kantianism became Weber's discursive vehicle. In evaluating Weber's polemical context, the 'Postscript' to Burger's (1987) new edition is illuminating, stressing the centrality of the metalevel as a renewal of 'historiography':

> For then as now, the development of sociology has received its main impetus from the conviction and hope that it is possible to devise a different and more powerful mode of analyzing social reality than that provided by historiography. As a negation of this hope, Weber's sociology has therefore been attractive mostly to the sceptical and disenchanted; for those who maintain this hope it may function as a challenge but cannot constitute a viable alternative. (p. xi)

Juxtaposing especially Burger (1976) and Oakes (1988) reveals different attitudes to the fruitful approach to the classics and how to interpret their endeavours retrospectively. Perhaps the best way to formulate the central question would be: is there a research programme to reconstruct, or is Weber's *œuvre* a gradual response to balls others put into play?

44   My translation. Lepsius's article originated as a commemorative address in Münchener Seestrasse, where Weber spent the last year of his life (close to the Englischer Garten).

45   Neo-Kantianism was not only heterogeneous, it was divided into different related branches. The so-called Baden school or Southwest

German school of Windelband and Rickert were the most important influences on Weber. For an overview of neo-Kantianism, Cassirer (1950) might be of help, as well as Köhnke (1986) and Ollig (1987). Bjarne Jacobsen (1999) has worked on Weber and early neo-Kantians, in particular F. A. Lange.

3 An Analysis of Weber's Solution

1   It was a good occasion for programmatic statements – together with Werner Sombart and Edgar Jaffé, Weber had taken over the editorship of *Archiv für Sozialwissenschaft und Sozialpolitik*. The essay touched on three major debates: the *Methodenstreit*, the proper way to distinguish the cultural from the natural sciences, and values and objectivity in social science.
2   'Peace' was clearly also in his own interest, if he wished to reach an audience and avoid becoming marginalized in the German scholarly community.
3   It is clear from Weber's first footnote that he selected Meyer because of his justified reputation as a historian: 'The errors which an outstanding author makes are more instructive than the correct statements of a scientific nonentity' (Weber 1949: 114).
4   When Weber makes a case for the rational economic actor as a conceptual historical tool with critical respect for the limits of the application of the concept, the use he has in mind, as seems clear from both his reference to 'empirical rules' and his footnote on Menger's 'theoretical schema', is that it should be a tool for comparison rather than a Procrustean bed.
5   This is in curious contrast to Weber's background in jurisprudence: 'It is natural that it was precisely the jurist and primarily the jurist specialized in criminal law who treated the problem since the question of penal guilt, insofar as it involves the problem: under what circumstances can it be asserted that someone through his actions has "caused" a certain external effect, is purely a question of causation. And, indeed, this problem obviously has exactly the same logical structure as the problem of historical "causality"' (Weber 1949: 168).
6   Weber (1990). These notes from his 1898 lectures in Heidelberg are from Weber's *Nachlass* and were published for the first time in 1990. They were actually already published in 1898 but only for a very limited circulation among students (Guenther Roth kindly informed me about this). I follow Tribe's translation in Hennis (1987: 121). The text had been picked up by Hennis at the Weber archives in Munich and Scaff also had used it before the German original was published.
7   Max Weber: 'Critique of Stammler', translated by Guy Oakes. Translation from *GAW*: 346–7; the pagination in this chapter refers to the 7th German paperback edition.

8   The Weber–Tönnies link has been dealt with, for instance, by Niall
Bond (1988). Weber does appropriate the central concepts of *Gemeinschaft* (community) and *Gesellschaft* (society) that Tönnies developed,
and comes close to Tönnies in several respects. For further elucidation
of ideal-typical 'rules' and actual causes, see Tenbruck (1987) on Weber
and his criticism of Meyer of 1906. See chapter 5.

9   'Some Categories of Interpretive Sociology', in *Logos*, 1913, translation
by Graber (1981: 151–80). This quotation seems to me another
example where Weber goes for the *Erklären*- rather than the *Verstehen*-
alternative. There is, admittedly, a basic Diltheyian concern with the
empathetic element, although Weber's creed in dealing with the problems of evaluating individuals is really unified science-inclined.

10 Which is indicated by the role it plays in the German and American
debate. The 'Objectivity' essay, however, is intrinsically the most
indispensable text since it contains the most elaborated view of the
ideal-type.

11 And is also part of the 'double historicity', that our selection should be
relevant today as well as to the actors under scrutiny.

12 'Psychological' might (in the sociological realm, defining away the
'Freudian' introspective and/or solipsist variations) refer to 'inner'
understanding between ego and alter, *einfühlende* – or: empathetic –
but also the the naturalist search for psycho-physical laws in the vein
of positivism. That 'psychology' might refer to both empathetic acts of
Verstehen, as well as to unified-science reductionism is bound to create
some misunderstanding by the neophyte reader in the study of the
history of social science doctrine. The label 'psychology' for Weber's
ideal-type methodology only applies to Weber insofar as the rational
actor model is included. However, Weber's industrial sociology from
around 1908 might be characterized as naturalist 'psychology',
although Weber explicitly denied the existence of the basic law of psychophysics, which several followers of the Menger school of marginalism adhered to.
  Another elementary source of misunderstanding is that the term *Verstehen* as such tends to lead our thoughts in the direction of empathetic
rather than rational understanding. Weber is by no means alien to transcending the limits of the 'fictitious puppets' of the rational actor type
in the search for explanatory hypotheses, involving *ad hoc* elements and
counterfactuals, certainly probabilities – but the very tool of the ideal-
type is non-empathetic and non-psychological. (See also *rationale
Evidenz* on pp. 20, 49, 76, 83. See also Eliaeson 2000d.)

13 *Verstehen* has a scent of empathy and what used to be called 'soft-data
sociology' to it, while Weber's *Verstehen* is less Diltheyian 'hermeneutic' and more rational economic actor-imprinted – yet embryonic also
in his debate with Meyer, about historical method, in 1906, where counterfactuals are part of Weber's explanatory strategy.

14 Although Weber accepts a necessarily limited role for *empathetic* interpretation, it is not, again, part of the verifiable stuff of sociology. (A

small indication of Weber's opinion here is that he writes 'evidence', in quotation marks, which suggests that it stands for something that still remains to be elucidated.)

15 Weber's anti-psychological stance is sometimes very explicit, as in ' "Energetische" Kulturtheorien', where he writes that 'Denn dass die reine "Theorie" unserer Disziplin auch nicht das mindeste mit "Psychologie" zu tun hat, weiss jeder an modernen Methoden geschulte Theoretiker (richtiger, sollte es wissen)' (*GAW*: 413–14). My translation: 'That the pure theory of our discipline has nothing at all to do with "psychology" is something which every theoretician schooled in modern methods knows (or rather: *should* know).' This neglected essay might teach us a few things about Weber's relation to unified science.

16 'Sinnhafte verstandene seelische Zusammenhänge' in the original, 'links in causal chains'. On this point the translation might be paradigmatically daring, in the sense that 'seelische' has connotations that are lost in Graber 's translation.

17 We might consider his notion by dividing psychological understanding into two categories. One would be interpretative (explanatory) understanding (*Verstehen*). The other would be the kind of non-interpretative (descriptive) understanding that might be thought to comprise some account of human nature – that is, a scientific form of philosophical anthropology, statistical or experimental psychology, or psychophysics. Weber is critical of the latter type of psychology, and attacks such scholars as Wundt in his essay on marginal utility and the fundamental laws of psychophysics.

18 The same holds for actions with a significance specific to a particular culture, such as greeting ceremonies. Europeans, out of old habit, cannot but respond seriously to the American greeting 'How are you?', which usually does not expect an answer, at least not a serious one. The American would say 'Fine, thank you' even if he were dying. The European would rather complain about poor digestion, sciatica, or worries over the environmental causes of health problems, partly because he would not want to create envy by looking too contented.

19 The wood-chopper is a popular illustration, also employed, for instance, by Howard Becker (1934; abridged version in Gurvitch and Moore 1945). My point here is the basic distinction between behaviour and meaningful action and the latter 's context-bound character.

20 Weber's posthumously published 'Die rationalen und soziologischen Grundlagen der Musik' is a good example of how he attempts rational explanations of cultural phenomena.

21 In the controversial translation by A. M. Henderson and Parsons. *Verstehen* by means of *Erklären* or *Erklären* by means of *Verstehen*: this is one of the passages that could be read either way, at first glance. It has to be put into context. It goes without saying that no uncontested translation could be made of such a passage; moreover, it seems to me that any translation almost requires a presupposed metaposition. Many fissures in Weber's image are due to Anglo-Saxon dependence on

translations; it is well known that there are a number of concepts that simply do not lend themselves to translation.

22 English translation by Louis Schneider in *Social Science Quarterly* 56(1) (June 1975), 21–36. The ideal-type has many formulations in Weber's *œuvre*, and in this essay yet another one.

23 Weber writes to Brentano (30 Oct. 1908, *MWG* II/5: 689): 'It is true that Menger might overestimate himself a lot, but he has very important good sides and he was basically right in the controversy with Schmoller' (my translation). Moreover: 'It is no accident that this essay contains a laudatory footnote on Carl Menger, the renowned Austrian economist and central figure in the late 19th century dispute about economic method (the so-called Methodenstreit)', Schneider writes in 'Translator's Introduction', p. 22. Weber, furthermore, writes: 'I do not really see the justification for the disparaging treatment of the "Austrians" by Brentano. Carl Menger proposed excellent views even if they were not methodologically finished. And as regards the question of "style", which is today usually overvalued at the expense of pertinent content of thought, even in this Böhm-Bawerk if perhaps not Menger, is a master' (*GAW*: 396; p. 33 in Schneider's translation).

24 Brentano was Weber's predecessor in Munich. His correspondence with Brentano is elucidating, since it deals with the Menger link (29 May 1908; 30 Oct. 1908; pp. 578, 688 in *MWG* II/5).

25 'That in all spheres of sensation the same law of dependence of sensation on stimulus asserts itself – the same law which Bernoulli had set up for the dependence of the sensation of happiness (which increase of a sum of money brings) on the amount of wealth of the one who experiences the sensation' (p. 25 in Schneider's translation of Weber's rendering of Brentano's summarizing).

26   But, now, let us consider again: In the economic theory of marginal utility and in every 'subjective' value theory – particularly if we refer back to the 'psychic ' appurtenances of the individual – there is, to begin with, not an external 'stimulus' but a 'need'. This is of course the reverse of the situation we have in the case of the fundamental law of psychophysics. Accordingly, if we wish to express ourselves in 'psychological' terms, we deal with a complex of 'sensations', 'feeling-states', states of 'tension', 'discomfort', 'expectations', and the like, which may at any time be of most intricate character. And these, moreover, combine with 'memory images', 'purposes' and perhaps conflicting' 'motives' of the most various kinds. (*GAW*: 388; p. 27 in Schneider's translation)

27 To use the term 'culture' in this way comes close to embracing 'historical relativism'. Weber is not only cognizant of the problem of historical relativism, but concedes a great deal to its claims. There are several indications, though, clearly pointing in my 'nihilist' direction, like the letter to Gottl of 28 March, also discussed by Bruun; the quotations from the end of 'Between Two Laws'; and the passages in Weber's *WuG*

and *GPS,* which W. Mommsen noted. It is an open question whether Weber concedes so much to historical relativism as to become a kind of nihilist. He avoids the vestiges of value-objectivism found in Rickert, but he is not, in my view, a fully fledged nihilist. Weber's term 'language community' (*GAW*: 455; p. 168 in Graber's translation) is crucial to understanding his conception of the scope and limits of cultural understanding. For Weber, religion and language seem to be the main components of a culture, though of course these are found together with a lot of 'habits', and what we might today call lifestyles, along with such things as climate.

28   Weber's choice of the term '*Utopie*' is rather misleading, since it gives leeway for some normative misinterpretations. Numerous circumstantial indications make clear that Weber did not intend the ideal-type as a normatively inclined construct. 'Utopia' is used more in the sense of *fictitious.*

29   The concept of the ideal-type is used with increasing explicitness in Weber's essays. It is clearly part of the discussion in the marginal utility essay, and the historical studies each employ ideal-types, both before and after Weber explicitly formulated the concept. Both the 'Protestant ethic' and the 'spirit of capitalism' are ideal-types of so-called historical individuals. It should be noted here that criticisms of Weber on the ground that the ideal-types he constructed deviate from reality are based on a misunderstanding. Ideal-types, Weber says, are deliberately accentuated (*Steigerung*) or intensified to aid the interpreter in depicting reality, without reflecting reality directly. The representation of reality given by the ideal-type is disproportionate, which serves to make the central features of reality more visible and intelligible. The *rational variation* of the ideal-type, however, works differently, since logic and rationality cannot be 'accentuated' more than they are already. Means–ends rationality is an absolute or limiting concept; a violation of the rules of logic in a chain of deductive reasoning would represent a flaw and a failure to match the ideal-type of rationality.

30   It is said that he was a favourite of Marx.

31   Sahay (1971) and Aron (1957, 1970) and others are helpful, the more so if we accept the limitations of any attempt to catch the ideal-type. My own interpretation stresses the historical significance of the rational marginalist and neo-Kantian elements.

32   By singular I mean the following: 'A', as one contributing factor out of many presumptive other factors, causes the unique phenomenon of 'B', which we are interested in explaining.

33   The ideal-type often appeared as the result of an act of '*verstehende Induktion*'. However, its most significant variation – from the point of view of the development of social science doctrine – functions well in a deductive context: the rational ideal-type, which utilizes rational economic actors as its central metaphor, formed under the influence of Menger's marginalist economics.

It is a matter of interpretation how much to emphasize the rational type with economic man as a prototype. In my view the rational type seems to be a sort of 'super type' corresponding with rational purposeful action in Weber's sociology. In Burger's (1976: 160) words, the ideal-type is 'the attempt of a *rational reconstruction* of a *procedure in use*'.

34 For the long line of secularization in social thought, from Machiavelli to Weber/Rickert and Myrdal/Hägerström, see 'Methodological Appendix'.

35 Understanding Weber requires a certain familiarity with early nine-teenth-century historicism and economics, as currents in the opposition to Enlightenment rationalism, as well as present-day strategies of history versus theory. The new controversies over method are not iden-tical but are, to a large extent, similar to those to which Weber had to respond.

36 There is a limit regarding intersubjectivity, in the Diltheyian tradition, and thus a limit to cumulativity in knowledge formation.

37 No immanent interpretation will ever be quite convincing, insofar as it aims at a reconstruction of a coherent – especially causal – approach. Still, immanent analyses are indispensable. If Weber insistently adheres to Rickert, insistently stresses the rule-like (rather than law-like) char-acter of the ideal-type construction of rational action, and never claims to proffer systematic theory, I feel we should take him seriously. But nuancing history *vs* sociology in the work of Max Weber is challeng-ing, since these supplementary antipodes are delicately balanced in a way that changes over time. I feel equally sceptical about the 'cultural-ist' stress on the Weber of the 1890s (Scaff 1984, 1988, 1989; Hennis 1988), as on the structural macrosociologist Weber of 1918–20 (Collins 1986b), in which only premature death prevented him from taking the sociologist salvation. Weber always had his identity as a historian, but from 1909 on, also increasingly as a sociologist; it is an unostentatious 'break' within brackets.

38 In his comparative sociology of world religions, Weber adopts a strat-egy that calls to mind J. S. Mill's methods of induction, although Mill's authority is related to it critically. Given Weber's function to adapt secular methodology to the historicist German ambience, any reference to British sources, in the aftermath of the *Methodenstreit* , would have been adventurous. Weber's famous letter to von Below indicates that the whole comparative sociology of religion, Weber's life project, is a venture in the vein of the neopositivist Mill, in order to bring about supportive evidence for Weber's basic thesis about the uniqueness of Western rationalism.

> This winter I intend to publish a rather extensive contribution to the outline of the Social Sciences series on the forms of political associations. It will deal with the subject in a comparative and normative manner. . . . For I think that one can only define the specific characteristics of, for example, the medieval city – and that is precisely the sort of thing which

is the historian's task (in that we are absolutely in agreement) – after one
has established which of these characteristics were lacking in other cities
(classical Chinese, Islamic). That is a general rule. The next task of historians is to give a causal explanation of those specific characteristics.
(letter of June 1914 printed in Below (1925: xxiv–xxv); here quoted from
Weber 1988: 21–2)

39   This is also quite explicit in his correspondence, as in some of the letters
     to Lujo Brentano mentioned above.
40   Some attempts have been made to extract a comprehensive all-
     inclusive definition of the ideal-type, like Arun Sahay's (1971) rational
     interpretation.
41   Weber later explicitly acknowledged Marx's two-class model of the
     capitalist mode of production as a good and inspiring example of early
     ideal-types (*GAW*: 204, see also Kozyr-Kowalsky 1968 and Janoska-
     Bendl 1965). Weber pays homage to Marx as a methodological pre-
     cursor, although Marx, as a pre-neo-Kantian unrelated to the more
     immediate influences on Weber's methodology, has no central role in
     the shaping of Weber's contribution to social science.
42   This stress on instrumentality (*Zweckrationalität*) as a component
     part of the basic concept of interpretative sociology is also clear from
     other instances of Weber's work, such as his 'Richtigkeitsrationalität'
     (1913). The *Richtigkeitstypus*, the type of functionally rational conduct,
     has a high significance for the evaluation of Weber (Mommsen 1989:
     127).
43   As Arun Sahay writes:

> An ideal-type is a logically consistent description, from a specific, or
> given, point of view which makes the means–end relationship of the
> action, event, process or interpretation of ideas, unambiguous, to enable
> one to translate disparate, fragmentary ideas, interpretations or correla-
> tion into scientifically explicable terms. The ideal-type concept, in fact, is
> the realization of the principle of sociological rationality, which is Weber's
> basic and original contribution to scientific analysis. (Sahay 1971: 72–3)

Raymond Aron's balanced judgement is: 'The theory of the ideal-
type is, no doubt, incomplete. Perhaps we should distinguish between
historical types (modern capitalism), general types (bureaucratic
power), and types of rational behaviour (economic theory)' (Aron 1970:
83). The latter is, rightly, emphasized as being of special relevance to
the methodological understanding of Weber.

4 Three Paradigmatic Conceptions of Weber

1   In philosophy Hume and Kant are both exponents of this new and inse-
    cure predicament, and later Kierkegaard and Nietzsche drew out the

existential consequences of this cognitive insecurity. There is an evident divide on the connotation of 'Nietzsche' between American ('Straussian') and European social thought, as is pointed out by Horst Baier (1987). Weber's 'competing Gods' at work in his selective abstraction from reality has a strong affinity with Nietzsche's philosophy. For a discussion of the methodological aspect of this see, for instance, Charles Turner (1992: esp. p. 65). And further, Bryan S. Turner (1992, esp. ch. 10), and also Arpád Szakolczai (1998). The thematic link to the recent debate over 'modernity' and 'post-modernity' is obvious, i.e. various reactions to post-Enlightenment polytheism and secularization. See for instance Whimster (1987).

2   As manifested in the reactions of Lukács and Strauss and others.

3   The distinction between value-relativism and scientific value-relativism is basically that the latter restricts itself to the realm of what we might claim as valid scientific truth, thus answering to the polytheist predicament in the post-Enlightenment, while mere 'value-relativism' might indicate for instance empirical sociology of knowledge, or anthropology.

4   In his opening address Topitsch emphasized the anti-metaphysical creed in Weber's work:

> In making the distinction between statements of fact and value-judgments, which was only dealt with in a very late phase of development of philosophical thought and was represented among Max Weber's contemporaries particularly by Georg Simmel, the neo-Kantian from Baden, and Werner Sombart, the fact comes to light that men's orientation of the world, as it appears in daily life but also in mythical, religious and metaphysical thought-structures, exercizes several simultaneous functions which, from a scientifically logical point of view, differ radically from each other. (Stammer 1971: 20, with explicit reference to Arnold Brecht 1959)

5   For an overview of Weber's reception, see, for instance, Mommsen (1989: ch. 11).

6   See also Fogt (1981) and Lassman and Velody (1989).

7   See Käsler and Turner 1991.

8   It also led directly to the heated academic disputes at the Heidelberg sociological congress in 1964, with Raymond Aron as arbiter.

9   Moreover, they displayed a great interest in what Germans call *Realbedingungen der Methode* – reducing methodology to its societal context, its genesis and consequences. Weber has, after all, often been described as 'a bourgeois Marx'.

10 Salomon coined the description of Weber's sociology as 'a long and intense dialogue with the ghost of Karl Marx', which was traded on by Irving Zeitlin (1968). An example of the Marx–Weber 'juxtaposition industry' is Jürgen Kocka's (1966) brilliant discussion of the methodologies of Marx and Weber. Yet another example of this partly erroneous vein relating Weber's work to that of Marx is Janoska-Bendl's (1965)

already almost classic booklet on Weber's methodological sources. See Eliaeson (1986). The Marx–Weber juxtaposition industry generated many contributions to the modern Weber renaissance, such as works by Johannes Weiss (1981), and John Lewis (1975), as well as readers by Böckler and Weiss (1987), Norbert Wiley (1987), and Antonio and Glassman (1985), to mention only a few. Of course the works of, for instance, Karl Wittfogel have an obvious relation to both Marx and Weber. The same is true of Jürgen Habermas, Anthony Giddens, Klaus Eder, C. Wright Mills, A MacFarlane, and so on; see also Dennis Wrong (1982). In retrospect, however, the link appears overestimated, at least from a contextualist perspective, and in urgent need of much nuancing. See also Schroeter (1985).

11   There are several steps in the Weber renaissance. Wolfgang Mommsen's (1959) re-evaluation of Weber as an ugly nationalist (from being a kind liberal) and the ensuing debate (see Eliaeson 2000b) was something German scholarship had to go through, in order to be once again able to scrutinize Weber's contribution, leaving the political shadows behind. The heated controversies at the Heidelberg centennial in 1964 somehow marked a shift, a catharsis, although some less noticed important works – often dissertations, some already written in the 1930s – had seriously dealt with Weber's methodological implications for quite some while (e.g. Mettler, Henrich, Girndt). In the wake of student revolt and unrest and a new alleged crisis of science the Marx–Weber nexus came into focus.

12   For instance, Burger (1976), Hennis (1987) and the debates they have generated about a Weberian 'programme', within or outside his methodology.

13   Although it is inherent also in his 1908 essays where the influences from the Menger school are strong.

14   We should note, however, that even if few fell under Weber's spell immediately, several nevertheless drew on his thought, among them influential scholars such as Karl Mannheim, Hans Morgenthau, Edward Shils, C. Wright Mills, Norbert Elias, Carl Schmitt, Joseph Schumpeter, Alfred Schutz, Alexander von Schelting and Hans Kelsen.

15   The full title of his dissertation is 'The Concept of Capitalism in Recent German Literature', available in two parts in *Journal of Political Economy* 36 (1928/29), 641–61 and vol. 37, pp. 31–51; both Sombart and Weber figure prominently in it. The reciprocity between European and American sociological scholarship is a striking and intriguing phenomenon in intellectual history.

16   In his *The Structure of Social Action*, a monumental historical work of the late 1930s, Parsons's presentation of Marx is less penetrating than that of other classics. Much of the criticism of Parsons's interpretation of Weber is anticipated by Lowell Bennion (1933); see also di Padova and Brower (1992).

17   Marxism somehow does not travel well to the United States, the country of classical liberalism. The conflict perspective vanishes. This also

happens to Weber's work. We may compare Scaff's article on 'Weber and Political Education' (1973), where 'middle class' as a translation of 'bourgeois' somehow appears merely linguistically correct. A term like 'political education' easily acquires an unintended idealistic stance not quite in concert with the Weberian context of class-conscious nation-building. Although there is nothing apparently wrong with the translation (in its context it implies a 'whiggish' view of political culture), considering the mutual influences between Weber himself and American sociology, matters of translation become crucial in avoiding misinterpretation. Agnes Erdelyi's *Max Weber in Amerika* (1992) discusses Weber's reception in the United States.

18   The respect for Parsons is prevalent also in many works, such as Vidich's and Lyman's (1985) account of the development of American sociology, with its specific religious background and preoccupation with urban ethnic cohesion; see also Giddens: 'Even the severest critic of Talcott Parsons must recognize the extraordinary nature of his contributions to social theory over a period of half a century. More than any other single scholar, Parsons has been responsible for introducing an Anglo-Saxon sociological audience to a sophisticated reading of the works of Durkheim and Max Weber' (Giddens 1982: 76). The case of Parsons in fact suggests a tension between the utility and the interpretation of the classics, since his successful annexation of Weber meant a great deal to modern sociological discourse and simultaneously obscured the genuine image of Weber. The respect for Parsons is hardly unanimous; Don Martindale is one exception.

19   As Parsons himself notes in his autobiographical reflections, it took quite some time for him to gain recognition as a theoretician within the behaviouralistically dominated academic community. Towards the end of his life, however, he became a respected doyen of American theoretical sociology. He died in Germany in the spring of 1979, only one day after the celebration of the half-centennial of his doctorate. He wrote a number of autobiographical articles (Parsons 1970, 1980, etc.).

20   In fact, Weber openly criticized the evolutionism that is constitutive of any functionalist approach, to stress just one obvious conflict between Weber and structural functionalism.

21   Although the concept of 'culture' is Americanized in a way that Tenbruck and Hennis (the two most spectacular opponents in the German *Gesamtdeutung* debate) both conceive of as out of place, given their common historicist inclination.

22   Parsons's and Roth and Wittich's translations are very similar, but Parsons evidently did not take notice.

23   Parsons's activity as a translator is more a matter of tendency than of errors. For instance, his translation of *Kasuistik* as 'theoretical differentiation' is really bending the text in the wrong direction, since 'casuistry' has anti-theoretical connotations. What arises out of the Weberian quarry of taxonomies is a polished and modernized Weber, 'updated' for specific purposes.

24 On Weber and causality, see for instance Turner (1985 and 1986), and Turner and Factor (1981). Since Weber never wrote any 'systematic treatise' on method – the 1904 essay on 'Objectivity' is as close as he ever came – immanent analyses are difficult, while matters of logic (of science) ought to be discussed in immanent terms. The danger of contextual reductionism, however, does not alter the fact that he wrote in a communicative culture and a language quite different from the present-day Anglo-Saxon debate in the philosophy of science. The proper interpretation calls for a balance between immanent analysis and contextual interpretation, which, in the case of the German classics, to some extent involves philology. Any exegesis of Weber's methodology thus appears daring, owing to the linguistic gulf as well as the fragile and somewhat scattered character of the primary discourse under scrutiny.

25 'People don't realize that we study the classics in order to learn something also about our present day society' (Jeff Alexander, conversation in Los Angeles, 4 June 1990). This viewpoint is characteristic of the Californian 'retrospectivists' and neo-Parsonsians, and is anathema to the pure contextualists who are not inclined to accept any meaning beyond the classic's own horizon.

26 Although he does not emphasize the inherent methodological individualism in Weber's position.

27 For a succinct discussion of Parsons's critique of Weber's ideal-type, see Martindale (1959: 82 *et passim*). It is noteworthy that both Parsons and Martindale seem to be well aware of the 'marginalist link', and the role the prototype of 'rational economic actor' played for the Weberian type.

28 Parsons does not scrutinize at any length the distinction between general abstract frameworks and conceptual apparatus, on the one hand, and explanatory theories, on the other. One might even say that Parsons is himself a modern product of the everlasting need to stress that important distinction, to oppose tendencies to *Model-Platonismus*, to use Hans Albert's tem, referring to a Platonic love of models where one never accomplishes the harmonious matching of structuring concepts to the reality to be explained, and thus the models never take the decisive step of becoming theories, i.e. statements that explain reality.

29 See Glossary.

30 Yet it remains true that without Parsons there would probably not be the living legacy of Max Weber today; in any case it would be another Weber, perhaps with an emphasis on political sociology, leadership legitimacy, organizational theory, forms of government and goal conflicts between democracy and efficiency, and so on. This Weber exists too, albeit in the shadow of the monumental 'social action' Weber of the several competing major paradigms. About the inhibited reception of Weber within German political science, see Hübinger et al. (1990).

31 Schutz is more influential than famous. Not until rather recently has his work become more widely recognized. His *Collected Papers* have

been edited by Maurice Natanson, Arvid Brodersen and Ilse Schutz (1962–6). Berger and Luckmann built upon Schutzean foundations, especially in *The Social Construction of Reality* (1966). The ethnomethodological approach of Harold Garfinkel is also influenced by Schutz, although Garfinkel himself was once a pupil of Parsons in New York. In Uppsala in 1978, at the World Congress in Sociology, Schutz was the topic of one of the few theoretical themes on the programme. In the 1980s thematic issues of *Human Studies* (1980, 1985) were dedicated to Schutz or his most prominent pupils, such as Helmut Wagner.

32 The New School's ancestry goes back to Charles A. Beard; Alvin Johnson and scholars like Arnold Brecht, Albert Salomon, Carl Mayer, Leo Strauss and Felix Kaufmann are its beneficiaries. The full history of the New School remains to be written, although some recent attempts have been made. There is much biographical material at hand, for instance only Arnold Brecht's *Lebenserinnerungen* (1966–7) and Alvin Johnson's own autobiography *Pioneer's Progress* (orig. 1952). See also Krohn (1987) and Scott and Rutkoff (1986). In the Constance archives there is a photo of the faculty in the early 1950s, which shows only one or two non-European (non-emigrant) members. This seems to be a fairly representative picture.

33 The perils of European pundits readjusting to the new context is well documented (for instance in Martindale 1982).

34 As Schutz himself remarks in the correspondence between them – and Parsons also endorses, in a letter to Voegelin, the 'hidden participant' in the Schutz–Parsons exchange (see Rehorick and Buxton 1986).

35 Unlike Weber, there seems to be only one Schutz, meaning that his legacy has not caused such controversies because it was 'monopolized' early on by Berger and Luckmann. This harmonious state of affairs may also be due to his approach being more unequivocal than Weber's. Maurice Natanson also contributed to the diffusion of Schutzean phenomenology but without generating any conflicts of interpretation.

36 This focus gives his sociology the character of a 'protosociology' (Luckmann 1990: 13–14). We have no reason to doubt that Schutz had been scrutinizing Weber in his youth in Vienna. However, in his later private library (his original library in Vienna was lost), now kept at the Sozialwissenschaftliches Archiv in Constance, there are not many signs of extensive reading in his copies of Weber's books, although he had several of Weber's most central works, like *WuG* and *GAW*. Several chapters of his first book (1932) deal with Weber and Weberian themes. Whether Schutz's later 'American pragmatist' phenomenology also reveals a living relationship to Weber is unclear. Younger phenomenologists tend to make little mention of Weber. Schutz focuses on all the basic philosophy – about the objective reconstruction of meaning and intersubjective transcultural validity – that has to be done *before* sociological research or theory construction really starts, which means that

he is stuck in the realm of philosophy of social science, which Weber and Parsons tried to avoid.

37   Husserl is, though, rather close to an empiricist position, since his descriptive psychology focuses on 'the world as encountered in every-day life and given in direct and immediate experience, especially per-ceptual experience and its derivatives' (Gurwitsch, in Natanson 1970: 35). Intersubjectivity rests upon revelations: a pair of young lovers might for instance believe they understand each other, yet they might wake up twenty years later, realizing they never really knew each other. Current phenomenological trends are visible in the journal *Philosophy and Phenomenological Research*, which had Schutz on its editorial board from 1941 (Grathoff 1989: 24). The journal was devoted to Husserlian phenomenology well before Schutz, whose work on 'multi-ple realities' was published there in 1945, in the same volume in which Marvin Farber made programmatic statements about the goal and nature of phenomenology. Current phenomenology has become a most cosmopolitan undertaking, thriving in locations from Toronto and Brandeis to Constance and Bielefeld, recognizing Schutz as a founding father of the modern paradigm and Luckmann and Berger as his apos-tles. See also about Schutz and the International Society of Phenome-nological Research (ibid.). Natanson's reader *Phenomenology and the Social Sciences* (1973) is a valuable collection of paradigmatic sources.

     Schutz in fact had an offer to become Husserl's assistant in Freiburg. The Husserl link is important for our understanding of Schutz's rela-tion to Weber. To judge from the journal *Social Research*, in which Schutz published an 'instant version' of his approach in 1960, phe-nomenology has one of its bases at the New School, although it is by no means dominant there.

38   Schutz did not solve the problem. Nobody did. One can either give pri-ority to human 'inner' understanding, or intersubjective knowledge with a higher degree of certainty, 'objectivity'. For a contribution on the Husserl link, see Muse (1981); see also Wagner (1983; esp. section VIII, p. 287 *et passim*). In fact the (at least superficial) affinity between Weber and Husserl might be a major cause of Schutz's misinterpretation of Weber. According to Muse, Weber used Husserl against Dilthey's psy-chologism, in his plea for constructive types of rational understanding, the validity of which is to be tested by causal analysis (see Muse 1981: 101 from Roscher and Knies 1975: 168).

39   The German roots are not always obvious, since 'the everyday' is a his-torically relativistic phenomenon. Moreover, in the United States much of the European legacy could be reformulated in terms of American pragmatism. This is especially true for Schutz, who was advised not to speak about Husserl and other obscure Europeans in his lectures but to use American pragmatists to make the same points; he frequently referred to William James.

40   My presentation of the phenomenological approach stresses the Husserlian legacy and rather neglects its prehistory. The roots of

phenomenology go way back in the history of ideas. Descartes is a central ancestor, and the Cartesian dilemma of how one can know anything more than *cogito ergo sum* is another way of expressing the intersubjectivity problem. There is an interesting relationship between the Cartesian dualism and the neo-Kantian conception of reality *vs* mind. See also Grathoff's systematization of the issues of the controversy between Parsons and Schutz (Grathoff 1978b: xx–xxi).

41 The solution of transcultural intersubjectivity through *Lebenswelt* – instead of the rational constructs of a more marginalist and Weberian kind – might sound more like Husserl than Schutz. For the Schutzean critique of Husserl, see Grathoff (1989). Schutz feels that Husserl provides what he does not find in Weber, although he is critical of Husserl.

42 It is with this background in mind that we have to understand Garfinkel's experimental approach, an empiricist phenomenology taken to its extreme, as when he and his pupils let loose thousands of live chickens at a street corner in Los Angeles during rush hour, in order to observe people's reactions. Something might be explored in this way about the boundaries of transcultural everyday-life understanding. The TV programme called *Candid Camera* is similar. The basic idea is – apart from making fun of people – to confuse them through mixing the trivial with the extraordinary, thus putting the trivial into perspective, relativizing it. For the connection between phenomenology and ethnomethodology, see for instance Dallmayr and McCarthy (1977; esp. part 4, on 'Phenomenology and Ethnomethodology'). See also Sprondel and Grathoff (1979), for a differentiation of *Lebenswelt*.

43 Historically the 'anti-positivist' vein in phenomenology is further underpinned by the focus on crisis, for which modern technology is to blame. There is an alleged connection between the crisis of science and the crisis of society, with which mere applied science cannot deal adequately. There is, moreover, an eschatological element in phenomenology – in the case of Schutz, in the sense that the 'Kakania' of his youth (the Austrian empire, after '*Kaiserlich-königlich*', in the official name of the 'double monarchy') really did disappear, dissolve into its component parts. On Schutz's antipathy to unified science, see Grathoff (1989: 213 and 180). One might say that Schutz engaged in a dialogue with the Vienna circle of logical positivism. However, his aim was rather to establish a unified science that also embraced economics and sociology (Prendergast 1986). The thematization of the crisis of science, in terms of 'cultural criticism', is by no means exclusive to the phenomenologists. It is rather a typical theme of the early 1920s, and typical of the early reactions to Weber, especially his famous 'gulf doctrine', restricting the scope of scientific reason (see Lassman and Velody 1989).

44 In our context some of Schutz's later work is also of interest, e.g. 'On Multiple Realities' (1944–5), 'Don Quixote and the Problem of Reality' (orig. 1955), and 'The Social World and the Theory of Social Action' (1960). The first article appeared in *Philosophy and Phenomenological Research*; 'Don Quixote' was originally published in Spanish in 1955;

Schutz's own original English version was not available until the publication of his *Collected Papers* ten years later; 'The Social World' appeared in *Social Research*. Another good introduction to Schutz's sociology is his 'The Social World and the Theory of Social Action', in Braybrooke (1965). Schutz's *Collected Papers* have been published by Natanson and Brodersen (1962–6). Schutz's private library is kept in Constance. The correspondence between Parsons and Schutz is published in both English and German by Grathoff (1978a, 1978b). See also Rehorick and Buxton (1986), for Voegelin's 'hidden participation' in the exchange.

45   As Richard J. Bernstein (1978: 146) writes: 'At any moment in an individual's life he finds himself in a biographically determined situation. He is not merely a physical being in an objective spatial-temporal world.'

46   What Schutz found missing in Weber is manifested in *Der sinnhafte Aufbau* (1974: 15). There is a parallel with Parsons's critique of Weber for not 'going all the way'; in Schutz's case he finds Weber – not surprisingly – crude in his lack of differentiation of the *Verstehen* concept. In my view Parsons is more of Weber's creed than Schutz's, although Schutz certainly deals with Weberian problems. Schutz's criticism of Parsons could equally well be aimed against Weber. Weber is more of an adherent of unified science than Schutz realizes. This might partly be because of Schutz's somewhat narrow interpretation of Weber. Schutz predominantly builds on the initial parts of *WuG*, rather than the polemical methodological essays. Since the initial parts of *WuG* became a sort of Magna Carta for the enterprise of anti-positivist sociology, this promotes such an interpretation, while the 1903–7 essays and the 'twin-lectures' give us another and much more complex picture.

47   'Schutz's intention was in a sense to extend and complete Weber's economic sociology rather than to transcend his work' (Holton and Turner 1989: 56). The boundary between mending and transcending is, of course, hard to discern, but Schutz no doubt liked to think of himself as a Weberian scholar.

48   Although I focus mainly on the 'Objectivity' essay, there are also passages in both the Roscher and Knies essays, the *Rationale Deutung* and *Deutungsschema* (interpretative scheme; *GAW*: 130), as well as the Stammler essay on the 'rules of the game' (*GAW*: 337), which I read as good evidence for my assertion that any empathic reading of Weber is a misrepresentation in the Diltheyian vein. It is a matter of interpretation to what extent Schutz is more Diltheyian than Weber, since both are critical of their common philosophical mentor. Schutz and Dilthey depart further down the road of *Verstehen*, while Parsons and Weber depart further down the road of *Erklären*.

49   However, if Muse (1981) is to be believed, some passages in Weber could be read as an endorsement of intuitionist evidence (as we find it in Husserl), although I do not find this convincing, because of the translation and other circumstantial evidence.

50 See for instance Bernhard Mann (1990).

51 One of Parsons's reflections on Schutz's insistence on reconsidering fundamentals was that no scientific revolution would have occurred if Newton had been like Schutz.

52 Parsons (1979/80: 14) offers some comments on Schutz and the concept of action and meaning.

53 To the extent that 'objective' is an appropriate term for a neo-Kantian.

54 According to Popper, empathy could only have heuristic functions. For a discussion of this, see Struan Jacobs (1990). See also Albrow (1990: 209).

55 The human predicament is thus important to Weber, although hardly in the sense argued by Hennis (1988).

56 Gouldner speaks of him as the established 'dean' of this line of research, whereas C. Wright Mills in *The Sociological Imagination* rails against his 'abstracted empiricism'.

57 This book was burned by the Nazis. Zeisel has published recollections about Lazarsfeld and Vienna in the 1920s, for instance, in Merton et al. (1979: 394–413). This volume also contains other recollections by close collaborators. See also Oberschall (1978).

58 Lazarsfeld probably became more Americanized than later participants in the diaspora, owing to this early emigration.

59 'But again the sociologist attracted by the atmosphere of critical theory could not learn how to proceed if he wanted to study a specific topic in its spirit' (Lazarsfeld 1972: 175).

60 Göhres was one of the few people he addressed on a familiar basis, saying *du* instead of *Sie*, and perhaps Weber's only non-academic friend outside the close family. Göhres was, however, 'adopted' by Helene as an honorary member of the Weber family.

61 See Wagner and Zipprian (1994: 10), documenting Weber's correspondence with Siebeck-Mohr in Tübingen. See also Schluchter (1999).

62 See for instance Lindenlaub (1967), who accounts for the different tendencies within the Social Policy Association.

63 Among their pupils, later to carry on their achievements, although in disparate ways and in very various surroundings, were Michels, Mannheim and Lukács. The foundation of the German sociological association in 1909 was partly due to opposition to the dominant tendency in the Verein.

64 Hilde Rigaudias-Weiss (1936) deals with these early French surveys. Quetelet (1848 and 1869) is hard to avoid in this context. There is now a huge historical literature on nineteenth-century statistics, owing to research projects in the 1980s.

65 On the ambiguous role of the German professor as simultaneously scholar and civil servant, see Hughes (1958: 49).

66 Guenther Roth (1963) deals with this problem of an entire social class at the crossroads in a hardly representative political system.

67 They are not the only scholars to deal with Weber's empirical vein, see for instance Heckmann (1979), Gert Schmidt (1980) and Gerth (1994: 530).

68 Recently published in *MWG*, with a sudden topical relevance, after the fall of the Berlin Wall and the westward mobility of the population of the former GDR and Poland.

69 Beetham (1974) notes Weber's Russophobia; see also Pipes (1955). Weber's essays on the Russian Revolution in 1905 have been republished in *MWG* with still accurate 'situational' (to borrow Roth's terminology) analyses of Russian affairs.

70 I prefer to characterize Weber's recommendations as early policy analyses, owing to their instrumental reasoning and political application value. They are value-oriented without allowing ideology to suffuse the analysis.

71 See Andreas Lindt (1973) on the Weber–Naumann relationship. See also Aldenhoff in Mommsen and Osterhammel (1987).

72 See Oberschall (1965: 128 *et passim*). Weber's text from 1908 is the one where his marginalist streak is manifest. Similar elements could be traced in other essays on 'industrial sociology' from around 1908, as well as in the East of Elbe studies from the 1890s.

73 Although he was a pioneer in the field of psychophysics, Weber was negative about the search for the basic law of psychophysics, which preoccupied many others in his day. Both 'Zur Psychophysik der industriellen Arbeit' and 'Die Grenznutzenlehre und das psychophysische Grundgesetz' appeared in the same year (1908) in *Archiv für Sozialwissenschaft und Sozialpolitik*.

74 See Lazarsfeld and Oberschall (1965: 190); see also Oberschall (1965), esp. ch. 6 (p. 111 *et passim*).

75 However, early surveys often only managed to get a return frequency of about 10–20 per cent.

76 Providing some ammunition for Wilhelm Hennis's natural law-inspired interpretation of Weber. See Hennis (1988: 55 *et passim*) and Scaff (1989: 141–2).

77 Here 'positivist' is used in the meaning of – roughly – 'empiricist'.

78 Of course one has to realize that a participant in a debate is captured by the terminology of the discourse he contributes to, as a medium of communication. Compare, for instance, Hobbes, who was accused of atheism, although, to a modern reader, at least half of *Leviathan* appears as Bible exegesis.

79 Turner and Factor (1994) are enlightening on this topic.

80 For instance, his first proper book was completed when he was still thinking of a career as a lawyer. There are not many references to Radbruch in *WuG*, but he was assumed by Weber to be well known to his readers.

81 See for instance Stephen Turner (1986, 1990) and Wagner and Zipprian (1985, 1987).

82 The formulation 'we' followed by a reference to Oberschall's book is indicative of the intellectual symbiosis Lazarsfeld and Oberschall develop in their interpretation of Weber. Since Oberschall was also a pupil of Lazarsfeld it is difficult to judge how far the affinities go –

co-written articles are hardly unusual and Lazarsfeld published several joint ventures.

83 The 'patron saint' formulation is found in Lazarsfeld's foreword to Oberschall (1965: v); see further Lazarsfeld (1972: 98):

> And here one is struck by the paradoxical convergence of two trends moving in opposite directions. In Germany the tradition of action schemes in the human sciences impeded the incorporation of empirical studies of action into the body of legitimate sociological endeavour. In the United States, empirical studies of social actions might have been the relief for latent intellectual tensions: protest against primitive behaviourism, desire to overcome the static side of early community surveys, opposition to irrelevant minutiae. The mere term 'action' was bound to start a crusade in the United States, and hardly anyone knew or noticed that here were two brothers with the same name and maybe the wrong one was anointed.

84 I have scrutinized Lukács's conception of Weber, as a 'pre-neo-Kantian' (Hegelian) reaction to Weber's nominalism; see Eliaeson (1990).

5 Beyond Appropriation: Weber Yesterday and Today

1 On this topic, see Smith (1986).
2 On Weber's influence within German history, on scholars such as Otto Hintze and Theodor Schieder, see Mommsen (1989: esp. last chapter).
3 The books by Fukuyama might be seen as a follow-up of a theme in Daniel Bell, who launched the idea of 'The End of Ideology'.
4 I made this observation in summer 1992, when a visiting DAAD scholar at Lehrstuhl Baier in Constance; Ilja Srubar drew my attention to this.
5 C. Wright Mills's 'Weber' has a lot in common with the 'critical theory' Weber with his overemphasis on empathetic understanding. Gerth also contributed to the diffusion of Weberian themes, not only as a translator but as a teacher in Madison, Wisconsin; see for instance Martindale (1982).
6 There is no clear-cut division between the eclectic and the paradigmatically flawed interpretations (the 'creative extensions'), as the example of Habermas embodies, neither between eclectic and 'ultimate' interpretations, nor between ultimate and paradigmatically flawed ones. The styles of interpretations are 'ideal-types', whereas real scholars are mixed cases and not ideal-types.
7 See for instance Müller (2000).
8 Hennis has also suggested the Christian American thinker Channing as an influence on Weber; but the latest key figure is Thucydides, according to Hennis.
9 It should be mentioned that no full biography of Max Weber yet exists. Bendix (1960) covered parts but neglected the methodology, and

Marianne Weber's (1926) biography is useful but evidently not complete. For example, there is almost no mention of the British family contacts that Roth reveals in recent works. No less than four scholars are now cited as working on Weber's biography, among them Dirk Käsler and Wolfgang Mommsen.

10   Zingerle (1974), Turner and Factor (1984), Mommsen (1989) and Erdelyi (1992) are examples of this. For an intriguing attempt at operationalization, see Adatto and Cole (1981).

11   For the more purely contextualist material, see for instance Wegener (1962). In Engisch et al. (1966) we find documentation on how Weber was conceived by his contemporaries and early followers.

12   Epistemological but not ontological relativist, I should add.

13   Hägerström's inaugural lecture as professor in practical philosophy at Uppsala in 1911 launches the doctrine of negative value ontology: 'There is no science *in* morals, only *on* morals.' See 'Appendix: The Radical Solution', pp. 118 *et passim.*

14   Jennifer Platt, Ron Eyerman and Paul Hoch have been doing research on the interdependence between especially US and European social science. Although Weber certainly has been important in America it might be noted that his influence on the Chicago school is not as important as one might expect.

15   Even Jürgen Habermas (1984) evidently feels that he has to relate to the tradition: 'there is no one among his contemporaries who developed a social theory of comparable complexity' and 'no social theory can be taken seriously today which does not, at the very least, clarify its relationship to Parsons' (Habermas, here quoted from Alexander 1984: 395).

16   Albrow's hints at Goethe as a key to Weber as a seeker or at a phenomenologist affinity are not quite justified; his theory on Weber is based on a rather marginal fringe of Weber's production as a whole, namely the 1907 essay on Stammler. The idea that Husserl should somehow contribute to Weber's concept-formation is hard to document and give supportive evidence for, although Weber *does* have some half a dozen favourable references to Husserl. To claim Weber for historical sociology as Bryan Turner does also seems to be a presentist reconstruction, and the 'politically correct' Weber who emerges out of Ringer's study is very unlike the original Weber (Ringer is excellent on context though, see Eliaeson 1999).

17   And, surprisingly, some are missing. There is a certain lack of recognition of the political Weber, which might sound strange considering the famous definition of the state, the concept of charisma, the legitimacy-types, etc. Yet it is true considering how much such scholars as Robert Dahl, J. G. A. Pocock as well as William Kornhauser actually are 'Weberian'. The Weber we saw in Reinhard Bendix's (1960) work as an American liberal was 'killed' by Mommsen's (1963) well-documented dissertation, and the link to Carl Schmitt remains a 'hot potato'. Palonen's recent work might reactivate Weber as a living legacy in political contingency analyses.

18   This might seem surprising considering the enormous secondary litera-
     ture (Runciman had noted more than 600 items), but is nevertheless
     true. Weber's methodological writings are rarely taken seriously as a
     whole and are either employed selectively or given condescending treat-
     ment in favour of other parts of his *œuvre*.

19   Hennis has been influential in the English-language world, the result
     being not only in collections of his main articles but also articles about
     him in *The History of the Human Sciences*.

20   For example Gangolf Hübinger, Niall Bond, Jürgen Osterhammel and
     Edith Hanke.

21   Hennis's interpretation is not without its paradigmatic aspirations, to
     retain Weber for classical political philosophy and humanist scholar-
     ship, but it is simultaneously the arch example of the 'ultimate' trend,
     in his case including a denial of Weber's methodology for the under-
     standing of his basic intention. His basic understanding of Weber has
     in fact a certain affinity to Tenbruck's, owing to a common historicist
     bias.

22   See Oakes and Vidich (1999), esp. pp. 99–100.

23   Weber was also the main emphasis at the World Congress in History
     in Stuttgart in 1985 (see Kocka 1986), and his lasting interest among
     historians is embodied, for instance, in readers, like the *Festschrift* to
     H.-U. Wehler, *Was ist Gesellschaftsgeschichte?* (1991).

24   For instance, they have to contemplate the possibility that the letters
     won't be available *in toto*, if those who are now Weber's legal heirs
     change their minds.

25   This notion is also stressed by Wolfgang Mommsen, who made the
     point at a historical seminar in Uppsala in the late 1980s. Weber's
     Randglossen (marginal notes) in Simmel's book on Schopenhauer and
     Nietzsche are available at the archives in Munich but are hard to inter-
     pret, owing to Baumgarten's additional notes (the handwriting is
     unfortunately similar to Weber's). Moreover, Simmel worked on value-
     philosophy early on, and his works were very probably more
     familiar to Weber than is made explicit in his texts.

26   Schroeder (1998) and Whimster (1999). The *Aldgate Papers in Social
     and Cultural Theory* might be mentioned in the same context.

27   'Serious attempts to uncover and demonstrate the systematic concep-
     tion of the WL [*Wissenschaftslehre*] as a whole have been rare . . . and
     have little impressed the profession', as Tenbruck wrote in his 'Outline
     for Session on Max Weber's Methodology' (mimeo on the occasion of
     a guest appearance at the University in Munich, 3 August 1988). One
     possible reason why Henrich's work did not cause a great stir at the
     time of its publication was probably that it was a dissertation. The same
     goes for Mettler and a few more dissertations from the 1930s.

28   Lowell Bennion (1933) is an example, since his book on Weber's
     method focuses on Weber's so-called Calvinist thesis, while Pfister
     (1928) is the first real contribution to Weber's explicit ideal-type
     methodology in its context.

29   Weber did not write a lot about such topics of today as the viability of the modern welfare state or gender issues (although he was supportive of his wife in her scholarly efforts). Yet books appear in those fields with Weber as 'ornament'.

30   Maybe Lash and Whimster (1987) broke the ice. In *The History of the Human Sciences* a number of very interesting articles also appeared, especially in 1995, for instance dealing with Weber's rather complex relation to the Leipzig school.

31   Paradoxically much in line with Lukács, as Riesebrodt (1980) remarks.

32   Baumgarten is easy to criticize, because of many errors in his huge documentary work *Max Weber. Werk und Person* (1964). The erroneous dating of Weber's letter to Troeltsch of February 1909 is merely one example.

33   See for instance Turner and Factor (1994).

34   Tenbruck (conversations in Munich and Tübingen, 1988) was unenthusiastic about a 'pure' sociology, striving instead for a cultural-historical sociology that falls back on a specifically German tradition. It was not until the mid-twentieth century that German historians lowered their defences against social science, and a Weber-inspired social history utilizing ideal-types came about, for instance in Bielefeld (see Mommsen 1989: 187). It is telling that all German interpretations – including those, like Burger's, which opposed any *Gesamtdeutung* so strongly – stress the historical dimension in Weber's work, the element least congenial for the later development of social science.

   The sociological approach has been promoted by the way in which *WuG*, especially in the Anglo-Saxon world, has been identified as Weber's main concern. But the matter is not a simple one. As early as 1906, Weber's correspondence makes it clear that he speaks about sociology as an important concern (*MWG* II/5, Briefe 1906–8, for instance p. 81, in a letter to Willy Hellpach of 18 April, original in Weber's *Nachlass*, ZStA Rep. 92, NI. Max Weber, Nr. 17, Bl. 45–6). The *Nachlass* has now been moved from Merseburg to Berlin-Dahlem, Geheime Preussiche Staatsarchiv in Archivstrasse, very close to parts of the Free University. The catalogue system has recently been reorganized but the old references still work. Moreover, the *Findbuch* for the Weber *Nachlass* is very instructive.

35   The natural inclination to stress the historical significance of an idea instead of the author's own intentions; see the various contributions by Quentin Skinner. Moreover, it might well be the case that an author cannot foresee the significance and originality of his own contribution.

36   A lethargy or indifference which Popper has called 'moral futurism'.

37   Viewing social science as merely a 'language-game' would not be helpful for the advancement of cumulative discourse; rather it would have the effect of pouring oil instead of water on the fire. The proponents of instrumental applied science (what Weber would call *Zweckrationalität* and I have called normative empirical theory – in itself a perfectly legitimate undertaking in the name of 'public' or 'social interest') as well as

the proponents of methodological anarchy and unreflected pluralism therefore threaten the balanced process of the pursuit of learning and growth of instrumental well-tested knowledge.

38 See Eden (1984).

39 We could speak of Eden (1984) *vs* the Germans, including the normative liberal Mommsen. Nietzsche has bad ideological connotations, which is detrimental to his image in the United States, where the natural law inclination is still prevalent. See Baier's (1985 and 1987) comments on this topic. American neo-Straussians typically ascribe to the Nietzschean elements in Weber an inappropriate moral dimension, since the very amoral and 'nihilist' character of post-Enlightenment polytheism is exactly the predicament we have to learn to accept and to live with.

40 Baier is editing the methodological work by Weber for *MWG*, while Hennis rather neglects the relevance of Weber's methodology for the understanding of his work as a whole. The same is true of Tenbruck. The polytheist interpretation, however, could be pleaded precisely from an interpretation of Weber's methodology, as an answer to the value-incommensurability problem. Science cannot replace the new gods ascending from their graves, which Weber speaks of.

41 For a critique of Schluchter's views of Weber's view on ethics, see for instance Charles Turner (1992: 163 *et passim*). Perhaps the best statement of his position is to be found in Schluchter (1996b: ch. 7).

42 Carl Schmitt and his sinister radical decisionism cast a shadow over this topic; I try to restrict my scope and comments to the methodological consequences, concerning the validity and partiality of social science, although there is an obvious link to the political theme of how Weber as 'a liberal in despair' responds to the problem of leadership and the rational conformity of modern mass politics (see for instance Aschheim 1992: 311–12).

43 *Polyarchie der Werte* is the German phrase.

44 More precisely a combination of non-cognitivistic value-sentence theory and negative value-ontology. Value judgements don't have any truth content and don't refer to reality. Hägerström had no distinct school but the Scandinavian school of legal realism (Olivecrona and Lundstedt) has exercised considerable influence and has great affinities also with American jurisprudence (Justice Oliver Wendell Holmes; Roscoe Pound). Hägerström has, alongside Weber, been a formative influence on Gunnar Myrdal, who wrestled with the problem of value-intrusion throughout his career.

45 Who indeed is well aware of the links between Weber and Nietzsche and Kierkegaard, which is manifest in several places, for instance his letter to Hanna Arendt of 29 April 1966 (in Jaspers 1989: 186). Jaspers indeed seems to be pioneering this particular connection, later to become a bone of contention between Schluchter and Roth against Hennis and Baier and others.

46 On Weber and Nietzsche, methodology, post-modernity and value-incommensurability, see further for instance Lassman and Velody

(1989: 172–5). Several of the contributions to Mommsen and Osterhammel (1987) touch upon the same topic, for instance those by Robert Eden (pp. 405–21) and Dieter Henrich (esp. p. 541).

47 The existentialist dilemma of post-Enlightenment humans is clearly manifest also in the last pages of the lecture on 'Science as a Vocation' (*GAW*: 609; Lassman and Velody 1989: 29).

48 Cf. Luther's famous words to Charles V: 'Here I stand and can do no other.' Weber's thoughts on the relation between science and value have gained a retrospective importance beyond his own possible horizons, to judge from recent works by Rorty (1984), MacIntyre (1981), Bloom (1987), Eyerman (1985), among others.

49 The example of Hägerström's reception in Sweden demonstrates the seamy sides of philosophical nihilism, in which top-heavy state and welfare bureaucracy thrive on a sort of empty state mysticism, almost an antipode to American extreme individualism. However, nothing prevents a combination of philosophical nihilism, understood as negative value-ontology, and subjective natural law, understood as a deliberately chosen standpoint, in matters of individual property rights, etc. The seamy side of empty state-utility (or collective utility) replacing objective norms based on natural law does not follow from Hägerström's nihilism as such. It was merely *one* alternative to fill the vacuum that appeared as natural to some of his followers, like the law scholar Vilhelm Lundstedt, whose ideas provide the basis for the so-called 'functional socialism' of the Swedish social democrats. See Eliaeson (1993 and 2000a).

50 See also Aron (1957), in his comments on Strauss's views on Weber. Further, see also Sadri and Sadri (1988).

Appendix: The Radical Solution?

1 Arnold Brecht's *Political Theory* (1959) has been much used in Swedish teaching, especially on 'scientific value relativism' and the painful area of scientific impotence ('the seamy side of scientific value-relativism'), constituted by value incommensurability.

2 His philosophical inspiration Axel Hägerström wrote his main works in the German language and the majority of the founders of Swedish social science had degrees from German universities.

3 This gulf opened up as early as 1933, when Mackenroth's *Deutsche Jugend in Aufbruch* was translated into Swedish and Myrdal and Mackenroth exchanged views about the Introduction, focusing on the character of nationalism, as well as on the shift to the right of National Socialism when entering government.

4 For an overview of the Myrdal *Nachlass* at ARAB in Stockholm, see Andersson (1999).

5 There are roughly 120,000 letters in the Myrdal *Nachlass*. The material is computerized and the letters are therefore easy to find; the staff at ARAB are very helpful.

6   Myrdal's own 'Max Weber and Myrdal' is printed in Andersson (1999). The statement is an appendix to a letter to Herman Wold (enclosure of letter to Wold, 21 March 1974), with whom he conducted a correspondence on the topic.

7   For an excellent introduction see Swedberg (1990).

8   Myrdal's correspondence is voluminous, to say the least, but it seems – to judge from the collections of letters at the archives in Stockholm – that Mackenroth and Ross were Myrdal's closest friends, apart from Richard Sterner and, late in life, Tore Browaldh, who belonged, though, to a younger generation. Already in 1926 Hägerström is mentioned in a letter from Ross to Myrdal.

9   However, two prominent refugee scholars in Sweden, Ernst Cassirer and Theodor Geiger, wrote books on Hägerström and his school. Two edited volumes have appeared in English.

10 My italics. Here quoted from Eliaeson (2000a: 19; orig. in Hägerström 1964).

11 They knew of each other and Hägerström was inspired by Westermarck. Hägerström and Kelsen never understood each other, but Hägerström's criticism must be understood as a criticism of lingering natural law in Viennese legal positivism, which basically covers the same ground as Scandinavian legal realism, which is more radical, denying any scientific meaning to concepts such as 'right' or 'wrong'.

12 A young Swedish philosopher, Hans Ruin Jr, has recently recorded that Hägerström in fact contemplated writing a book on Nietzsche, drawing on letters to his brother in the 1890s as well as the drafts for Hägerström's lectures of 1926. There are no less than 25,000 unpublished manuscript pages in the Hägerström *Nachlass* at the Carolina Rediviva in Uppsala.

13 Stellan Andersson's account for the correspondence between Herman Wold and Myrdal is illuminating. In his statement on his relation to Weber, Myrdal says that he read Weber's work on capitalism and Protestantism as a student – and that he read *GAW* before writing *The Political Element*. The reference in this book to Weber, however, does not really reflect any more intimate acquaintance. In a letter to Sissela Bok of 30 November 1981 the elderly Myrdal tried to play down the Weberian influence on his thinking. See Eliaeson (2000c), esp. p. 340, n. 3.

14 Myrdal (1958, 1970 and 1990) documents his life-long concern with this particular core problem in social science. Parts of *An American Dilemma Revisited* which Myrdal worked on in his last years with deteriorating eyesight and never managed to bring to fruition (it was never published – but a Swedish preliminary version was, *Historien om An American Dilemma* (The History about *An American Dilemma* (1997); this MS was written in English but as yet only published in Swedish translation). Gunnar Myrdal is here critical of his own last chapter of 1944, the Enlightenment optimism of which is out of tune with the methodological creed of the investigation as a whole, with its clearly

defined value premisses. He even implies that he never saw this last chapter in its final guise. However, the MS copy of this chapter kept at ARAB is identical with the one published, as far as I can see. In the last few years Myrdal's memory was no longer reliable, for natural reasons. He was nearly ninety years old when the book MS was finalized. It has been slightly edited by the publisher.

15 Myrdal was engaged in a project to modernize society and had several careers. He was a prominent Swedish politician, member of parliament and sometimes of the government. Although his sociological career was more American than Swedish, he also had a crucial role in the foundation (institutionalization) of Swedish sociology, for instance through advice to Professor Einar Tegen in Lund and helping displaced emigrant scholars, such as Fritz Croner, who held a sociological seminar at Lund, to find meaningful outlets for their talents. Myrdal's importance for social science method on a more global scale is reflected in Immanuel Wallerstein (1991) and Ulrich Beck (1974).

16 Letter of 19 September 1932, kept in the Myrdal *Nachlass* in ARAB. The letter is phrased with great reverence and thus stands out in Gunnar's correspondence, which tends to be far more straightforward.

17 Sissela Bok mentioned this in an e-mail to me. About the less happy relation between Gunnar and Jan, see Martin Bulmer (2001). See further Eliaeson (2000a) and (2000c).

18 I refer to Myrdal's personal copy of the biography written by Hägerström's daughter, Margot Waller. The book is kept at ARAB. There are indications that Myrdal's marginal notes were made during his last couple of years in the apartment in the Old Town in Stockholm. The handwriting suggests that he had Parkinson's disease and there is a note elsewhere in the book that he should ask Janken (the grandson) for assistance in contacts with a locksmith (Janken, Jan's son, was one of the few relatives who visited Myrdal during his last years on a regular basis; the daughters lived in America and Germany). Myrdal underlines, on the same page, 'jenseits von Gut und Böse' (although in its Swedish translation) and also the famous formulation in Hägerström 'not in morals but instead about morals', the core formulation from 1911.

19 Very many new problems in society are really generated by science itself, genetic techniques, information techniques, nuclear power, creating issues that neither Marx nor Mill had ever heard of. But science is in itself unable to provide the existential solutions, to help us in our ultimate choices.

Choice is the destiny of modern man. Science cannot help. The responsibility is thus back with the individual, unless something unexpected happens 'around the corner', like a fundamentalist revival in the West. It would be very difficult for a modern scholar to communicate immediately with an Augustinian or Thomist, still it is the background against which Weber (and his contemporaries Simmel, Nietzsche, Hägerström, Kelsen, Westermarck) has to be understood, from the long view of the history of ideas.

Methodological Appendix

1 These attitudes could be illustrated by Muse (1977) and for instance Collins's (1986b) interpretation.
2 'Each sees what is in his heart', as Weber writes at the end of his central 'Objectivity' essay (*GAW*: 209; Weber 1949: 107). This sounds very much like existentialism to me. Moreover, immediately after, he summarizes the argument for a clear distinction between value and value-orientation, his regret about the confusion caused by 'the term value' – 'that unfortunate child of misery of our science, which can be given an unambiguous meaning only as an ideal type' (ibid.) – and an outline of the necessary predicament of conflicting instrumental means–end hierarchies.
3 This comparison is questionable, insofar as it implies a unified-science view of 'normal science', which might well be impossible within the realm of social science; perhaps comparison with paradigmatic scholars such as Tocqueville or Hobbes would be more appropriate. Alexander (1987) offers an interesting discussion on the discursive role of the classics in social science.
4 Also reflecting a transatlantic gulf as well as a paradigmatic one, since the American Weber is mostly presented without his roots; German scholars are now reviving those roots, with a natural risk of returning the 'bathwater with the baby'.
5 For the role of Alfred and Max Weber in early German sociology, see for instance the statistics in Käsler (1984). It was jokingly remarked that the amount of time the Weber brothers should be allowed to speak ought to be restricted to some 50 per cent or so, in order to give other scholars a chance.
6 Schluchter 1998, esp. p. 334 *et passim*.
7 In the current California seminars a more interesting 'Weber' than the original one might be created, by Goldman, Bellah and Alexander. But when they believe they have returned to the real Weber we must keep in mind that they take a longer route to get there than, for instance, the German scholars contributing to Mommsen and Osterhammel (1987). However, a lack of access to the original context might in fact promote bold attempts to see things with fresh eyes; see, for instance, Collins (1993). To me 'Weber the macro-theoretician' and 'Weber the historian' are two equally problematic revisions, from the point of view of intellectual history.

Short Biographies

Adorno, Theodor (1903–69) A co-founder of the so-called Frankfurt school of critical theory. Emigrated to the USA during the Nazi years, returned later to the Frankfurt Institute. Famous as one of the authors of *The Authoritarian Personality*. Worked on music theory.

Bagehot, Walter (1826–77) Famous for *The English Constitution* (1867), but also author of an introduction to sociology.

Below, Georg von (1858–1927) Medieval historian, contemporary of Weber, whose famous letter to von Below reveals basic traits in Weber's views on the method of comparative sociology, much in line with J. S. Mill's methodological canons from *A System of Logic*.

Bergson, Henri (1859–1941) French philosopher, a founder of existentialism and a fashionable lecturer. Nobel laureate in literature in 1927. His thoughts on time and free will are an important background to Schutz.

Bismarck, Otto von (1815–98) Prussian politician and *Junker*, implemented the *kleindeutsche Lösung* (a unified Germany with Austria left outside) and modern social insurance. Defeated France and Austria. 'Bribed' Ludwig II of Bavaria to switch sides and enter a Prussian-dominated unified Germany.

Brentano, Lujo (1844–1931) German historian (with Italian roots), Weber's predecessor in Munich. Adherent of the historical school and a left-liberal co-founder and member of Verein für Sozialpolitik.

Buckle, Henry Thomas (1821–62) British historian of the mid-nineteenth century. Tried to write positivistic history in the vein of Comte, resulting in the *History of the Civilization of England I–II* (1857–61). It is this sort of positivistic history writing that Popper for some reason confusingly labels 'historicism' (in *The Poverty of Historicism*).

Carlyle, Thomas (1795–1881) Mediator of German thought (Kant and Goethe) to the English-speaking realm and vice versa; inspired Weber's concept of charisma and romantic 'exceptional personalities'. *The French Revolution* is probably his most well-known work.

Carnap, Rudolf (1891–1970) 'Viennese' philosopher (important representative of the so-called Vienna circle, together with Schlick. Early career in Freiburg and Jena, transferred to the USA. *Der logische Aufbau der Welt* (1928) is a discursive background to Schutz's *Der soziale Aufbau.*

Comte, Auguste (1798–1857) French sociologist, founder of 'positivism' (he invented the term), used the term 'sociology' for a master science of society. There is a statue of him outside the Sorbonne, where he never held an academic post.

Condorcet, Marquis de (1743–94) French scholar, launched 'the idea of progress', the idea that the history of mankind is a progress to higher degrees of civilization, also meaning an optimistic and scientistic conception of Enlightenment and the scope of scientific reason. Typical of his time. Forerunners include Lessing, d'Alembert and Turgot. Followers include Hegel and Marx, and, some would argue, Norbert Elias.

Descartes, René (1596–1650) French philosopher. Dualism, mind versus body. 'I think, therefore I exist.' Died of pneumonia at the royal castle in Stockholm, where Queen Christina urged him to give private lessons in the middle of the night. Perhaps the most relevant philosopher for the methodology, or rather epistemology, of social science before Kant and J. S. Mill.

Dilthey, Wilhelm (1833–1911) German neo-idealist philosopher, emphasized biography and the peculiarity of the object of knowledge (actors with values) as the main demarcation line against the natural sciences. Works on the *Geisteswissenschaften*, which in fact is a translation of J. S. Mill's term 'moral science'. Weber took over his view on the demarcation and the specificity of the cultural/social sciences, but developed Rickert's method for its study.

Droysen, Johann Gustav (1808–84) A pioneer of German historicism, of its so-called Prussian school. His most relevant work in our context is *Historik: Vorlesungen über Enzyklopädie und Methodologie der Geschichte.* Was much engaged in the preservation of German identity in Danish-ruled Schleswig-Holstein. Academic positions in Jena and Berlin.

Durkheim, Emile (1858–1917) French educator and sociologist, known for, among other things, the concept of 'social fact'. Inspired Parsons's interpretation of Weber. Main difference between Durkheim and Weber is that as a positivist Durkheim did not actually adhere to the doctrine of methodological individualism, which makes quite a difference, in matters of testability and verification, etc.

Fichte, Johann Gottlieb (1762–1814) Historicist and nationalist philosopher famous for his *Reden an die deutsche Nation* (1807). One of the most influential early historicists. Nation-building was his project.

George, Stefan (1868–1933) Neo-romantic bohemian character known from Schwabing (Munich's literary part of town) and Heidelberg. Known for the so-called cosmic circle of devoted followers. He moved in some of the same circles as Weber, who found contacts with anarchists and bohemian characters refreshing. (See Martin Green 1974 and 1986.)

Goethe, Johann Wolfgang von (1749–1832)   German poet. Initially part of the romantic *Sturm und Drang* movement. He was perhaps more of a formative influence on Weber than has hitherto been noticed. Goethe studied in Leipzig and Strasburg. Became *Geheimerat* in Weimar. He had scientific ambitions, manifested in his *Farbenlehre* (theory of colour). Inspired by Spinoza.

Gottl-Ottlilienfeld, Friedrich (1868–1958)   Contemporary of Weber with whom he had an important correspondence on value-intrusion in the social sciences. Most of the crucial letters, touching upon the relationships between Weber and Rickert and between Weber and Schmoller, are published as parts of *MWG*. Gottl (as his name originally was, before his father was ennobled) was also engaged in *Grundriss der Sozialökonomik*.

Gouldner, Alvin (1920–73)   American sociologist with works on dialectical and reflexive sociology. Famous for his criticism of the functionalist tradition (*The Coming Crisis of Western Sociology*, 1971). After studying at Columbia in New York and sojourns at Harvard and in Buffalo and other places, he became professor at Washington University in St Louis. He also taught at the Free University in Berlin and in Jerusalem.

Guizot, François (1787–1874)   French historian and politician. Works on the English and French revolutions. Left France for England after 1848.

Hägerström, Axel (1868–1939)   Swedish 'nihilist' philosopher, founder of the Uppsala school of 'value-nihilism'. Famous inaugural lecture in Uppsala (1911) in which the negative value-ontology was launched for the first time as a coherent doctrine: 'There is no science in morals, only on morals.' Influential in jurisprudence and founding father of Scandinavian legal realism. Hägerström is a manifestation of radical anti-metaphysics. He also played a role in Swedish theological debate, defining the demarcation line between faith and scientific knowledge. Inspired Theodor Geiger, who criticized him on details but shared his general views. He has also played a role in the political culture of Sweden. Several leading social democrats were inspired by his thoughts, resulting in, for instance, 'functional socialism', i.e. that concepts such as property rights could be gradually dismantled. Gunnar Myrdal regarded Hägerström as his main influence in value-philosophy.

Hegel, G. W. F. (1770–1831)   Professor of philosophy in Berlin, born near Stuttgart, in Swabia. Famous for his vision of history, the dialectical method, and also for his early thoughts on civil society. Influenced both Marxians as well as Prussian state idealists.

Hellpach, Willy (1877–1955)   Psychologist and 'sociobiologist' who thought that phenomena such as 'hysterical women' were culturally relative. Career in Karlsruhe and Heidelberg. Works: *Sozialpsychologie* (1933) and *Völkerpsychologie* (1938).

Hempel, Carl (1905–97)   German philosopher in US exile from 1937. Works on the logic of science. The Popper–Hempel covering law means that an explanation is to subsume a phenomenon under a general law, such as 'Famine causes revolution. Famine in France in the late eighteenth century: thus revolution.' This does not exhaust the topic of explanation and Popper himself did not adhere to this crude view in the social sciences and humanities.

Herder, Johann Gottfried (1744–1803)   German co-founder of historicism; indeed, regarded as the first to launch the concept. Emphasized cultural belonging as the basis for identity, expressed for instance as folk poetry.

Heuss, Theodor (1884–1963)   The Heuss brothers (Theodor and Alfred) were both pupils of Weber. Theodor Heuss became the first president of the Federal Republic of Germany and wrote the preface to the 2nd edn of *GPS*.

Honigsheim, Paul (1885–1963)   Max Weber's 'Boswell', French-German scholar, emigrated to the USA. His book *On Max Weber* contains several anecdotes about Weber in 'unbuttoned' mood – what he said after seminars, what took place at the Sunday receptions in Ziegelhäuser Landstrasse, and what Marianne felt about the young Lukács, etc.

Horkheimer, Max (1895–1973)   Together with Adorno, first generation of the Frankfurt school and co-founder of the Institut für Sozialforschung in Frankfurt and co-editor of *Zeitschrift für Sozialforschung*. His article, 'Traditional *vs* Critical Theory' (1937) is regarded as the programmatic statement of Frankfurt critical theory, later carried on by Habermas. Like Adorno, he emigrated to the USA and later returned to the FRG.

Hume, David (1711–76)   Famous for his radical scepticism. Affinity with Viennese empiricism (logical positivism). For instance, causality was, in Hume's thinking, reduced to a chain of sense data. The very important distinction between 'is' and 'ought' (the so-called gulf-doctrine, crucial for Weber and later Arnold Brecht) is part of his legacy, but could be traced also to other scholars.

Husserl, Edmund (1859–1938)   Born in Moravia. Career in Berlin, Vienna, Halle, Göttingen and Freiburg. Founder of phenomenology (although Hegel of course had used the term). Inspired, among others, Heidegger and Schutz, the latter on concept-formation. In Weber's *œuvre* there are very few (about half a dozen), but quite appreciative, references to Husserl. The concept of the 'crisis of science' was coined by Husserl and later traded on by the 1968 generation of student revolt, also returning to the classics in order to widen the scope of social science. Husserl might fill a lacuna in Weber's more 'formal' view on concept-formation.

Jaffé, Edgar (1866–1921)   Bought *Archiv für Sozialwissenschaft und Sozialpolitik* and edited the journal together with Weber and Sombart. Married to Else von Richthofen, Weber's true love later in life, but also a good friend of Marianne Weber.

Jaspers, Karl (1883–1969)   Pupil of Max Weber and also a good friend of his wife Marianne and a participant in the Weber circle. Saw Weber as the man who could have led Germany during the Weimar era. 'The lost option of Max Weber's leadership' is a chapter in his book on Weber from the 1930s. An existentialist philosopher, he specialized in medicine and psychiatry. Dealt with the proper balance between subject and object. Disagreed with Rickert's view of Weber as a philosopher in his own right. Destroyed Weber's self-diagnosis (autopathology) soon before the end of the Second World War, after consultation with Marianne.

Jellinek, Georg (1851–1911)   German (Moravian) scholar in political science and jurisprudence with chairs at Basle and Heidelberg. His *Allgemeine Staatslehre* (1900) became very influential. He used a type concept and is thus part of the background to Weber's central methodological device.

Kant, Immanuel (1724–1804)   Philosopher in Königsberg, a town he never left. He inspired both Hegelian and neo-Kantian modes of thought (about concepts and reality) and is perhaps the most important Enlightenment philosopher.

Kelsen, Hans (1881–1973)   Professor in jurisprudence in Vienna. The classic scholar of legal positivism. Thoughts in line with Weber, Hägerström and Westermarck, on the proper relation between law and justice, following up the distinction between *jus* and *lex* in Bentham.

Kierkegaard, Sören (1813–55)   Danish existentialist philosopher. His thoughts on the anguish of existential choice make him a forerunner of Nietzsche, the later Sartre and others.

Kjellén, Rudolf (1864–1922)   Social conservative Swedish political scientist, founder of geopolitics, chairs in Gothenburg and Uppsala, also a participant in the German debate of 1914–15 on culture versus civilization. Works in international politics. The concept of 'the people's home' is associated with Kjellén but has many roots. Kjellén also spoke of a 'national socialism', which in his case should lead our thoughts more in the direction of Friedrich Naumann than Hitler. Kjellén also inspired Gunnar Myrdal throughout his life. He has been a controversial thinker owing to an alleged Nazi connection, but there is now a revival of interest, because of a recent 'communitarian' focus on what socialism and conservatism have in common.

Knies, Karl (1821–98)   Economist in Heidelberg. Weber took over his chair in 1896. Weber's critique of Roscher and Knies is his first step in methodological polemics after recovery from his nervous breakdown.

Lamprecht, Karl (1856–1915)   Historian in Leipzig. A contemporary of Weber, he tried to accommodate history and theory, albeit in a 'different key' (grand synthesis rather than ideal-type methodology).

Lask, Emil (1875–1915)   Pupil of Windelband. Neo-Kantian. Fell in the war as a volunteer. Close to the Webers in Heidelberg.

Lazarsfeld, Paul F. (1901–76)   Austrian-Jewish émigré scholar. Moved from Vienna to New York (Columbia), as a Rockefeller scholar, in 1933. Famous pioneer in electoral behaviour (survey), often organized as team work. *Die Arbeitslosen in Marienthal*, co-written with his first wife Marie Jahoda, is an important classic in the tradition of participant observation. His active search for the intermediary variable and his interest in psychology make him less an 'empiricist' than he appears in C. Wright Mills's unfavourable portrait in *The Sociological Imagination*. Work on the reception of Weber together with Anthony Oberschall, a younger Habsburg (Hungarian) immigrant to the USA.

Levenstein, Adolf (1870–1942) Writer and sociologist. Friend of Weber, who gave him advice about the design of surveys. Emphasis on *die Arbeiterfrage* (workers' question). Died in Theresienstadt.

List, Friedrich ('Freddy') (1789–1846) German economist, born in Reutlingen. His academic background was the Evangelisches Stift (seminary) in Tübingen (Baden-Württemberg), which was also Hegel's background. List spent several years in the USA. Became US consul in Germany after 1832, having helped Andrew Jackson in his presidential campaign. Pleaded for protectionism in the early phases of industrialization. A critic of pure laissez-faire. His most famous work is *The National System* (1841), translated into many languages.

Lukács, György (1885–1971) Hungarian-Jewish scholar and friend of the Webers in Heidelberg. Lukác's *Geschichte und Klassenbewusstsein* (1922) is inspired by Weber's views on rationality and Marx's on reification. Lukács's work on *Die Zerstörung der Vernunft* (1953) is a partly 'Stalinist' piece of scholarship, a contribution to the Cold War; yet a remarkable work in the history of ideas, especially of the German *Sonderweg*. Lukács's interpretation of Weber has some affinity with Friedrich Tenbruck's slightly 'anti-sociological' interpretation.

Machiavelli, Niccolò (1469–1527) Pioneer in secularized political science and history. He was also a playwright and diplomat in Florence but was dismissed after the return of the Medicis and spent his last fifteen years as a country gentleman in St Andrea in Percusina, outside Florence, near Fiesole. He employed in embryonic form the rational actor model in his manual for statecraft. Anticipated central themes in the works of Hobbes, Parsons and Weber. The first 'theorist' of modernity. *The Prince* (1513) is his most well-known work. A more republican and less 'Machiavellian' Machiavelli appears in his historical works.

Malinowski, Bronislaw (1884–1942) Polish-British anthropologist, pioneer of structural functionalism. His sojourns on the Trobriand islands generated a number of classic works. Academic posts in London and at Yale.

Mannheim, Karl (1893–1947) Born in Budapest. Main works written in German. Founding father of the sociology of knowledge with *Ideologie und Utopie* (1936). Launched the concept of the free-floating intellectual. Exiled in England during the war. Often misinterpreted as relativizing the concept of truth. Inspired Edward Shils.

Marx, Karl (1818–83) German (secularized) Jewish political economist from Trier. Wrote *Das Kapital* in the British Library in London. A left-wing Hegelian. Inspiring source of Weber's ideal-type. Most quoted classical theorist in social science, he was also politically active. He published *The Communist Manifesto* in 1849 and was a co-founder of the first communist international. His ideological and scientific theories formed the basis of state doctrines across a third of the globe between 1949 and 1989. Considering the role he has played in methodological debate in the twentieth century (and especially for the 1968 generation), he wrote surprisingly little about method (perhaps a dozen pages around 1850), a problem area in which he is out of date, while his theories survive as fresh as ever, today mainly in the USA (analytical Marxism). It is hard to say whether Marx is a positivist or a historicist; he belonged to the mid-nineteenth century generation, with its typical 'merge' or 'flirtation', before the frontlines in the famous *Methodenstreit* were defined.

Meinecke, Friedrich (1862–1954) Historicist scholar. Took initiative for the foundation of Goethe institutes all over the world after the Second World War. First Rector of the Free University in Berlin in 1948.

Menger, Carl (1840–1921) Career in Prague and Cracow, later Vienna. Austrian marginalist economist. Opponent of Schmoller and the younger historical school in the famous *Methodenstreit*, from a positivist theoretical position (which Popper confusingly described as 'historicism').

Meyer, Eduard (1855–1930) Historian, a main influence on Weber whose criticism of Meyer of 1906 is very formative and crucial for the understanding of Weber's methodology as a whole and its sources. Tenbruck has written on this.

Michels, Robert(o) (1876–1936) Close friend of Weber (until 1915) and his protégé. Pupil of Droysen. Career in Brussels, Basle, Chicago, and at Italian universities. The 'iron law of oligarchy' catches the slow shift in organization, from a means to the original end, to an end in itself, in a way that anticipates modern themes in the sociology of parties and organizations, and concepts, such as 'iron triangles' in the discussion of neo-corporatism. A very important scholar for the proper understanding of Weber's political sociology.

Mill, John Stuart (1806–73) British positivist, developed the comparative method in *A System of Logic* and launched the concept of 'moral sciences' (*Geisteswissenschaften*), taken over by the Germans (e.g. Dilthey). Mill was not only a political economist but also a liberal political philosopher, emphasizing freedom of opinion and expression.

Mills, C. Wright (1916–62) Texan educated in Madison, Wisconsin, later professor in sociology at Columbia. Cooperated with H. H. Gerth on *From Max Weber* from the late 1940s, though it is not known who actually wrote the Introduction. *The Sociological Imagination* (1962) is still a readable guide to social theory and research. Other works include *White Collar* and *The Marxists*. Participated in the debate on non-decision-making (against Robert Dahl and others). In general, C. Wright Mills's approach might be described as a synthesis between Marx and Weber, much in the vein of later European critical theory. Like H. H. Gerth, he became a legend.

Mises, Ludwig von (1881–1973)   Austrian economist born in Lemberg (Lvov). Wrote on the history of the *Methodenstreit*. A critic of positivism.

Mommsen, Theodor (1817–1903)   Very famous historian from a huge and well-known family of Danish origin, opting for Germany during the Schleswig-Holstein crises. Chairs in Zurich, Breslau and Berlin. Specialized in Roman law and ancient history. Nobel Prize laureate in literature in 1902, for his *Römische Geschichte*; he might have needed the prize since he had eighteen children. His son Ernst was married to Weber's sister Clara. Grandfather of Wolfgang Justinianus Mommsen, co-editor of *MWG*, together with Schluchter, Baier and Lepsius (originally also Johannes Winckelmann, the founder of the Weber archives in Munich, as well as editor of posthumous editions of *WuG*).

Myrdal, Gunnar (1898–1987)   Swedish social scientist, who applied a modified version of Weber–Rickert on value-relation. Myrdal was inspired by and developed both Weber and Hägerström. Famous for *An American Dilemma* (1944), a huge Carnegie-financed project on the 'Negro-question', involving such famous later scholars as Edward Shils, Sam Stouffer, Arnold Rose and Ralph Bunche. The work was cited by Justice Earl Warren in the US Supreme Court's decision in Brown *vs* Board of Education in Topeka in 1954, which ended legal segregation in the US educational system.

Myrdal worked on the problem of uncontrolled value-intrusion all his scholarly life, building on the foundations laid by Rickert's and Weber's *Wertbeziehung* (value relation).

Although Myrdal was born in Skattungbyn in Orsa, his roots were in Solvarbo in Gustats. He had strong local roots but was mobile from an early age, since his father made a career as a building contractor, before finally settling in Gesta, close to Mariefred. Myrdal grew up in Falun, Köping, Stockholm. He took his student examination (*Abitur*) in 1918 and studied jurisprudence at Stockholm University College (later to become Stockholm University). He married Alva (*née* Reimer) in 1924. They raised three children, who are all still alive and have written books about their famous parents and childhood experiences. Myrdal switched to economics (*Volkswirtschaftslehre*) although still within the faculty of law. He took his doctorate in law in 1927 and became a *docent* (a tenured position) in the same year. Among his youthful experiences, a term as acting mayor of the city of Mariefred ought to be mentioned. During the early 1930s he was, for a short period, professor at the Institut Universitaire des Hautes Études Internationales in Geneva. In 1933 he was appointed to the Lars Hierta chair in economics and finance at Stockholm. Myrdal's early work focused on monetary topics. He examined Dag Hammarskjöld's dissertation. He also wrote on housing and agricultural policy and he was much in demand for state-promoted investigations, resulting in and combined with a political career. The very modernistic home of the Myrdals in a western suburb of Stockholm actually became a radical *salon* in the 1930s, where many students, scientists and politicians exchanged ideas, including the young Erik Dahmén (later professor of economics) and Uno Åhrén, the architect. Myrdal was elected a senator in 1935 for the social democrats. Between 1938 and 1942 he spent most of his time in the USA with a ten-month interruption following the occupation of Norway and Denmark. He returned to the USA in 1943 as a Swedish diplomat, an attaché trying to study to what extent Sweden could draw on American experiences in post-war planning. His warnings against being too optimistic about peace are still a matter of debate, since methodologically they appear as self-falsifying. Myrdal's dark pessimism proved false but his predictions might have been well founded 'under the circumstances' – and his warnings efficient. After his return to Sweden he was much absorbed by politics for some years, both as a secretary of state for trade and commerce and as the leader of the so-called Myrdal Commission, which was rather unpopular since it prolonged wartime regulations, with restrictions on the purchase of consumer goods, rather parsimonious rations of coffee, etc.

However, he soon accepted a position in the UN post-war planning commission for Europe in Geneva (1947–57), after spending some time with his wife in Paris, where Alva had been appointed to a high position in UNESCO. He was the leader of the Twentieth Century Fund's investigation of the South-East Asian economy in 1957–67. He held a personal chair in international economics at Stockholm between 1960 and 1967 and chaired the recently established Stockholm Peace Research Institute (SIPRI), as well as the LAI (Latin America Institute) in Stockholm. It is impossible to list all his contributions to 'community service'; he was a very useful and dutiful citizen.

Myrdal followed Alva to India when she was appointed Swedish ambassador to New Delhi. He worked for a decade on his *Asian Drama*, a gigantic work which was not quite as successful as *An American Dilemma*. He founded the Institute of International Economy in Stockholm (1961). He also spent time at various American universities. He was a member of several foreign academies of science and received some thirty honorary doctorates from different universities.

In some respects he became Sweden's 'grumpy old man', although it might equally well be argued that he provided the increasingly ahistorical Swedish welfare state with much-needed and not yet fully appreciated 'psychoanalysis'.

Naumann, Friedrich (1860–1919)   Close friend of Weber. The concept of *Mitteleuropa* (Central Europe) is associated with his name. He was a theologian and Christian reformer and leader of the National Social Association (the Nationalsozialer Verein). Weber was his adviser. He was a parliamentarian, and was engaged in several Christian liberal party formations, such as the Christlich-Soziale Bewegung, the Nationalsozialer Verein (which he founded), Freisinnige Vereinigung, Fortschrittliche Volkspartei and finally the Deutsche Demokratische Partei (of which he was the chairman after the war). Naumann had a close exchange not only with Max Weber but also with Weber's mother Hélène (who was a very crucial and life-long influence on her son).

Nietzsche, Friedrich (1844–1900)   Born near Leipzig. Philosopher, originally a philologist in Basle (professor at the age of 24). There has been a

Nietzsche revival. He is also viewed today as an inspirer of post-modernist thought. Archives in Weimar, where his sister 'realigned' some of his texts in accordance with Nazi ideology. Nietzsche knew Richard Wagner. He inaugurated several very important slogans, such as Death of God, *Übermensch*, the Gay Science, *Wille zur Macht*, some of them book titles as well, often pinpointing post-Enlightenment themes. Among his many famous works: *Jenseits von Gut und Böse* (1886) and *Zur Genealogie der Moral* (1887) deserve special mention in our context. Many echoes of Nietzsche are found in Weber and Axel Hägerström. Nietzsche was inspired by Schopenhauer and himself inspired much later thinking, including such strange bedmates as fascism and post-modernism. Hospitalized during the last decade of his life; insane probably because of syphilis. Saw Christian morality as a slave morality, just as Machiavelli did.

Ostwald, Wilhelm (1853–1932)   Philosopher and natural scientist. Professor in Riga and Leipzig in physical chemistry. One of the most important and perhaps also most neglected parts of Weber's *GAW* is his polemics with Ostwald.

Parsons, Talcott (1902–79)   Extremely influential, not only in sociology but also in political science (David Easton, Karl Deutsch). Parsons linked Pareto, Durkheim and Weber into a synthesis which served as an alternative to Marxism – but also made it possible for Americans to deal with Marxian themes in the days of the Cold War. Accused of conservative bias, owing to his emphasis on stability and his alleged neglect of dysfunctions. Inspired by Alfred Whitehead. Inspiration also from Hobbes and from medicine. Wrote several autobiographical works (see References). Died in Munich in 1979, soon after visiting Heidelberg, fifty years after receiving his doctorate there. Much criticized 'sparring partner' of several scholars, but still relevant. Back on the intellectual scene because of revived neo-functionalism. Admired also by Habermas.

Popper, Karl (1902–94)   Austrian-British-Jewish philosopher of science. Exiled in 1939. *The Open Society and its Enemies* is a criticism of totalitarian thought from Plato to Marxism. *The Poverty of Historicism* is directed against historical determinism (which Popper calls 'historicism' with a daring definition, influenced by mid-nineteenth-century political situation). His fallibilism or falsificationism offers a way out of pure empiricist fragmentation and solipsism. *Logik der Forschung* (1934) is a pathbreaking work, with ideas later elaborated in several follow-ups. Took part in the *Positivimusstreit* of the 1960s, with Adorno and others. Shared an interest in natural science and formal logic with the Viennese school, but departed from their anti-theoretical position, favouring 'bold conjectures' that could in principle be refuted. Debate with T. S. Kuhn on the growth of knowledge. Inspired among others George Soros, who was a student of Popper.

Procrustes   In Greek mythology a person who cut off or stretched out visitors so they should fit into his Procrustean bed.

Quesnay, François (1694–1774)   French physiocrat. Inspired Marx's (and Engels's) second volume of *Das Kapital*.

Quetelet, Adolphe (1796–1874)   Belgian demographer. Pioneered empirical social investigation.

Radbruch, Gustav (1878–1949)   Law scholar, professor in Heidelberg, Königsberg and Kiel. Attorney-general during the Weimar period. One of many examples of the crucial role of legal scholarship in shaping Weber's methodology and his concept of causality in particular.

Radcliffe-Brown, Alfred Reginald (1881–1955)   British anthropologist and pioneer of structural functionalism, an approach allowing us to study any society, for instance for comparative purposes, without any pre-existing Western bias at the level of conceptualization. Inspired by Durkheim. Best-known work: *Structure and Function in Primitive Society* (1950). Positions in Cape Town, Sydney, Oxford and Chicago.

Ranke, Leopold von (1795–1886)   German historian, he was an historicist who studied 'wie es eigentlich gewesenist' and cultivated a merely Platonic love for macro-theoretical constructions and methodology, but who wrote many works characterized by idiographic mastery, especially dealing with various aspects of German history. Teacher with many followers because of his longevity. His *Nachlass* is kept at Syracuse in New York.

Rickert, Heinrich (1863–1936)   German philosopher, chairs in Freiburg and Heidelberg, founder of Baden school of neo-Kantianism. Very important and probably also formative in the shaping of Weber's ideal-type, although the finer details are a matter of recent dispute, between Thomas Burger, Guy Oakes, and others.

Roscher, Wilhelm (1817–94)   Follower of List and Comte. Works on method. Scholar in history and political science. Positions in Göttingen and Berlin. Chair in Leipzig, a university with a special legacy, with less of a historicist hegemony than the rest of Germany. Together with Knies, he was a target for Weber's early *études* in methodology after the recovery (which took place roughly 1902–3). Together with Knies and Bruno Hildebrand, Roscher is regarded as the main representative of the older historical school. *Grundriss zu Vorlesungen über die Staatswissenschaft nach geschichtlicher Methode* (1843) is one of his works. He did not really fulfil his own programme. Reflected on the 'is' versus 'ought' problem.

Schlick, Moritz (1882–1936)   Important representative of the Vienna circle, with stress on sense data and 'protocol sentences' as crucial for testability, in the form of verificationism. Early influences were Mach and Poincaré; a later influence was Wittgenstein. Schlick provides a link between neo-Kantianism and the Vienna school.

Schmitt, Carl (1888–1985)   German legal and political theorist. There has been a revival following works by Ellen Kennedy, Joseph Bendersky and Gary Ulmen. Enjoyed a high profile (despite his absence) at the Heidelberg centennial in 1964, when Habermas accused Weber (guilt by association) because Schmitt was his natural or legitimate child, while Weberians, rather, see Schmitt as a cuckoo in the Weberian nest.

Schmitt's decisionism is seen as a development of Weber's scientific value-relativism. Schmitt was undoubtedly influenced by Weber and his concepts of friend versus foe are still relevant to issues of how to define the scope of community. Schmitt was a critic of modern parliamentary democracy and emphasized contingency in politics, developing a crucial theme already discernible in Machiavelli and Weber, as well as later political philosophers, such as Pocock.

Schmitt legitimized Hitler's assassination of Ernst Röhm and many of his SA followers in 1934. Nevertheless Schmitt was an important scholar, although with romantic traits. Schmitt was a friend of Ernst Jünger and – like Jünger – did not fall in with Nazi ideology in the long run.

Schmoller, Gustav (1838–1917)   German historian and political scientist, co-founder of the Verein für Sozialpolitik. Chairs in Halle, Strasburg and Berlin and editor of *Schmollers Jahrbuch*.

Schopenhauer, Arthur (1788–1860)   *Die Welt als Wille und Vorstellung* is his most famous work. He influenced Nietzsche and also vitalism and voluntarism especially in the 1920s, when the *Zeitgeist* was an optimistic mode of his thought, the creative individual, exceptional personalities etc, trying to overcome what Weber had called 'the iron cage' (of rationality). (In the 1920s this is a recurring theme in literature, the revolt against the 'machine society' etc.). Schopenhauer himself was a pessimist. He stressed the will as the basic element and analytical unit. He was a morose bachelor with a less than happy relationship to his mother, who was a famous novelist. He scheduled his lectures in Berlin to be held at the same time as Hegel's and had, as a result, very few students.

Schumpeter, Joseph Alois (1883–1950)   Austrian-American economist, born in Moravia; career in Vienna and at Harvard, where he was a faculty member until his death. In recent years Richard Swedberg has published extensively on Schumpeter. Schumpeter was secretary of finance in the republic of Austria after the First World War. He was not only an economist but was also very relevant in sociology and political philosophy. *The Crisis of the Tax State* and *Capitalism, Socialism and Democracy* (1942) are among his most famous works. Quarrelled with Weber in a coffee-house in Vienna in 1918, about socialism and a planned economy. Their thought did not differ a lot, but their temperament did: Weber carried the tensions of the world within himself, while Schumpeter never took anything very seriously; he cultivated an image of himself as a sophisticated gentleman standing at a certain distance from mundane affairs.

Schutz (or Schütz), Alfred (1899–1959)   Austrian-Jewish social theorist in exile at the New School for Social Research in New York. Main guru of the phenomenological paradigm. Banker. His *Nachlass* is kept at the Sozialwissenschaftliches Archiv in Constance, where his legacy is cultivated by Berger and Luckmann.

Shils, Edward (1910–85)   Sociologist born in Philadelphia, where his family, eastern Jewish immigrants, made their living working in cigar factories. He started out as a social worker and contributed to Gunnar Myrdal's team work on *An American Dilemma*. He was an admirer of Karl Mannheim. For many years he was also the editor of *Minerva* (from 1962 until his death) and defended intellectual freedom and the autonomy of science all over the world. He divided his time between the University of Chicago (Committee for Social Thought) and Cambridge, UK (Peterhouse). He translated (together with Henry Finch) Weber's central methodological essays (1949). He cooperated with Parsons at Harvard, trying to establish structural functionalism as the hegemonic paradigm around 1950. He was a scholar in a very Weberian vein and an Anglophile, and was also quite at home in the German-language world. His main works are *The Constitution of Society* (1972) and *Tradition* (1981). His concepts of centre and periphery inspired Stein Rokkan's comparative studies.

Mrs Christine Schnuzenberg, his secretary, and Steven Grosby kept Shils going; he was still planning new courses only a few months before he died. Shils had a worldwide network and talking with (or rather listening to) him was an intellectual feast.

Simmel, Georg (1858–1918)   German-Jewish philosopher and sociologist, Weber's contemporary and protégé. Creator of 'formal sociology'. His legacy has a high profile especially in Chicago and Bielefeld.

Sombart, Werner (1863–1941)   German economic historian and colleague of Weber. Co-editor of *Archiv für Sozialwissenschaft und Sozialpolitik*, together with Weber and Jaffé. Member of Verein für Soziologie. His book *Händler und Helden* (1915) is typical of the hatred of England that was cultivated in Germany after the outbreak of the war. Sombart later 'accommodated' with the Nazis, in a sort of inner emigration. Most famous work: *Der moderne Kapitalismus*.

Spencer, Herbert (1820–1903)   Social Darwinist liberal, very popular in the USA. A classic author in sociology. Although today not widely read in academia, his ideas have had immense importance in the formation of, especially, American society. Buried at Highgate cemetery, less than ten yards from Karl Marx, whose theories could be seen as an antipode to his own.

Stammler, Rudolf (1856–1938)   An editor of *Zeitschrift für Rechtsphilosophie*. Neo-Kantian. Chairs in Marburg, Giessen, Halle and Berlin. Weber's criticism of Stammler reveals an otherwise not very virulent theoretical streak in Weber's work.

Strauss, Leo (1899–1973)   German-Jewish-American political philosopher (Munich and Chicago) and critic of Weber's value-philosophy. Eloquent conservative critic of mass society. Strauss has many followers in the USA, such as Harvey C. Mansfield jr at Harvard. Famous works on Hobbes and Machiavelli. *Natural Right and History* (1953) has a chapter on Weber. Strauss sees modernity as a gradual demise of the moral dimension.

Thiers, Adolph (1797–1877)   French politician and historian, aiming at large synthesis. President of the Third Republic. Inspiration for some of Balzac's characters.

Tönnies, Ferdinand (1855–1936) German sociologist. Wrote on the United Kingdom, in which he spent much time and where he also had family ties. His *Nachlass* is kept in Kiel, in the Schleswig-Holsteinisches Landesarchiv. The paired concepts of *Gemeinschaft* and *Gesellschaft* are associated with his name. His collected works are now being edited, in Kiel.

Treitschke, Heinrich von (1834–96) Prussian nationalist, but born in Dresden. A conservative who took part in the *Kulturkampf* against the Catholics. Influential as a teacher of teachers and an archetype for the politicizing sort of *ex cathedra* thinking which Weber despised. His *History of Germany in the Nineteenth Century* (1879–94) is a magisterial work, manifesting and expressing Prussian virtues, such as discipline, as a triumph over egoism, combined with a disdain for South German (e.g. Bavarian, Austrian) attitudes and culture. Chair in Berlin.

Troeltsch, Ernst (1865–1923) German evangelical theologian from Augsburg and neighbour of the Webers in Heidelberg, in Ziegelhäuser Landstrasse 17, as well as their travelling companion to America and the St Louis exhibition in 1904. In fact Troeltsch defines the predicament to which Weber's work is a response, i.e. the crisis of historicism and the problems of polytheism and theodicy.

Veblen, Thorstein (1857–1929) Famous American sociologist and economist in Chicago, of Norwegian ancestry. Veblen never managed to launch a 'full' career but became famous, esp. for his work on *The Leisure Class*. His book on *Imperial Germany and the Industrial Revolution* (1915) deals with what is later called the German *Sonderweg* (see the entry in Glossary).

Voegelin, Eric (1901–85) Austrian political philosopher (though born in Cologne), with posts in Vienna and Baton Rouge, brought to the USA by the Laura Spelman Rockefeller Foundation. His – rather negative, yet admiring – reception of Weber is pretty close to Strauss's, imprinted by value-objectivism and natural law. Voegelin tried to recover what had been lost and interpreted modern political thought in the light of pre-modern, especially ancient, thought.

Wagner, Adolph (1835–1917) Political scientist in Berlin. Pioneer in the study of the public sector. 'Wagner's law' says that the public sector and state power (state interventionism, we might say) grow with economic development. 'Socialist of the chair' and member of Verein für Soziologie.

Weber, Alfred (1868–1958) Chairs in Prague and Heidelberg. Member of Weber circle after Max's death. Prominent – together with his brother Max – in Deutsche Gesellschaft für Soziologie, which was founded in 1909. Economist and sociologist, but perhaps best known for his achievements in cultural geography.

Weber, Max (1864–1920) A descendant of a merchant family with factories outside Bielefeld (Oerlinghausen). Born in Erfurt, childhood in Berlin-Charlottenburg. Studies in Berlin and Strasburg. Military service in Poznan. Academic positions in Berlin, Freiburg, Heidelberg, Vienna and Munich. Weber was very German (although with a Huguenot heritage), but as

Guenther Roth has documented in recent years in several essays and a huge book (on Weber family history), he also belonged to a rather cosmopolitan extended family, with members also in the United Kingdom and Argentina. He also had 'hillbilly-relatives' in Mt Airy, in the American South, not far from the Smoky Mountains. He was very close to his mother, Hélène, who lived until 1919. His father died in 1897, following a quarrel in the family over what we would today call 'women's rights'; father and son were never reconciled after the clash. Max Jr suffered a severe nervous breakdown and was a neurasthenic 'tourist in life' for a few years, slowly recovering and returning to more active scholarship in 1902–3. His early career in commercial law never 'took off'. Inhibited political career. Historian and economist (his chairs were in *Nationalökonomie* or *Volkswirtschaftslehre*). Gradually became a sociologist (but perhaps was less a sociologist than Durkheim or Simmel) and was co-founder of DGS (Deutsche Gesellschaft für Soziologie) in 1909.

Weber is often retrospectively characterized as a 'present-day relevant theoretical classic author in sociology', none of which is quite true. He was an extremely influential mediator, influenced by the German *Sonderweg* (the peculiarities of German history), rather than a genuine classic author, and has a very strategic position 'at the crossroads' in the history of social thought. Weber manifests, together with such thinkers as Machiavelli, Hobbes and Bentham, and later Gunnar Myrdal and Axel Hägerström, the gradual secularization of social thought in modernity and, in Weber's case, the reciprocity of social thought across the Atlantic. The uniqueness of Western civilization and the birth of rational modern capitalism are his most famous theme, but he also wrote extensively on such topics as German agrarian history (in reality a form of political sociology), and was a pioneer of parliamentary democracy adjusted to German circumstances (delayed nation-building). His methodological essays and especially the tool of the ideal-type have been the target of 'paradigmatic hijacking' (e.g. by Schutz and Parsons) or rejection (e.g. Lazarsfeld and Oberschall, and Lukács).

His wife **Marianne**, née Schnitger (1870–1954), achieved fame in her own right, as editor of her husband's posthumous works in various fields, together with Melchior Palyi and later Johannes Winckelmann. She was a feminist pioneer and chairperson for the Bund deutscher Frauen. Wrote on women's rights within the family and in society. Friend of Karl Jaspers. The Webers had a non-sexual marriage, although they shared a bedroom in Freiburg. Weber was sexually inhibited and only late in life experienced more 'earthy' relationships, although he had contacts with anarchists and Bohemians, such as Otto Gross, the father of Else Jaffé-von Richthofen's child. These connections (experimental forms of living and eroticism, etc.) must have been a frustrating contrast to the religious influences from his mother.

Weber has resisted many attempts at interpretation. In politics he has been seen as a forerunner of National Socialism (because Hitler was an example of charismatic leadership) as well as a pioneer of parliamentary democracy. (pleading for modernized and more democratic forms of government, a *Volksstaat* instead of a *Machtstaat*). Both views are partly correct. He has also been seen as both a positivist (the fact-value distinction) and an anti-positivist (the concept of *Verstehen*). Again both views are in part correct. Actually in both cases the same concept has been a victim of selective reception, in politics the concept of 'plebiscitary leadership democracy' and in methodology the ideal-type.

Late in life Weber had to return to active teaching, since he lost his inherited fortune, which his mother Hélène had invested in war bonds.

Weber had a somewhat problematic relationship with his younger brother Alfred. For one thing, they loved the same woman, Else Jaffé-von Richthofen, who became Alfred's partner.

Westermarck, Edvard (1862–1939)   Finnish anthropologist and sociologist. Studied moral relativism, especially regarding marriage. Spent long sojourns in Morocco and the UK. Inspired Axel Hägerström's value nihilism. Westermarck was already a *docent* in sociology in the 1890s (in Helsingfors/Helsinki) and the Finnish sociological association is still today called the Westermarck Society.

Windelband, Wilhelm (1848–1915)   German philosopher. Belonged to the so-called Baden school (or South-West School) of neo-Kantianism. He launched the paired concepts of idiographic and nomothetic sciences in his *Rektoratsrede* in Strasburg (1893). Chairs also at Zurich, Freiburg and Heidelberg.

Wundt, Wilhelm (1832–1920)   German psychologist and philosopher. Chairs at Zurich and Leipzig. Weber's psychophysics in industrial sociology navigates between Wundt and Hellpach.

Glossary

Adäquate Verursachung (adequate cause) Crucial term for the interpretation of Weber's views on explanation, for instance in 'Critique of Meyer' (1906).

AGIL (LIGA) scheme Talcott Parsons's famous basic scheme. AGIL stands for adaptation, goal-attainment, integration and latency.

Anti-Enlightenment While Enlightenment could indicate cold reason and belief in the idea of progress – or humanism and a broader vision of reason – anti-Enlightenment historically indicates the search for historical roots, romantic nation-building, belief in Utopian projects. Evidently the broader humanist vision of Enlightenment overlaps anti-Englightenment.

Calvinist thesis A term for Weber's view on the origin of modern capitalism: 'Der Puritaner wollte Berufsmensch sein, wir müssen es sein' (The Puritan wanted to have a vocation, we have to). We are predestined for eternal salvation or the reverse, and success especially in economic life is a sign of God's grace. The Protestants are so to speak through their work – and accumulation of capital – collecting credits for Doomsday.

Causality The idea that a phenomenon (event or change) has a cause and a cause has an effect, that an event could be explained by a factor, like the apple falling to the ground because of gravity.

Civil society A central notion in secular (post-theological) social thought, developed by, among others, Samuel Pufendorf, G. W. F. Hegel and modern communitarians, such as Sandel and Etzioni. The concept is controversial because it is ideologically suffused, especially in debates between market liberals, socialists and neo-conservatives. In social policy civil society often discussed in terms of the Titmussian triad (a conceptual triangle with the individual, the market and the state – in one of its formulations).

Cognitive Cognition, to conceive of reality. Transcendental and deontic notions are non-cognitive.

Commensurability The comparison or translation of different paradigms, often meaning that a general method or 'language' is in principle possible. See also *Value-incommensurability*.

Contextualism To understand in its context, historicize a phenomenon. A crucial term in the debate over Quentin Skinner's methodological tools for the proper pursuit of intellectual history.

Covering law (Popper–Hempel) This is a normal deductive pattern for theoretical explanation in the natural sciences. Popper does not himself believe in its application in the cultural/social sciences.

Decisionism There is a separation between the political will and the scientific striving for truth, and both activities, depending upon each other, have to be purified of the other in order to be efficient. The Weberian paradox is that in order to promote means–end rationality and an ethic of responsibility, the scientist himself has to cling to an ethic of conviction and value-rationality, in his search for truth as a value in its own right, which must not be corrupted by various forms of politicizing intrusion (such as Lysenkoism). The term 'decisionism' has a sinister association, since it is sometimes associated with Carl Schmitt.

Deduction Logical inference (syllogism) of statements about reality from axioms and general laws, 'theory from above'.

Dialectical Plato used the concept but in modern usage it is connected with Hegel and Marx. Friedrich Engels in his so-called *Anti-Dühring* developed a rigid notion of the dialectical method as something to apply also in nature and to replace formal logic.

Dogmengeschichte History of doctrines.

Empathy *Einfühlung*, re-experiencing or even reliving, trying by means of the ego to access the inner meaning of the alter.

Epistemology Theory of knowledge, how we can know anything about anything, not to be confused with methodology, which is the manual for how we actually produce and 'verify' (confirm) scientific knowledge.

Erklären Explanation.

Essentialism The idea of *Ding an sich*, the true core, 'the real thing', an essence.

Ethnomethodology An approach used by Harold Garfinkel and others. Experimental extension of Schutz's phenomenology, close to descriptive psychology.

Existentialism Sartre, the earlier Kierkegaard and Nietzsche. Deals with the anxiety of man in his post-Enlightenment predicament, when 'God is dead and we have many churches'.

Functionalism A term with several meanings. In social science it refers to a tradition in anthropology and macro-sociology, with such classic authors as Malinowski and Radcliffe-Brown. Literature on functionalism by Bertalanffy, Erwin Laszlo, Buckley, etc.

Gemeinschaft (community) Concept taken from Tönnies, but really common goods recurring in many guises.

German *Sonderweg* The peculiarity or exceptionalism of German development, often seen as a romantic reaction against Enlightenment reason. The concept has generated much debate, in terms of the legacy of Bismarck, the role and nature of historicism, the delayed nation-building 'from above', the theme of civilization *vs* culture, etc. There is a lot of literature on this theme, for instance works by Eley and Blackbourn, Sheehan, Barkin, Elias, Veblen, Plessner, and many others.

Gesamtdeutung My term for an all-inclusive interpretation that explains the whole of Weber's *œuvre*.

Gesellschaft (society) A more large-scale rational and less civic form of *Gemeinschaft*. Impersonal and mostly applies to modern industrial societies.

Gesetz Law.

Gestalt 'Form', a phenomenon caught in its individuality.

Handlung Action, act. An act differs from mere behaviour since it has an intentional meaning – and if it is related to other humans it is a social act, at least insofar as it relates to expected cultural patterns (to distinguish it from pure biological or mechanical interaction, like making love or war with strangers).

Hermeneutics Hermes was the messenger of the gods and gave his name to the tradition of interpretation of cultural phenomena. In general it refers to the art of interpretation (mostly of texts). In the social sciences it more specifically refers to an empathetic tradition of interpretative understanding. Hermeneutics has a long tradition, including names such as Schleiermacher, Droysen, Dilthey, Schutz, K.-O. Apel, Habermas, Ricoeur and Gadamer. The concept for obvious reasons plays a crucial role in the 'demarcation debate' between positivism and various forms of anti-positivism, about the peculiarities of cultural-, spiritual-/social sciences, as compared to the natural sciences and the limits of the positivistic ideal of unified science. Emphasis on understanding rather than explanation and the denial of universal methods for establishing knowledge, valid in all fields of enquiry.

Heuristics Tools for knowledge formation, tentative tools. A model might serve heuristically to establish a theory. So might the ideal-type.

Historicism Complex current with many definitions. It has an inherent relativism and is an obscure and confusing term with several – partly contradictory – meanings. Basically the core of historicism is the denial of eternal laws and norms, while Karl Popper says it is the belief in historical determinism. Nicos Poulantzas says that it is the belief in a driving force in history. Moreover, in the debate on methodology in the history of ideas, historicism is often used as a synonym for **contextualism.**

   The concept was launched by Herder and the current is a virulent one, especially in the German-speaking world. It plays a significant role in nation-building movements in the nineteenth century. Such historical retrievals as

Ossian's songs in Scotland, Kalevala epos in Finland (or Karelia), as well as the Grimm brothers and their interest in folklore, are typical expressions of early historicism, which, nevertheless, also meant a development of the methods of history writing (modern source criticism etc.).

Ideal-type   Max Weber's central methodological device, developed in various essays from, in particular, 1904, 1906 and 1908, but already discernible in his works from the 1890s. The concept has generated much debate. It has the rational economic actor as a prototype, but with *Steigerung* (accentuation) as a central tenet.

Idiographic   Individualizing. Idiographic versus nomothetic: Windelband launched these concepts in 1894. Idiographic studies aim at giving *Gestalt* while nomothetic studies try to achieve *Gesetz*.

Induction   Generalizations from observations (or more general 'sense data', 'theory from below').

Intersubjectivity   That different observers can see the same thing (at least that it is possible in principle, by means of documentation, etc.). Prerequisite for establishing common knowledge and cumulative scientific discourse.

Iron cage   A congenial misinterpretation, a metaphor catching the increasing rationality in the modern world and the diminishing sphere of meaning, i.e. one of Weber's dominant themes. The provenance of the term was discussed in *Sociological Inquiry* in the early 1980s.

Junker   Prussian landed gentry. The *Junker* class was the recruiting base for officers and civil servants. Bismarck is one famous example. The concept has a wider relevance than the geography would suggest. Von Stauffenberg is sometimes seen as a representative, although he came from south-west Germany.

Lebensphilosophie   A philosophy characterized by vitalism and the role of the will. Schopenhauer is one early manifestation; Simmel a later one. This mode of thinking was very popular in the 1920s and it should *not* be confused with *Lebenswelt*.

Lebenswelt   Everyday life provides an instance of comparison that establishes intersubjectivity. Not to be confused with *Lebensphilosophie*. That such confusion sometimes occurs might be due to Dilthey, who could be seen as a representative of both.

Marginalist economics   The core of this theory is the idea of marginal utility, the explanation of preferences and/or market behaviour by use of the rational economic actor model.

Means–end rationality   What Weber called *Zweckrationalität*. Instrumental analysis that builds on rational calculation.

Metaphysics   Philosophy of what is beyond our senses and transcendental.

Methodenstreit   The battle over method. Basically the conflict between Schmoller and Menger in the 1880s, but often used metaphorically for recent conflicts as well (Swedberg) and/or a constructed dialogue (based on real differences) between Ranke and Schmoller. Basically, theory versus history, *Gesetz* versus *Gestalt*, nomothetic versus idiographic, positivism versus anti-positivism.

Methodological individualism Testability is tied to individual actions. Schumpeter, Carl Menger and J. S. Mill are connected to this broad tradition which is almost a standard position in social science. Steven Lukes has written on methodogical individualism.

Moral realism Tricky term, which in the USA might indicate a position of value-objectivism, while to most Scandinavians (certainly in Sweden) it would refer to legal positivism, which holds that objective norms are non-cognitivistic, that regularities of deed and punishment are what we might observe, and that laws have little to do with justice and have more the character of traffic regulations.

Natural law The idea of a timeless normative standard, anchored in God or nature. Natural law reached its peak in the works of Thomas Aquinas, where we also find the embryo of its demise, since 'positive law' might vary, over time and between cultural contexts.

Natural right The idea of universal (human) rights, anchored in natural law, or accepted as a 'useful social fiction' (as Axel Hägerström's pupils would put it).

Neo-functionalism Functionalism, structural functionalism, revitalized, as in the works of Jeffery Alexander, Richard Münch, and many others.

Nihilism A position which denies the objective validity of ethical norms (latin *nihil* = nothing). Often described (in value-philosophy) as non-cognitivism or emotivism. The word as such could also refer to a variety of less technical strands, such as radical revolutionaries in pre-communist Russia, a rejection of all moral restraints, a rejection of the very concept of truth, a callous ignorance of worldly affairs, etc. Hägerström's inaugural lecture (1911) on the truth of moral values is a classic text, expressing the non-cognitivist value ontology, or more specifically, a combination of negative value ontology and non-cognitivistic value-sentence theory.

Nominalism In our context: concepts are names we construct, not something we discover. Compare universalism and belief in universal concepts, as adversaries.

Nomothetic Searching for law/*Gesetz*.

Normative (as opposed to cognitive) Normativism might indicate for instance ideological and Utopian modes of thinking. It is not value-neutral or value-free. But it could also refer to means–end rationality with a top value, *Wertobjektive* as points of departure which could not be subject to intersubjective proof – but once it is accepted the rest follows, intersubjectively and testable. Bentham's utilitarian principle is one example of such an ultimate value.

Ontology The philosophy of what is real, the nature of reality, adversary to metaphysics – which makes it a bit confusing, since both concepts could refer to the borderline between what is reality and what is non-real.

Paradigm Nebulous concept made famous by Thomas Kuhn (1962) and ensuing debates, with a prehistory in works by N. R. Hansen and T. K. Merton. According to Margaret Masterman the concept has no fewer than twenty-two different definitions in Kuhn's original book *The Structure of Scientific Revolutions*. Basically it refers to a pattern of internalized methodological procedure, forming a tradition of research, a school, but including elements of old *Gestalt* psychology.

Pattern variables Central to Parsons; his pattern variables for normative orientation carry on a tradition from Hobbes and Durkheim; in particular the dichotomy between traditional and modern is a recurrent phenomenon in various guises.

Phenomenology A tradition starting with Husserl and Schutz, although the term also is to be found in Hegel.

Polytheism The worship of many gods, also metaphorical, used about competing world views and/or ideologies: 'God is dead and there are many churches'. The predicament of polytheism is typical of the post-Enlightenment and one way to express the predicament of value-incommensurability, which is the background to Weber's 'value-aspect–choice' methodology.

Positivism Comte's term, originally indicating a tradition that tried to establish theoretical laws, later referring to empiricism. Verificationism and Vienna anti-metaphysics and unified science are tenets that are common to old and new positivism, while attitudes to theory differ, between Comte and the Vienna circle (so-called logical positivism).

Presentism Compare retrospectivism and chronocentrism. The adversary to **contextualism** and/or **historicism** (in one of its meanings).

Procrustean bed Procrustes had a bed which guests were forced to fit by being stretched out or cut down to size.

Psychologism Could refer to both empathetic and natural science ways to explain human acts, i.e. 'hermeneutical' efforts in various forms as well as the search for the basic law of psychophysics, by extreme followers of the marginalist school.

Psychophysics The idea that our mentality is biologically determined, important at the turn of the century and for the understanding of Weber, especially his criticism of Ostwald and the way he positions himself between Hellpach and Wundt.

Rationale Evidenz Rational proof, what makes Weber's ideal-type differ from pure empathy.

Rationality A broad concept that resists brief explanation. However, in the case of Weber a distinction is made between value-rationality and means–end rationality. The first indicates a strong propensity to fulfil certain norms and ideals in all circumstances, as in the Hippocratic oath (always save lives), while means–end rationality has the propensity to accomplish certain specified aims by various means, like stability being established by various means of latency.

Such a conflict as 'is it OK to kill one person in order to save ten?', is one illustration. To the value-rational pro-life person the answer is already given, while the means–end rational person would give the matter serious thought.

Rationalization   A process found in Weber studies, especially in his comparative sociology of religions, which is often expressed in the metaphor of the 'iron cage'.

Scientific value-relativism   Weber's position, which enables instrumental normative theory, i.e. investigations of which means are rational, to bring about specific goals. We have to start from a top value or ultimate value, the validity of which we cannot prove, owing to the value incommensurability characteristic of secularized post-Enlightenment thought. Compare Bentham, Hobbes and Machiavelli. The concepts of value relevance or value orientation (*Wertbeziehung*) and the differences between Rickert, Weber and Myrdal are ongoing concerns in the history of ideas. Arnold Brecht's (1959) account of the so-called gulf doctrine is perhaps the most authoritative statement of this standard position (although never uncontested).

Sinnzusammenhang   Context of meaning.

Socialists of the chair   German pundits pioneering debate about the public sector, within the Verein für Sozialpolitik.

Sociology   Originally a French term (a mixture of Greek and Latin), coined by Comte, which is part of the reason Weber hesitated to adopt it for quite some while. The river Rhine is a broad divide in some matters, and Weber – sociologist or not – was not eager to adopt foreign terminology.

Solipsism   Being alone, aware only of one's own existence. Being captured in a private world. The consequence is multiple realities and no intersubjectivity, between alter and ego, the idea that you cannot know anything for sure outside your own mind, but are caught in a Cartesian predicament. The epistemology of Hume, Berkeley – and Schutz – cannot easily avoid the risk of solipsism.

Steigerung   Accentuation. See **ideal-type**.

Structural functionalism   A major tradition in social science during the twentieth century. Parsons and his followers (in political science Easton and Deutsch) belong to this tradition.

Taxonomy   Chains or systems of classifications, like those of Linneaus – or Weber (in *WuG*).

Teleological   There is a goal or purpose at hand, as when functionalism and system theory aim at system maintenance. Aristotle pioneered teleological analyses.

Tentative   Provisory. A tentative theory means that it is not yet confirmed.

Theodicy   Theological concept – with implications for the problem of evil.

Understanding   Complex concept often differentiated according to the type of evidence and type of 'feeling', such as explanatory or direct understanding, with rational or empathetic kind of evidence. Understanding is often characterized by various modes of interpretation. The specificity of the human/cultural sciences depends upon values and evaluating individuals being part of the object under study, which calls for interpretative methods of understanding.

We must know the abstract concept of money in order to understand how scraps of papers could be exchanged for various consumer goods. There is a mutual understanding that builds on common abstractions – if you have never heard of money you cannot survive in capitalist society, when entering the store or the market place. Society is full of such common abstractions, the seminar room and the concept of a scientific seminar being another example. We must know the concept of the seminar as an institution in order to comprehend what is going on. The concept of legal institutions such as law and courts makes some activities comprehensible that otherwise would appear as strange, esp. when we watch American movies. Many of these conceptualized institutions are culturally relative, such as burial ceremonies, to mention only one classic example.

Weber's mode of understanding is a rational non-empathetic variation, with the rational economic actor as a 'blueprint' for comparison and a prototype for the ideal-type. With the help of such models value-hierarchies could be rationalized and made more lucid, at the service, for instance, of policy decisions.

Universalism See **nominalism**.

Uppsala school (in philosophy) Refers to Axel Hägerström and his school, characterized by radical anti-metaphysics, especially in value-philosophy.

Utilitarianism A concept associated with Bentham and J. S. Mill – and, from a retrospective perspective, even Hobbes and Machiavelli. If an action produces the greatest happiness to the greatest number of people, it conforms with the utilitarian principle. Today, consequentialism is sometimes used synonymously, meaning that the value of an act depends on the result (rather than the intentions).

Value-incommensurability Various ultimate values or 'top-values' in a rational means–end hierarchy cannot be chosen on purely rational scientific grounds.

Value-rational For instance value-rational social action. See **rationality**.

Value-relativism See **scientific value-relativism**.

Verein für Sozialpolitik Social policy association. A group of reform-minded establishment scholars, promoting the study of the public sector and reform policy, through state interventionism.

Verificationism Basic element in Vienna circle and their logical positivism. Compare Popper's fallibilism/falsificationism, which is a more theoretical and less empiricist approach, in which bold conjectures should be tested against reality. Reality should have the chance to 'kick back' and falsify the theory. Scientific theories should be falsifiable, while ideologies are not, they are belief-systems with mixed elements of faith and secure knowledge.

Verstehen   See **understanding**.

Vienna school   Carnap, Wittgenstein, Schlick, Neurath and others. Analytic philosophy in Britain (e.g. Bertrand Russell; and also in Sweden, as pursued by Hägerström's followers) has a high degree of affinity with Viennese philosophy.

Volksstaat   German word for a state with a democratic order. Compare *Machtstaat* and (Prussian) *Obrigkeitsstaat*.

Wertbeziehung   Value-relation or value-orientation or point of view. Rickert's *Gesichtspunkt* is basic to Weber's *Wertbeziehung*.

'Whiggish'   (interpretation of history) History from the retrospective or presentist perspective of our own time, rather than on its own terms. 'Whiggism' is hard to avoid, although it invites chronocentrism and overinterpretation. The term itself comes from Butterfield, who wrote the political history of England as if everything that had happened moved towards the same ultimate goal.

Wirklichkeitswissenschaft   Could be translated as 'empirical science'. The term was used by Weber as a label for his own and the historicists' common ambitions, as well as with a slightly condescending tone of something that was a bit methodologically 'crude' and in need of realignment, which Weber offered.

Wissenschaftslehre   'Theory of science' or 'methodology', but really untranslatable. The term *Wissenschaft* has a broader meaning than the English 'science' and includes also the humanities.

Vitalism   There is a special 'life force' which marks the difference between natural science and the humanities. Basically rooted in German romanticism. In France Bergson spoke about *élan vital* (vital impulse). The voluntarism of (e.g.) Schopenhauer is a philosophical 'relative'.

Zeitgeist   Important concept for early historicists, Herder and others.

Zweckrationalität   Instrumental means–end rationality.

References

Adatto, K. and Cole, S. (1981) 'The Functions of Classical Theory in Contemporary Sociological Research. The Case of Max Weber', in *Knowledge and Society. Studies in the Sociology of Culture, Past and Present*, 137–62.

Adorno, Th. W. et al. (1969) *Der Positivismusstreit in der deutschen Soziologie*. Darmstadt and Neuwied: Luchterhand.

Albert, H. and Topitsch, E. (eds) (1971) *Werturteilsstreit*. Darmstadt: Wissenschaftliche Buchgesellschaft.

Albert, H. (1964) *Theorie und Realität*. Tübingen: Mohr.

Albrow, Martin (1970) *Bureaucracy*. London: Pall Mall.

——(1990) *Max Weber's Construction of Social Theory*. London: Macmillan.

Aldenhoff, R. (1991) 'Nationalökonomie, Nationalstaat und Werturteile. Wissenschaftskritik in Max Webers Freiburger Antrittsrede im Kontext der Wissenschaftsdebatten in den 1890er Jahren', *Archiv für Rechts- und Sozialphilosophie*, Beiheft 43, 79–90.

Alexander, Jeffrey (1983) *Theoretical Logic in Sociology, Volume Three. The Classical Attempt at Theoretical Synthesis. Max Weber*. Berkeley and Los Angeles: University of California Press.

——(1984) 'The Parsons Revival in Germany', *Sociological Theory*.

——(1987) 'The Centrality of the Classics', in A. Giddens and J. H. Turner (eds), *Social Theory Today*. Cambridge: Polity, 11–57.

——(1989) *Structure and Meaning. Rethinking Classical Sociology*. New York: Columbia University Press.

Alexander, Jeffrey (ed.) (1985) *Neofunctionalism*. Beverly Hills: Sage.

Andersson, Stellan (1999) 'On the Value of Personal Archives', in *Nordeuropaforum* 1, 15–32.

Andreski, Stanislav (1964) 'Method and Substantive Theory in Max Weber', *The British Journal of Sociology*, 15.

——(1984) *Max Weber's Insights and Errors*. London: Routledge and Kegan Paul.

Antoni, Carlo (1959) *From History to Sociology*. London: Merlin Press; originally in Italian 1940.

Antonio, Robert J. (1989) 'The Normative Foundations of Emancipatory Theory: Evolutionary versus Pragmatic Perspectives', *AJS*, 721–48.

——(1995) 'Nietzsche's Antisociology: Subjectified Culture and the End of History', *AJS* 101, 1–43.

Antonio, R. J. and Glassman, R. (eds) (1985) *A Weber-Marx Dialogue*. Lawrence, KA: University Press of Kansas.

Aron, Raymond (1957) *German Sociology*. Glencoe: Free Press.

——(1965) 'Max Weber und die Machtpolitik', in Otto Stammer (ed.), *Max Weber und die Soziologie heute. Verhandlungen des 15. deutschen Soziologentages*. Tübingen: Mohr.

——(1970) *Main Currents in Sociological Thought. II*. Garden City, NY: Doubleday (orig. published in English by Weidenfeld and Nicolson, 1968, also in Penguin and Pelican books).

Aschheim, Steven E. (1992) *The Nietzsche Legacy in Germany 1890–1990*. Berkeley: University of California Press.

Ay, Karl-Ludwig (1987) 'Die Max Weber Gesamtausgabe', in Walther Jaeschke et al. (eds), *Buchstabe und Geist. Zur Überlieferung und Edition philosophischer Texte*. Hamburg: Felix Meiner.

Baier, Horst (1969) 'Von der Erkenntnistheorie zur Wirklichkeitswissenschaft. Eine Studie über die Begründung der Soziologie bei Max Weber'. Mimeo. Münster. (Available through the Arbeitsstelle und Archiv der Max Weber-Gesamtausgabe, Kommission für Sozial- und Wirtschaftsgeschichte an der Bayerischen Akademie der Wissenschaften).

——(1982) 'Die Gesellschaft – ein langer Schatten des toten Gottes. Friedrich Nietzsche und die Entstehung der Soziologie aus dem Geist der Décadence', *Nietzsche-Studien. Internationales Jahrbuch für die Nietzsche-Forschung* 10(11), 6–32.

——(1985) 'Friedrich Nietzsches "neue Aufklärung" – oder: Das "metaphysische Bedürfnis" im Traumschatten der Vernunft', in *Der Traum der Vernunft. Vom Elend der Aufklärung*. Darmstadt: Luchterhand, 263–94.

——(1987) 'Friedrich Nietzsche und Max Weber in Amerika', *Nietzsche-Studien. Internationales Jahrbuch für die Nietzsche-Forschung* 16, 430–6.

Barber, Michael (1988) *Social Typifications and the Elusive Other. The Place of Sociology of Knowledge in Alfred Schutz's Phenomenology*. London and Toronto: Associated University Presses.

Baumgarten, Eduard (1964) *Max Weber. Werk und Person*. Tübingen: Mohr.

Beck, Ulrich (1974) *Objektivität und Normativität/Die Theorie-Praxis-Debatte in der modernen deutschen und amerikanischen Soziologie*. Reinbek bei Hamburg: Rowohlt.

Becker, Howard (1934) 'Cultural Case Study and Ideal-typical Method', *Social Forces*, 399–405.

——(1945) 'Interpretive Sociology and Constructive Typology', in Gurvitch and Moore 1945: 70–95.

Beetham, David (1974) *Max Weber and the Theory of Modern Politics*. London: Allen & Unwin.

——(1986) 'Die Max Weber Gesamtausgabe – Implikationen für ein neues Werkverständnis', *Soziologische Revue* 9.

Bellah, R. (1957) *Tokugawa Religion*. Glencoe, Ill.: Free Press.

——(1991) *Beyond Belief*. Berkeley: University of California Press.

Below, Georg von (1914) *Der deutsche Stadt des Mittelalters. Eine Grundlegung der deutschen Verfassungsgeschichte*, Bd 1. Leipzig: Quelle and Meyer.

Bendersky, J. W. (1983) *Carl Schmitt, Theorist for the Reich*. Princeton, NJ: Princeton University Press.

Bendix, Reinhard (1960) *Max Weber. An Intellectual Portrait*. Garden City, NY: Doubleday.

——(1984) *Force, Fate, and Freedom. On Historical Sociology*. Berkeley: University of California Press.

——(1987) 'Values and Concepts in Max Weber's Comparative Studies', *European Journal of Political Research* 15, 493–505.

Bendix, Reinhard and Roth, Guenther (1971) *Scholarship and Partisanship: Essays on Max Weber*. Berkeley, Los Angeles and London: University of California Press.

Bennion, L. (1933) *Max Weber's Methodology*. Paris: Les Temps Modernes.

Bergner, Jeff (1981) *The Origin of Formalism in Social Science*. Chicago and London: University of Chicago Press.

Berger, Peter L. and Luckmann, Thomas (1967) *The Social Construction of Reality*. Harmondsworth: Penguin, 1967; orig. in the USA 1966.

Bernstein, Richard (1978) *The Restructuring of Social and Political Theory*. Philadelphia: University of Pennsylvania Press.

Bittman, Michael (1986) 'A Bourgeois Marx? Max Weber's Theory of Capitalist Society: Reflections on Utility, Rationality and Class Formation', *Thesis-Eleven*, 81–90.

Blackbourn, D. and Eley, G. (1984) *The Peculiarities of German History*. Oxford: Oxford University Press.

Blegvad, M. (1982) 'Natural Law and Social Science. A Study of Thomas Hobbes and Adam Smith', *Danish Yearbook of Philosophy* 19, 7–62.

——(1991) ' "Value" in Turn-of-the-Century Philosophy and Sociology', *Danish Yearbook of Philosophy* 26, 51–96.

Bloom, A. (1987) *The Closing of the American Mind*. New York: Simon and Schuster.

Blum, Fred H. (1944) 'Max Weber's Postulate of "Freedom" from Value Judgments', *American Journal of Sociology* 50(1).

Bond, Niall (1988) 'Ferdinand Tönnies und Max Weber', in *Soziologisches Jahrbuch*. Trento: Università degli Studi di Trento.

——(1991) *Sociology and Ideology in Ferdinand Tönnies' Gemeinschaft und Gesellschaft*. Diss. Freiburg.

Bosse, Hans (1970) *Marx, Weber, Troeltsch*. Munich: Kaiser.

Bostaph, Samuel (1978) 'The Methodological Debate between Carl Menger and the German Historicists', *Atlantic Economic Journal* 6(3), 3–17.

Braybrooke, David (ed.) (1965) *Philosophical Problems of the Social Sciences*. London and New York: Macmillan.

Brecht, Arnold (1959) *Political Theory: The Foundations of Twentieth-Century Political Thought*. Princeton: Princeton University Press.

——(1966–7) *Lebenserinnerungen* I–II. Stuttgart: Deutsche Verlagsanstalt.

Breuer, Stefan (1991) *Max Weber's Herrschaftssoziologie*. Frankfurt am Main: Campus.

Breuer, Stefan and Treiber, Hubert (eds) (1984) *Zur Rechtssoziologie Max Webers. Interpretation, Kritik, Weiterentwicklung*. Opladen: Westdeutscher Verlag.

Brugger, Winfried (1980) *Menschenrechtsethosik und Verantwortungspolitik*. Munich: Alber.

Bruun, H. H. (1972) *Science, Values and Politics in Max Weber's Methodology*. Copenhagen: Munksgaard.

——(2001) 'Weber on Rickert: From Value Relation to Ideal Type', in *Mirrors and Windows. Essays in the History of Sociology*, ed. Janusz Mucha, Dirk Kaesler and Wlodzimierz Winclawski. Torun: Nicholas Copernicus University Press, 93–106.

Bulmer, Martin (2001) 'Problematical Parents and Critical Children: What is the Significance of Gunnar and Alva Myrdal's Chequered Family History?', *International Journal of Politics, Culture, and Society*, 14(3), Spring 2001, in Stanford M. Lyman and Sven Eliæson (eds), *Alva and Gunnar Myrdal: A Symposium on Their Lives and Works*.

Burger, Thomas (1976) *Max Weber's Theory of Concept Formation: History, Laws and Ideal Types*. Durham, NC: Duke University Press; 2nd edn with new Preface and Postscript, 1987.

Butts, Stewart (1975) 'Parsons, Weber and the Subjective Point of View', *Sociological Analysis and Theory* 5(2).

——(1977) 'Parsons' Interpretation of Weber: A Methodological Analysis', *Sociological Analysis and Theory*, 7(3).

Buxton, W. (with Rehorick, D.) (1986) 'Recasting the Parsons-Schutz Dialogue: The Hidden Participation of Eric Voegelin'. Mimeo. Paper presented at the Meetings of the Society for Phenomenology and the Human Sciences. Athens, Ohio, 21–2 June 1986. Published (slightly revised) in L. Embree (ed.), *Worldly Phenomenology. The Continuing Influence of Alfred Schutz on North American Human Science*. Lanham, MD: The University Press of America, 1988.

Böckler, Stefan and Weiss, Johannes (eds) (1987) *Marx oder Weber. Zu Aktualisierung einer Kontroverse*. Opladen: Westdeutscher Verlag.

Cahnman, Werner J. (1964) 'Weber and the Methodological Controversy in the Social Sciences', in Cahnman and Boskoff (eds), *Sociology and History*. Glencoe, Ill.: Free Press.

Cassirer, Ernst (1950) *The Problem of Knowledge*. New Haven: Yale University Press.

Cerny, Carl (1964) 'Storm over Heidelberg', *Encounter* 23.

Chapman, Mark D. (1993) 'Polytheism and Personality: Aspects of the Intellectual Relationship Between Weber and Troeltsch', *History of the Human Sciences* 6(2), 1–33.

Ciaffa, Jay A. (1998) *Max Weber and the Problem of Value-Free Social Science*. Cranbury, NJ: Associated. University Presses.

Cohen, Jere, Hazelrigg, Lawrence E., Pope, Whitney (1975) 'De-Parsonizing Weber: A Critique of Parsons' Interpretation of Weber's Sociology', *American Sociological Review* 40(2).

Colletti, Lucio (1972) *From Rousseau to Lenin. Studies in Ideology and Society.* London: New Left Books; originally in Italian 1969.

Collins, R. (1975) Reassessments of Sociological History: The Empirical Validity of the Conflict Tradition', *Theory and Society*, 147–78.

—— (1986a) *Max Weber. A Skeleton Key.* Beverly Hills and London: Sage.

—— (1986b) *Weberian Sociological Theory.* Cambridge: Cambridge University Press.

—— (1989) 'Toward a Theory of Intellectual Change: The Social Causes of Philosophies', *Science, Technology, and Human Values* 14(2), 107–40.

—— (1993) Review of Mommsen and Osterhammel 1987, *Theory and Society* 22 (Dec.), 861–70.

Critique and Humanism: Phenomenology as a Dialogue. Special Issue, 1990. Dedicated to the 90th anniversary of Alfred Schutz.

Dahrendorf, R. (1987) 'Max Weber and Modern Social Science', in Mommsen and Osterhammel (eds), *Max Weber and his Contemporaries.* London: Unwin Hyman, 574–80.

Dallmayr, Fred and McCarthy, Thomas (eds) (1977) *Understanding and Social Inquiry.* Notre Dame and London: University of Notre Dame Press.

Davis, Murray S. (1986) ' "That's Classic!" The Phenomenology and Rhetorics of Successful Social Theories', *Philosophy of the Social Sciences* 16, 285–301.

Derks, Hans (1989) 'Das Ende eines einmaligen Phenomens? Die Max Weber-Literatur 1920–1988', *ZfS*, 282–96.

Dilthey, Wilhelm (1883) *Einleitung in die Geisteswissenschaften.* Leipzig: Duncker & Humblot.

DiPadova, Laurie Newman and Browler, Ralph S. (1992) 'A Piece of Lost History: Max Weber and Lowell L. Bennion', *The American Scholar* 3(23), 37–51.

Dronberger, Ilse (1971) *The Political Thought of Max Weber.* New York: Appleton-Century-Crofts.

Eden, Robert (1986) *Political Leadership and Nihilism.* Tampa, FL: University Press of Florida.

Eldridge, J. E. T. (ed.) (1971) *Max Weber. The Interpretation of Social Reality.* London: Nelson.

Elias, N. (1939) *Über den Prozess der Zivilisation: Soziogenetische und psychogenetische Untersuchungen. Band 1: Wandlungen des Verhaltens in den weltlichen Obersichten des Abendlandes.* Basle: Haus zum Falken.

—— (1996) *The Germans.* Cambridge: Polity Press.

Eliaeson, S. (1986) 'Kommentaren zu den Beiträgen von W. Küttler, G. Lozek und H.-U. Wehler', in Jürgen Kocka (ed.), *Max Weber. Der Historiker.* Göttingen: Vandenhoeck und Ruprecht.

—— (1990a) 'Influences on Max Weber's Methodology', *Acta Sociologica*, 1–16.

——(1990b) 'Max Weber and his Critics', *International Journal of Politics, Culture and Society* 3(4), 513–37.

——(1991) 'Between Ratio and Charisma. Max Weber's Views on Plebiscitary Leadership Democracy', *Statsvetenskaplig Tidskrift* 94(4), 317–39.

——(1993a) 'GEIGER, the Uppsala-school of Value-Nihilism – and WEBER. An Encounter between Continental Sociology and Nordic Philosophy. A Lost Link', in Fazis, Urs and Nett, Jachen C. (eds), *Gesellschaftstheorie und Normentheorie*. Symposium zum Gedenken an Theodor Geiger. Basle: University of Basle.

——(1993b) 'Interpreting the Classics. Max Weber's Contribution to the Secularization of Social Science', 23–45, in Matthies, Jürgen and Palonen, Kari (eds) *Max Weber. Stadt, Politics, History*. Contributions from a Symposium at the University of Jyväskylä 19 and 20 February 1993.

——(1995) 'The Utility of the Classics. The Estate of Weber Unsettled', in *Jahrbuch für Soziologiegeschichte 1993*. Opladen: Leske and Budrich, 45–78.

——(1999) Review of Fritz Ringer, *Max Weber's Methodology. The Unification of the Cultural and Social Sciences*. Cambridge, MA: Harvard University Press, 1997, *Acta Sociologica*, 389–92.

——(1998) 'Max Weber and Plebiscitary Democracy', in R. Schroeder (ed.), *Max Weber, Democracy and Modernization*. London: Macmillan, 47–60.

——(2000a) 'Axel Hägerström and Modern Social Thought', *Nordeuropaforum*, Summer.

——(2000b) 'Constitutional Caesarism: Weber's Politics in their German Context', in S. Turner (ed.), *The Cambridge Companion to Weber*. Cambridge: Cambridge University Press, 131–48.

——(2000c) 'Gunnar Myrdal: A Theorist of Modernity', *Acta Sociologica* 43(4), 331–41.

——(2000d) 'Max Weber's Methodology. An Ideal-Type', *Journal of the History of the Behavioural Sciences* 36(3), 241–63.

Embree, Lester (1980) 'Methodology is Where Human Scientists and Philosophers Can Meet: Reflections on the Schutz-Parsons Exchange', *Human Studies*, 367–73.

Embree, Lester (ed.) (1988) *Worldly Phenomenology. The Continuing Influence of Alfred Schutz on North American Human Science*. Washington, DC: Center for Advanced Research in Phenomenology and University Press of America.

Engisch, Karl, Pfister, Bernhard, and Winckelmann, J. (eds) (1966) *Max Weber. Gedächtnisschrift der Ludwig-Maximilians-Universität München*. Berlin.

Erdelyi, Agnes (1992) *Max Weber in Amerika. Wirkungsgeschichte und Rezeptionsgeschichte Webers in der anglo-amerikanischen Philosophie und Sozialwissenschaft*. Vienna: Passagen.

——(1993) 'Das "Fremde" als eine fremde philosophische Tradition. Die verschiedenen Interpretationsmöglichkeiten der originalen Texte Max Webers und deren englischer Übersetzung', in *Übersetzen, verstehen, Brücken bauen. Geisteswissenschaftliches und literarisches Übersetzen im internationalen Kulturaustausch. Teil 1.* Ed. Armin Paul Frank, Kurt-Jürgen Maass, Fritz Paul and Horst Turk. Berlin: Erich Schmidt Verlag, 420–6.

Esser, Hartmut (1993) 'The Rationality of Everyday Behavior. A Rational Choice Reconstruction of the Theory of Action by Alfred Schütz', *Rationality and Society* 5, 7–31.

Eyerman, Ron (1985) 'Rationalizing Intellectuals', *Theory and Society* 14, 777–808.

Factor, R. and Turner, S. (1982) 'Weber's Influence in Weimar Germany', *Journal of the History of the Behavioral Sciences,* 147–56.

Farber, Marvin (1966) *The Aims of Phenomenology. The Motives, Methods, and Impact of Husserl's Thought.* New York: Harper.

Fleischmann, Eugène (1964) 'De Weber à Nietzsche', *Archives européennes de sociologie* 5(2).

Fogt, S. (1981) 'Max Weber und die deutsche Soziologie der Weimarer Republik: Aussenseiter oder Gründungsvater', *KZfSS,* 245–72.

Francis, Emerich (1966) 'Kultur und Gesellschaft in der Soziologie Max Webers', in *Max Weber. Gedächtnisschrift der Ludwig-Maximilians-Universität München zur Wiederkehr seines Geburtstages 1964.* Berlin: Duncker & Humblot.

Freund, Julien (1968) *The Sociology of Max Weber.* New York: Pantheon Books; orig. in French 1966.

Friedrichs, Robert W. (1970) *A Sociology of Sociology.* New York and London: Free Press.

Gay, William C. (1978) 'Probability in the Social Sciences: A Critique of Weber and Schutz', *Human Studies* 1, 16–37.

Gerth, H. H. (1982) 'The Reception of Max Weber's Work in American Sociology', in Bensman, Vidich and Gerth (eds), *Politics, Character, and Culture: Perspectives from Hans Gerth.* Westport, Conn.: Greenwood Press.

——(1994) 'The Development of Social Thought in the United States and Germany: Critical Observations on the Occasion of the Publication of C. Wright Mills' *White Collar', IJPCS* 7(3), 525–68.

Gerth, H. H. and Mills, C. Wright (eds) (1948) *From Max Weber.* London: Free Press; orig. publ. 1946.

Giddens, Anthony (1972) *Politics and Sociology in the Thought of Max Weber.* London: Macmillan.

——(ed.) (1974) *Positivism and Sociology.* London: Heinemann.

——(1976) 'Classical Social Theory and the Origins of Modern Sociology', *AJS* 81, 703–29.

——(1977) *Studies in Social and Political Theory.* London: Hutchinson.

——(1979) 'Schutz and Parsons: Problems of Meaning and Subjectivity', *Contemporary Sociology,* 682–5.

——(1982) *Profiles and Critiques in Social Theory.* London: Macmillan.

Girndt, Helmut (1967) *Das soziale Handeln als Grundkategorie erfahrungswissenschaftlicher Soziologie.* Tübingen: Mohr.

Glassman, Ronald M. (1983) 'The Weber Renaissance', *Current Perspectives in Social Theory*, 239–51.

Glassman, Ronald M. and Murvar, Vatro (eds) (1984) *Max Weber's Political Sociology. A Pessimistic Vision of a Rationalized World*. Westport, Conn. and London: Greenwood Press.

Glassman, R. M. and Swatos, William H. Jr (eds) (1986) *Charisma, History, and Social Structure*. Westport, Conn. and London: Greenwood Press.

Gneuss, Christian and Kocka, Jürgen (eds) (1988) *Max Weber. Ein Symposion*. Munich: Deutscher Taschenbuch Verlag.

Goldman, H. (1988) *Max Weber and Thomas Mann. Calling and the Shaping of the Self*. Berkeley, Los Angeles, London: University of California. Press.

——(1992) *Politics, Death, and the Devil. Self and Power in Max Weber and Thomas Mann*. Berkeley: University of California Press.

Goodman, Mark Joseph (1975) 'Type Methodology and Type Myth. Some Antecedents of Max Weber's Approach', *Sociological Inquiry* 45(1).

Gordon, Scott (1991) *The History and Philosophy of Social Science*. London: Routledge.

Gouldner, Alvin (1970) *The Coming Crisis of Western Sociology*. New York: Basic Books.

——(1972) 'Anti-Minotaur: The Myth of a Value-Free Sociology', *Social Problems* 9 (Winter). Also in I. L. Horowitz (ed.), *The New Sociology. Essays in Social Science and Social Theory in Honor of C. Wright Mills*. London: Oxford, 1964.

Graber, Edith (1981) 'Translator's Introduction to Max Weber's Essay on Some Categories of Interpretive Sociology', *The Sociological Quarterly* 22, 145–50.

Grathoff, Richard (1978a) 'Alfred Schütz', in Käsler (ed.), *Klassiker des Soziologischen Denkens. Band II*. Munich: Beck.

——(ed.) (1978b) *The Theory of Social Action. The Correspondence of Alfred Schutz and Talcott Parsons*. Bloomington and London: Indiana University Press; orig. in German 1977.

——(1989) *Milieu und Lebenswelt. Einführung in die phänomenologische Soziologie und sozialphänomenologische Forschung*. Frankfurt am Main: Suhrkamp.

Greeley, Andrew M. (1964) 'The Protestant Ethic: Time for a Moratorium', *Sociological Analysis*, 25, 20–33.

Green, Martin W. (1974) *The von Richthofen Sisters: The Triumphant and the Tragic Modes of Love*. New York: Basic Books; 2nd edn Albuquerque: University of New Mexico Press, 1988.

——(1986) *The Mountain of Truth. The Counterculture Begins, Ascona, 1900–1920*. Hanover, NJ and London: University Press of New England.

Green, Robert W. (ed.) (1959) *Protestantism and Capitalism. The Weber Thesis and its Critics*. Boston: Heath; 2nd edn 1973.

Gurvitch, George and Moore, Wilbert E. (eds) (1945) *Twentieth Century Sociology*. Freeport, NY: Books for Libraries Press.

Gustav Schmoller in seiner Zeit: die Entstehung der Sozialwissenschaften in Deutschland und Italien. Hrsg. von Pierangelo Schiera-Friedrich Tenbruck. Berlin and Bologna: Duncker & Humblot and Società editrice il Mulino, 1988.

Gutting, G. (ed.) (1980) *Paradigms and Revolutions.* Notre Dame, Ind. and London: University of Notre Dame Press.

Habermas, Jürgen (1967) *Zur Logik der Sozialwissenschaften.* Tübingen: Mohr.

——(1982) *Theorie des kommunikativen Handelns.* Bd 1. Frankfurt am Main: Suhrkamp (Engl. transl. 1984).

Haferkamp, Hans (ed.) (1989) *Social Structure and Culture.* Berlin: de Gruyter.

Hägerström, A. (1953) *Inquiries into the Nature of Law and Morals*, tr. C. D. Broad. Stockholm: Almqvist and Wiksell.

——(1964) *Philosophy and Religion.* London: Allen and Unwin.

Hall, John (1981) 'Max Weber's Methodological Strategy and Comparative Lifeworld Phenomenology', *Human Studies* 4, 131–43.

Hanson, N. R. (1965) *Patterns of Discovery.* Cambridge: Cambridge University Press; orig. publ. 1958.

Hayek, F. (1978) 'The Place of Menger's *Grundsätze* in the History of Economic Thought', in Hayek, *New Studies in the Philosophy, Politics, Economics and the History of Ideas.* Chicago: University of Chicago Press, ch. 17; orig. publ. 1973.

Heckmann, Friedrich (1979) 'Max Weber als empirischer Socialforscher', *ZfS* 8(1).

Heiskanen, Ilkka (1967) 'Theoretical Approaches and Scientific Strategies in Administrative and Organizational Research. A Methodological Study', *Commentationes Humanarum Litterarum*, 39(2).

Hekman, Susan J. (1983) *Max Weber and Contemporary Social Theory.* Notre Dame, Ind. and Oxford: University of Notre Dame Press and Robertson.

Hennis, Wilhelm (1963) *Politik und praktische Philosophie. Eine Studie zur Rekonstruktion der politischen Wissenschaften.* Neuwied: Luchterhand.

——(1983) 'Max Weber's "Central Question"', *Economy and Society* 12, 135–80.

——(1985a) 'Im langen Schatten einer Edition. Zu Erscheinen des erstes Bandes der Max-Weber-Gesamtausgabe (MWG)', *Zeitschrift für Politik* 32, 208–17.

——(1985b) 'Die Spuren Nietzsches im Werk Max Webers. Vortrag gehalten in der öffentlichen Sitzung am 22. November 1985', *Jahrbuch der Akademie der Wissenschaften in Göttingen.* Göttingen: Vandenhoeck & Ruprecht.

——(1988) *Max Weber. Essays in Reconstruction.* London: Allen and Unwin; German edn 1987.

——(1991) 'The Pitiless Sobriety of Judgement': Max Weber between Carl Menger and Gustav von Schmoller – The Academic Politics of Value Freedom', *History of the Human Sciences* 4, 27–59.

Henrich, Dieter (1952) *Die Einheit der Wissenschaftslehre Max Webers.* Tübingen: Mohr.
——(1988) 'Einführung', in Jaspers 1988.
Heuss, Theodor (1958) 'Geleitwort' to Max Weber's *GPSe*, 2nd edn.
Hilbert, Richard A. (1992) *The Classical Roots of Ethnomethodology: Durkheim, Weber, and Garfinkel.* Chapel Hill, NC: University of North Carolina Press.
Hinkle, Gisela J. (1986) 'The Americanization of Max Weber', *Current Perspectives in Social Theory*, 87–104.
Hodges, H. A. (1952) *The Philosophy of Wilhelm Dilthey.* London: Routledge and Kegan Paul.
Holton, Robert J. and Turner, Bryan S. (1989) *Max Weber on Economy and Society.* London: Routledge.
Homann, Harald (1990) 'The Limits of Logic in Sociology', *IJPCS* 3, 555–8.
Honigsheim, Paul (1968) *On Max Weber.* New York and London: Free Press and Macmillan.
Hübinger, G. Osterhammel, J. and Welz, W. (1990) 'Max Weber und die wissenschaftliche Politik nach 1945. Aspekte einer theoriegeschichtlicher Nicht-Rezeption', *ZfP* 37(2), 181–204.
Hudson, W. D. (ed.) (1969) *The Is/Ought Question. A Collection of Papers on the Central Problem in Moral Philosophy.* London: Macmillan.
Huff, Toby (1980) 'On the Methodology of the Social Sciences. A Review Essay', Part I, *Philosophy of the Social Sciences*, 11(4), 461–75.
——(1982) 'On the Methodology of the Social Sciences. A Review Essay', Part II, *Philosophy of the Social Sciences* 12(2), 205–19.
Hufnagel, Gerhard (1971) *Kritik als Beruf.* Frankfurt am Main, Berlin and Vienna: Propyläen.
Hughes, H. Stuart (1958) *Consciousness and Society.* New York: Vintage.
——(1960) Review of Bendix, *Max Weber. An Intellectual Portrait*, *American Historical Review* 66.
——(1975) *The Sea Change.* New York: Harper and Row.
Hungar, Kristian (1971) *Empirie und Praxis. Ertrag und Grenzen der Forschungen Max Webers im Licht neuerer Konzeptionen.* Meisenheim am Glan: Anton Hain.
Husserl, Edmund (1954) *Die Krisis der europäischen Wissenschaften und die transzendentale Phänomenologie. Eine Einleitung in die phänomeno-logische Philosophie*, in *Husserliana Bd VI.* The Hague: Martinus Nijhoff.
Iggers, Georg G. (1968) *The German Conception of History.* Middletown, Conn.: Wesleyan University Press.
——(1984) 'The "Methodenstreit" in International Perspective. The Reorientation of Historical Studies at the Turn from Nineteenth to the Twentieth Century', *History of Historiography* 6, 21–31.
——(1973) 'Historicism', in *Dictionary of the History of Ideas. Studies of Selected Pivotal Ideas*, vol. II. New York: Charles Scribner's Sons.
Isajiw, W. W. (1968) *Causation and Functionalism in Sociology.* New York: Schocken.
Jacobs, Struan (1990) 'Popper, Weber and the Rationalist Approach to Social Explanation', *BJS*, 41(4), 559–70.

Jacobsen, Bjarne (1999) *Max Weber und Friedrich Albert Lange. Rezeption und Innovation.* Wiesbaden: Deutscher Universitätsverlag/DUV.

Janoska-Bendl, Judith (1965) *Methodologische Apsekte des Idealtypus. Max Weber und die Soziologie der Geschichte.* Berlin: Duncker & Humblot.

Jaspers, Karl (1946) *Max Weber. Politiker, Forscher, Philosoph.* Bremen: Johs Storm; orig. 1932, 2nd edn 1958. (Also in Karl Jaspers, *Max Weber.* Introduction by Henrich Dieter. Munich: Piper, 1988.)

——(1989) *Karl Jaspers on Max Weber.* Edited with an introduction and notes by John Dreijmanis, trans. Robert J. Whelan. New York: Paragon House.

Jay, Martin (1973) *The Dialectical Imagination.* Boston and Toronto: Little Brown.

——(1985) *Permanent Exiles. Essays on the Intellectual Migration from Germany to America.* New York: Columbia University Press.

Jellinek, Georg (1900) *Allgemeine Staatslehre.* Berlin: Häring.

Johnson, Alvin (1952) *Pioneer's Progress.* University of Nebraska Press; reprint as Bison Book (by arrangement with The Viking Press), 1960.

Jules-Rosette, Benetta (1980) 'Talcott Parsons and the Phenomenological Tradition in Sociology: An Unresolved Debate', *Human Studies* 3, 311–30.

Kaesler: see Käsler.

Kalberg, Stephen (1979) 'The Search for Thematic Orientations in a Fragmented Oeuvre: the Discussion of Max Weber in Recent German Sociological Literature', *Sociology* 13(1).

——(1987) 'The Origin and Expansion of Kulturpessimismus: The Relationship between Public and Private Spheres in Early Twentieth Century Germany', *Sociological Theory* 5, 150–64.

——(1994) *Max Weber's Comparative Historical Sociology.* Cambridge: Polity.

Käsler, Dirk (1972) *Max Weber. Sein Werk und seine Wirkung.* Munich: Nymphenburg.

——(1975) 'Max Weber-Bibliographie', *KZfSS*, 27(4) in collaboration with Helmut Fogt).

——(1978) 'Max Weber', in Käsler (ed.), *Klassiker des soziologischen Denkens, Band II, Von Weber bis Mannheim.* Munich: Beck.

——(1983) 'In Search of Respectability: The Controversy over the Destination of Sociology during the Conventions of the German Sociological Society, 1910–1930', in *Knowledge and Society: Studies in the Sociology of Culture Past and Present*, vol. 4, Greenwich, Conn.: Jai Press, 227–72.

——(1984) *Die frühe deutsche Soziologie 1909 bis 1934 und ihre Entstehungs-Milieus. Eine wissenschaftliche Untersuchung.* Opladen: Westdeutscher Verlag.

——(1988a) *Max Weber. An Introduction to his Life and Work.* Cambridge: Polity Press; orig. German edn 1979.

——(1988b) 'Unbefangenheit und Hingabe. Das Webersche Konzept der "Werturteilsfreiheit" und die Verantwortung des heutigen Sozialwissenschaftlers', in H. Maier et al. (eds), *Politik, Philosophie, Praxis.* (Festschrift für Wilhelm Hennis). Stuttgart: Klett-Cotta.

——(1991) *Sociological Adventures. Earle Edward Eubank's Visits with European Sociologists.* London: Transaction; orig. German version 1985.

——(1992) *Sociology Responds to Fascism.* Ed. with S. Turner. London and New York: Routledge.

Kassab, E. S. (1991) *The Theory of Social Action in the Schutz-Parsons Debate.* Fribourg, Switzerland: Universitätsverlag Freiburg Schweiz.

——(1992) ' "Paramount Reality" in Schutz and Gurwitsch', *Human Studies* 14, 181–98.

Kaufmann, Felix (1936) *Methodenlehre der Sozialwissenschaften.* Vienna: Springer.

Kendall, Patricia L. (ed.) (1982) *The Varied Sociology of Paul F. Lazarsfeld.* New York: Columbia University Press.

Kluback, William (1956) *Wilhelm Dilthey's Philosophy of History.* New York: Columbia.

Kocka, H. Jürgen (1966) 'Karl Marx und Max Weber. Ein methodologischer Vergleich', *Zeitschrift für die gesamte Staatswissenschaft,* 122; English version in Antonio and Glassman (eds) *A Weber-Marx Dialogue.* Lawrence: University Press of Kansas, 1985, 134–66.

——(1976) 'Kontroversen über Max Weber', *Neue politische Literatur,* 21, 281–301.

——(1980) 'Theory and Social History: Recent Developments in West Germany', *Social Research* 47, 426–57.

Kocka, Jürgen and Gneuss, Chr. (eds) (1968) *Max Weber. Ein Symposion.* Munich: DTV.

Kocka, J. and Nipperdey, T. (eds) (1979) *Theorie und Erzählung in der Geschichte.* Munich, vol. 3 in *Theorie der Geschichte. Beiträge zur Historik.*

Kocka, J. and Peukert, D. (1991) 'Max Weber und die Geschichtswissenschaft. Neuere Entwicklungen in der Bundesrepublik'. Berlin: mimeo.

Köhnke, K. C. (1986) *Entstehung und Aufstieg des Neukantianismus.* Frankfurt am Main: Suhrkamp.

König, René (1964) 'Einige Überlegungen zur Frage der "Werturteilsfreiheit bei Max Weber" ', *KZfSS* 16, also in König 1987: 201–29.

——(1987) *Soziologie in Deutschland.* Munich and Vienna: Carl Hanser.

König, René and Winckelmann, Johannes (eds) (1963) *Max Weber zum Gedächtnis, Sonderheft 7,* in *KZfSS.* Cologne and Opladen.

Koslowski, Peter (ed.) (1997) *Methodology of the Social Sciences, Ethics, and Economics in the Newer Historical School. From Max Weber and Rickert to Sombart and Rothacker.* Berlin: Springer.

Kozyr-Kowalsky, S. (1968) 'Weber and Marx', *The Polish Sociological Bulletin* 9, 5–17.

Krohn, Claus-Dieter (1993) *Intellectuals in Exile. Refugee Scholars and the New School for Social Research.* Amherst: University of Massachusetts Press; orig. in German in 1987.

Kronman, Anthony T. (1983) *Max Weber.* Stanford, Calif.: Stanford University Press.

Kruse, Volker (1990) 'Von der historischen Nationalökonomie zur historischen Soziologie. Ein Paradigmwechsel in den deutschen Sozialwissenschaften um 1900', *KZfSS* 19(3), 149–65.

Kunz, Jürgen (1986) 'Max Weber. Die Wechselbeziehung zwischen der Lebensgeschichte und dem soziologischen Werk Max Webers (1864–1921)'. Mimeo, University of Constance.

Lachmann, L. M. (1970) *The Legacy of Max Weber.* London: Heinemann.

Lakatos, I. (1970) 'Falsification and the Methodology of Scientific Research Programmes', in Lakatos and Musgrave 1970: 91–195.

Lakatos, I. and Musgrave, A. (eds) (1970) *Criticism and the Growth of Knowledge.* London and New York: Cambridge University Press.

Lassman, Peter (1980) 'Value-Relation and General Theory: Parsons' Critique of Weber, *Zeitschrift für Soziologie,* 9(1).

Lassman, P. and Velody, I. (eds) (1989) *Max Weber's 'Science as a Vocation'.* London: Unwin Hyman.

Laudan, Larry et al. (1986) 'Scientific Change: Philosophical Models and Historical Research', *Synthese* 69, 141–223.

Lazarsfeld, Paul F. (1962) 'Philosophy of Science and Empirical Social Research', in E. Nagel, P. Suppes and A. Tarski (eds), *Logic, Methodology and Philosophy of Science.* Stanford: Stanford University Press, 463–73.

——(1972) *Qualitative Analysis. Historical and Critical Essays.* Boston: Allyn and Bacon.

Lazarsfeld, P. and Oberschall, A. (1965) 'Max Weber and Empirical Social Research', *American Sociological Review* 30.

Lecky, W. E. H. (1910) *The Rise and Influence of the Spirit of Rationalism in Europe.* London, Bombay, Calcutta: Longmans, Green, and Co.; orig. 1865.

Lefèvre, Wolfgang (1971) *Zum historischen Character und zur historischen Funktion der Methode bürgerlicher Soziologie.* Frankfurt am Main: Suhrkamp.

Lepenies, W. (1988) *Between Literature and Science: The Rise of Sociology.* Cambridge: Cambridge University Press.

Lepsius, Rainer, M. (1977) 'Max Weber in München. Rede anlässlich der Enthüllung einer Gedenktafel', *ZfS,* 6(1), January 1977.

——(1986) 'Interessen und Ideen. Die Zurechnungsproblematik bei Max Weber', *KZfSS,* Suppl. 27, 20–31.

Levine, Donald (1981) 'Rationality and Freedom: Weber and Beyond', *Sociological Inquiry* 51, 5–25.

——(1985) *The Flight from Ambiguity. Essays in Social and Cultural Theory.* Chicago: University of Chicago Press.

——(1989) 'Parsons' Structure (and Simmel) Revisited', *Sociological Theory* 7, 110–17.

——(1995) *Visions of the Sociological Tradition.* Chicago and London: The University of Chicago Press.

Lewis, John (1975) *Max Weber and a Value-Free Sociology*. London: Lawrence and Wishart.

Lichtblau, Klaus (1991) 'Causality or Interaction? Simmel, Weber and Interpretive Sociology', *Theory, Culture and Society*, 33–62.

Liebersohn, H. (1988) *Fate and Utopia in German Sociology, 1870–1923*. Cambridge, Mass.: MIT.

Lindenlaub, Dieter (1967) *Richtungskämpfe im Verein für Sozialpolitik, Beiheft in Vierteljahresschrift für Sozial- und Wirtschaftsgeschichte*. Wiesbaden: Steiner.

Lindt, Andreas (1973) *Friedrich Naumann und Max Weber*. Munich, 1973, no. 174 in *Theologische Existenz heute*.

List, Frederick (1856) *National System of Political Economy*. Philadelphia: J. B. Lippincott.

Loos, Fritz (1970) *Zur Wert- und Rechtslehre Max Webers*. Tübingen: Mohr.

Löwith, Karl (1939–40) 'Max Weber und seine Nachfolger', *Mass und Wert*, 3.

Lübbe, Weyma (1992) 'Die Theorie der adäquaten Verursachung. Zum Verhältnis von philosophischem und juristischem Kausalitätsbegriff', *Konstanzer Berichte. Philosophie der Geistes- und Sozialwissenschaften* 1.

Luckmann, T. (ed.) (1978) *Phenomenology and Sociology*. Harmondsworth: Penguin.

——(1983) *Life-World and Social Realities*. London: Heinemann Educational.

——(1990) 'Towards a Science of the Subjective Paradigm: Protosociology', *Critique and Humanism*, Special Issue.

Luethy, Herbert (1964) 'Once Again Calvinism and Capitalism', *Encounter* 22.

Lukács, G. (1954) *Die Zerstörung der Vernunft*. Berlin: Aufbau Verlag.

MacFarlane, A. (1987) *The Culture of Capitalism*. Oxford: Basil Blackwell.

Machlup, Fritz (1970) 'Homo Oeconomicus and his Class Mates', in Natanson 1970: 122–39.

Manicas, Peter T. (1987) *A History and Philosophy of the Social Sciences*. Oxford: Blackwell.

——(1991) 'The Social Science Disciplines: The American Model', in Wagner, Wittrock and Whitley (eds), *Discourses on Society. The Shaping of the Social Science Disciplines*. Dordrecht and Boston and London: Kluwer, 45–72.

MacIntyre, A. (1984) *After Virtue*. Notre Dame. Ind.: University of Notre Dame Press; orig. 1981.

Mann, Bernard (1990) *Anpassungsqualitäten behinderter Volljähriger in der stationären Altenhilfe*. Frankfurt am Main: Haag and Herchen.

Mannheim, Karl (1936) *Ideology and Utopia: An Introduction to the Sociology of Knowledge*. London: Routledge and Kegan Paul.

Martel, Martin U. (1979) 'Parsons, Talcott', in *International Encyclopedia of the Social Sciences*, vol. 18, Biographical Supplement. New York and London.

Martindale, Don (1959) 'Sociological Theory and the Ideal Type', in Llewellyn Gross (ed.), *Symposium on Sociological Theory*. New York: Row, Peterson.

—— (1960) *The Nature and Types of Sociological Theory*. Boston: Houghton Mifflin.

—— (1982a) *The Monologue: Hans Gerth (1908–1978), a Memoir.* Ghaziabad, India: Intercontinental Press.

—— (1982b) *Personality and Milieu: The Shaping of Social Science Culture.* Houston, Tex.: Cap and Gown Press.

—— (1979) 'Ideologies, Paradigms, and Theories', in W. E. Snizek, E. R. Fuhrman and M. K. Miller (eds), *Contemporary Issues in Theory and Research. A Metasociological Perspective*. London: Aldwych.

Masterman, Margaret (1970) 'The Nature of a Paradigm', in Lakatos and Musgrave (eds), *Criticism and the Growth of Knowledge*. London and New York: Cambridge University Press.

Mayer, J. P. (1944) *Max Weber and German Politics*. London: Faber and Faber.

McKinney, John C. (1966) *Constructive Typology and Social Theory*. New York: Appleton-Century Crofts.

Meinecke, F. (1911) *Weltbürgertum und Nationalstaat. Studien zur Genesis des deutschen Nationalstaates*. 2nd edn. Munich: Oldenburg.

—— (1936) *Die Entstehung des Historismus*. Munich.

Meja, V., Misgeld, D. and Stehr, N. (eds) (1987) *Modern German Sociology*. New York: Columbia University Press.

Menger, Carl (1884) *Die Irrthümer des Historismus in der deutschen Nationalökonomie*. Vienna.

—— (1985) *Investigations into the Method of the Social Sciences. With Special Reference to Economics*. New York and London: New York University Press.

Merquior, J. G. (1980) *Rousseau and Weber. Two Studies in the Theory of Legitimacy*. London: Routledge and Kegan Paul.

Merton, Robert K. (1970) *Science, Technology and Society in Seventeenth-Century England*. New York; orig. published in 1938, also in *Osiris* 1949.

—— (1951) *Social Theory and Social Structure*. Glencoe, Ill.: Free Press.

Merton, R. K., Coleman, J. S. and Rossi, P. H. (eds) (1979) *Qualitative and Quantitative Social Research. Papers in Honor of Paul F. Lazarsfeld*. New York and London: Free Press and Macmillan.

Merz, Peter-Ulrich (1990) *Max Weber und Heinrich Rickert. Die erkenntniskritischen Grundlagen der verstehenden Soziologie*. Würzburg: Königshausen and Neumann.

Mettler, Artur (1934) *Max Weber und die philosophische Problematik in unserer Zeit*. Leipzig: Hirzel.

Metz, Karl H. (1984) '"Der Methodenstreit in der deutschen Geschichtswissenschaft (1891–99)": Bemerkungen zum sozialen Kontext wissenschaftlicher Auseinandersetzungen', *History of Historiography*, 3–19.

Meyer, Willi (1975) 'Values, Facts, and Science: On the Problem of Objectivity in Economics', *Zeitschrift für die gesamte Staatswissenschaften* 131.

Midgley, E. B. F. (1983) *The Ideology of Max Weber. A Thomist Critique.* Aldershot: Gower.

Mill, J. S. (1973) *A System of Logic.* Toronto and Buffalo. Vol. VII in *Collected Works.*

Mills, C. Wright (1970) *The Sociological Imagination.* Harmondsworth: Penguin; orig. 1959.

Mises, Ludwig (1929) 'Soziologie und Geschichte. Epilog zum Methoden-streit in der Nationalökonomie', *Archiv für Sozialwissenschaft und Sozialpolitik* 61.

Mitchell, William C. (1967) *Sociological Analysis and Politics: The Theories of Talcott Parsons.* Englewood Cliffs: Prentice Hall.

Mitzman, Arthur (1970) *The Iron Cage. An Historical Interpretation of Max Weber.* New York: Knopf.

Momigliano, A. (1982) 'From Mommsen to Weber', in *New Paths of Classicism in Nineteenth Century, History and Theory,* Supplement 21.

Mommsen, W. (1963) 'Zum Begriff der "plebiszitären Führerdemokratie" bei Max Weber', *KSfSS* 15.

—— (1974a) *The Age of Bureaucracy.* Oxford: Basil Blackwell.

—— (1974b) *Max Weber und die deutsche Politik 1890–1920.* 2nd edn. Tübingen: Mohr; orig. publ. 1959. Engl. trans. 1984, University of Chicago Press.

—— (1983b) 'Max Weber und die historiographische Methode in seiner Zeit', *Storia della Storiografia/History of Historiography,* 3, 28–42.

—— (1983a) 'The Antinomian Structure of Max Weber's Political Thought', *Current Perspectives in Social Theory,* 4, 289–311.

—— (1989) *The Political and Social Theory of Max Weber.* Chicago and Cambridge: University of Chicago Press and Polity.

Mommsen, W. and Osterhammel, J. (eds) (1987) *Max Weber and his Contemporaries.* London: Allen and Unwin. German version 1988: *Max Weber und seine Zeitgenossen.* Göttingen: Vandenhoeck and Ruprecht, ed. Wolfgang Mommsen and Wolfgang Schwentker.

Moon, Donald J. (1977) 'Understanding and Explanation in Social Science. On Runciman's Critique of Weber', *Political Theory,* 5(2).

Morgenthau, Hans J. (1948) *Politics among Nations: The Struggle for Power and Peace.* New York: Knopf.

Müller, Hans-Peter (2000) 'Romantischer Realismus. Isaiah Berlins Botschaft', *Merkur* 599, 157–62.

Muller, Jerzy Z. (1987) *The Other God that Failed. Hans Freyer and the Deradicalization of German Conservatism.* Princeton, NJ: Princeton University Press.

Münch, Richard (1980) 'Über Parsons zu Weber: Von der Theorie der Rationalisierung zur Theorie der Interpretation', *ZfS* 9(1).

—— (1988) *Understanding Modernity.* London: Routledge; orig. in German 1982.

Murvar, Vatro (1975) 'Toward a Sociological Theory of Religious Movements', *Journal of the Scientific Study of Religion* 14, 229–56.
—— (1983) *Max Weber Today – An Introduction to a Living Legacy: Selected Bibliography*. Brookfield, WI: Max Weber Colloquia and Symposia at the University of Wisconsin-Milwaukee.
—— (ed.) (1985) *Theory of Liberty, Legitimacy and Power: New Directions in the Intellectual and Scientific Legacy of Max Weber*. London, Boston, Melbourne and Henley: Routledge and Kegan Paul.
Muse, Kenneth R. (1977) 'Critique and Hermeneutics: Habermas and Weber'. Chicago: University of Chicago, unpublished dissertation submitted to the Faculty of the Divinity School, available in Regenstein Library, call no. HM 999.M96.
—— (1981) 'Edmund Husserl's Impact on Max Weber', *Sociological Inquiry* 51(2), 105–11.
Myrdal, Gunnar (1933) 'Ends and Means in Political Economy', *Zeitschrift für Nationalökonomie*, 4 (3), a Swedish variation of this article was published in *Ekonomisk Tidskrift* [Journal of Economics] 1931).
—— (1944) *An American Dilemma*. New York: Harper and Row.
—— (1958) *Value in Social Theory*. New York: Harper and Brothers.
—— (1970) *Objectivity in Social Research*. London: Gerald Duckworth, orig. in Swedish 1968.
—— (1987) *Historien om An American Dilemma* (*The History of An American Dilemma*, translation into Swedish from Gunnar Myrdal's English manuscript). Stockholm: SNS.
—— (1990) *The Political Element in the Development of Economic Theory*. New Brunswick, NJ: Transaction; orig. in Swedish 1930.
Natanson, Maurice (ed.) (1963) *Philosophy of the Social Sciences*. New York: Random House.
—— (ed.) (1970) *Phenomenology and Social Reality. Essays in Memory of Alfred Schutz*. The Hague: Martinus Nijhoff.
—— (ed.) (1973) *Phenomenology and the Social Sciences*. 2 vols. Evanston, Ill.: Northwestern University Press.
Nau, Heino Heinrich (1996) *Der Werturteilsstreit. Die Äußerungen zur Werturteilsdiskussion im Ausschuss des Vereins für Sozialpolitik*, ed. and with Introduction by H. H. Nau. Marburg: Metropolis.
—— (1997) *Eine 'Wissenschaft vom Menschen'. Max Weber und die Begrundung der Sozialökonomik in der deutschsprachigen Ökonomie 1871–1914*. Berlin: Duncker & Humblot.
Nedelmann, Birgitta (1988) ' "Psychologismus" oder Soziologie der Emotionen? Max Webers Kritik an der Soziologie Georg Simmels', in Otto Rammstedt (ed.), *Simmel und die frühen Soziologen. Nähe und Distanz zu Durkheim, Tönnies und Max Weber*. Frankfurt am Main: Suhrkamp, 11–35.
Nippel, Wilfried (1991) 'Max Weber, Eduard Meyer und die "Kulturgeschichte" ', in *Was ist Gesellschaftsgeschichte? Positionen, Themen, Analysen*, ed. Manfred. Hettling, Claudia Huerkamp, Paul Nolte, Hans-Walter Schmul. Munich: Beck.

Nipperdey, Thomas (1990) *Germany from Napoleon to Bismarck: 1800–1866*. Trans. Daniel Nolan. Princeton: Princeton University Press.

Nusser, Karl-Heinz (1984) 'Hermeneutik als offene Theorie bei Max Weber', in *Tradition und Innovation. XIII. Deutscher Kongress für Philosophie. Bonn 24.–29. September 1984*. Hamburg: Felix Meiner.

——(1986) *Kausale Prozesse und sinnerfassende Vernunft*. Munich: Alber.

——(1987) 'Der Baum der Erkenntnis', *Zeitschrift für Politik* 34, 293–300.

Oakes, G. (1975) 'Introductory Essay', in Max Weber, *Roscher and Knies: The Logical Problems of Historical Economics*. New York and London: Free Press and Macmillan.

——(1977) 'Introductory Essay', in Max Weber, *Critique of Stammler*. New York and London: Free Press and Macmillan.

——(1987) 'Max Weber and the Southwest German School: Remarks on the Genesis of the Concept of the Historical Individual', *IJPCS* 1, 115–31.

——(1988) *Weber and Rickert. Concept Formation in the Cultural Sciences*. Cambridge, Mass.: MIT.

Oakes, Guy, and Vidich, Arthur J. (1999) 'Collaboration, Reputation, and Ethics', in Hans H. Gerth and C. Wright Mills (eds), *American Academic Life*. Illinois: University of Illinois Press.

Oberschall, Anthony (1965) *Empirical Social Research in Germany 1848–1914*. Paris and The Hague: Mouton.

—— (ed.) (1972) *The Establishment of Empirical Sociology. Studies in Continuity, Discontinuity, and Institutionalization*. New York, Evanston, San Francisco and London: Harper and Row.

——(1978) 'Paul F. Lazarsfeld and the History of Empirical Social Research', *Journal of the History of the Behavioral Sciences* 14, 199–206.

Oexle, Otto Gerhard (1986) ' "Historismus". Überlegungen zur Geschichte des Phänomens und des Begriffs', in *Braunschweigische Wissenschaftliche Gesellschaft, Jahrbuch 1986*.

Olivecrona, Karl (1971) *Law as Fact*. 2nd edn. London: Stevens and Sons; 1st edn London and Copenhagen: Oxford University Press and Munksgaard, 1939.

Ollig, Hans-Ludwig (1979) *Der Neukantianismus*. Stuttgart: Metzler.

—— (ed.) (1987) *Materialien zur Neukantianismus-Diskussion*. Darmstadt: Wissenschaftliche Buchgesellschaft.

Oppenheimer, Hans (1925) *Die Logik der soziologischen Begriffsbildung. Mit besonderer Berüksichtigung von Max Weber*. Tübingen: Mohr.

Ostrogorski, M. (1902) *Democracy and the Organization of Political Parties*. London: Macmillan.

Owsley, Richard M. (1985) 'Wagner and the Intellectual Biography of Alfred Schutz', *Human Studies* 8, 307–13.

Owen, David (1991) 'Autonomy and "Inner Distance": A Trace of Nietzsche in Weber', *History of the Human Sciences* 5, 79–91.

Palonen, Kari (1994) *Politics, Rhetoric and Conceptual History. Studies on Modern Languages of Political Theory*. Jyväskylä: Julkaisuja Publications.

——(1998) *Das 'webersche Moment'*. Opladen: Westdeutscher Verlag.

Palyi, Melchior (ed.) (1923) *Erinnerungsgabe für Max Weber*, I–II. Munich and Leipzig: Duncker & Humblot.

Parkin, Frank (1982) *Max Weber.* London: Tavistock.

Parsons, Talcott (1936) Review of von Schelting, *Max Webers Wissenschaftslehre* (1934), *ASR* 1.

——(1948) *Essays in Sociological Theory. Pure and Applied.* Glencoe, Ill.

——(1951) *The Social System.* London: Routledge and Kegan Paul.

——(1965) 'Wertfreiheit und Objektivität', in Stammer 1965.

——(1968) *The Structure of Social Action*, vols I and II. New York and London; orig. published 1937.

——(1970) 'On Building Social System Theory: A Personal History', *Dædalus*, 99.

——(1979/80) 'On Theory and Metatheory', *Humboldt Journal of Social Relations* 7(1) Fall/Winter 1979/80, 5–16.

——(1980) 'The Circumstances of My Encounter with Max Weber', in R. K. Merton and M. White Riley (eds), *Sociological Traditions from Generation to Generation. Glimpses of the American Experience.* Norwood, NJ: Ablex, 37–43.

——(1981) 'Rationalität und der Prozeß der Rationalisierung im Denken Max Webers', in Sprondel and Seyfarth 1981.

Parsons, Talcott and Shils, Edward (eds) (1951) *Toward a General Theory of Action. Theoretical Foundations for the Social Sciences.* Cambridge, Mass.: Harvard University Press.

Passmore, John and White, Hayden (1974) *Essays on Historicism*, Supplement 14, *History and Theory* 14(4), 30–47.

Peukert, Detlev J. K. (1989) *Max Webers Diagnose der Moderne.* Göttingen: Vandenhoeck & Ruprecht.

Pfister, Bernhard (1928) *Die Entwicklung zum Idealtypus. Eine methodologische Untersuchung über das Verhältnis von Theorie und Geschichte bei Menger, Schmoller und Max Weber.* Tübingen: Mohr.

Phillips, Derek L. (1973) 'Paradigms, Falsification, and Sociology', *Acta Sociologica* 1.

——(1975) 'Paradigms and Incommensurability', *Theory and Society* 2(1).

Pipes, Richard (1955) 'Max Weber and Russia', *World Politics* 7, 371–404.

Pippin, Robert B. (1983) 'Nietzsche and the Origin of the Idea of Modernism', *Inquiry*, 26, 151–80.

Platt, Jennifer (1985) 'Weber's Verstehen and the History of Qualitative Research: The Missing Link', *British Journal of Sociology*, 448–66.

Plessner, Helmut (1988) *Die verspätete Nation.* Frankfurt am Main: Suhrkamp; orig. 1974.

Plotke, David (1975–6) 'Marxism, Sociology and Crisis: Lukács' Critique of Weber', *The Berkeley Journal of Sociology* 20.

Poggi, G. (1986) 'Max Weber: A Monumental Edition in the Making', *British Journal of Sociology*, 297–303.

——(1989) 'Max Weber's Work; Its Intellectual Context, its Main Concerns', review article in *History of the Human Sciences* 37, 235–40.

Popper, Karl (1957) *The Poverty of Historicism*. London: Routledge and Kegan Paul.

Portis, E. B. (1983) 'Max Weber and the Unity of Normative and Empirical Theory', *Political Studies* 31, 25–42.

——(1986a) *Max Weber and Political Commitment*. Philadelphia: Temple University Press.

——(1986b) 'Theoretical Interpretation from a Social Scientific Perspective: An Example from Max Weber', *Social Science Quarterly* 66, 505–18.

Poulantzas, N. (1982) *Pouvoir politique et classes sociales de l'état capitaliste*. Paris: Maspero; orig. 1968.

Prendergast, Christopher (1986) 'Alfred Schutz and the Austrian School of Economics', *AJS* 91, 1–26.

——(1993) 'Rationality, Optimality, and Choice, Esser's Reconstruction of Alfred Schutz's Theory of Action', *Rationality and Society* 5, 47–57.

Prewo, Rainer (1979) *Max Webers Wissenschaftsprogramm: Versuch einer neumethodischen Neuerschliessung*. Frankfurt am Main: Suhrkamp.

Rammstedt, Otthein (1988) 'Klassiker der Soziologie – was is das eigentlich?', *Soziologische Revue*, 269–76.

Rehbinder, Manfred and Tieck, Klaus-Peter (eds) (1987) *Max Weber als Rechtssoziologe*. Berlin: Duncker & Humblot.

Rehorick, David (1980) 'Schutz and Parsons: Debate or Dialogue?', *Human Studies*, 347–55.

Rehorick, David and Buxton, William (1986) 'Recasting the Parsons-Schutz Dialogue: The Hidden Participation of Eric Voegelin', mimeo, paper for the Meeting of the Society for Phenomenology and the Human Sciences, Athens, Ohio, 21–2 June 1986. Slightly revised version published in Embree 1988.

Rickert, Heinrich (1913) *Die Grenzen der naturwissenschaftlichen Begriffsbildung*. Tübingen: orig. 1902.

——(1926) 'Max Weber und seine Stellung zur Wissenschaft', *Logos* 11, 222–37.

——(1986) *The Limits of Concept Formation in Natural Science. A Logical Introduction to the Historical Sciences*. Abridged English version. Cambridge: Cambridge University Press.

Riesebrodt, Martin (1980) 'Ideen, Interessen, Rationalisierung: Kritische Anmerkungen zu F. H. Tenbrucks Interpretation des Werkes Max Webers', *KZfSS* 32, 93–110.

Rigaudias-Weiss, Hilde (1936) *Les Enquêtes ouvrières en France entre 1830 et 1848*. Paris.

Ringer, Fritz K. (1969) *The Decline of the German Mandarins. The German Academic Community, 1890–1933*. Cambridge, Mass.: Harvard University Press.

——(1997) *Max Weber's Methodology. The Unification of the Cultural and Social Sciences*. Cambridge, Mass.: Harvard University Press.

Ritzer, George (1993) *The McDonaldization of Society*. London: Pine Forge Press.

Robertson, R. and Turner, Bryan S. (eds) (1991) *Talcott Parsons. Theorist of Modernity.* Newbury Park: Sage.

Rocher, Guy (1975) *Talcott Parsons and American Sociology.* New York: Barnes and Noble.

Roscher, Wilhelm and Knies, Karl (1975) *The Logical Problems of Historical Economics*, tr. Guy Oakes. New York: The Free Press.

Rorty, Richard (1984) 'The Historiography of Philosophy: Four Genres', in R. Rorty, J. B. Schneewind and Q. Skinner (eds), *Philosophy in History. Essays on the Historiography of Philosophy.* Cambridge: Cambridge University Press.

Rose, Gilian (1976) 'How is Critical Theory Possible? Theodor W. Adorno and Concept Formation in Sociology', *Political Studies* 26.

Rossides, Daniel (1973) 'The Legacy of Max Weber: A Non-Metaphysical Politics', in Andrew Effrat (ed.), *Perspectives in Political Sociology.* Indianapolis, New York: Bobbs-Merrill.

Roth, Guenther (1963) *The Social Democrats in Imperial Germany*, Totowa, NJ: Bedminster.

——(1971): see Bendix and Roth 1971.

——(1976) 'History and Sociology in the Work of Max Weber', *The British Journal of Sociology*, 27(3).

——(1979) 'Abschied oder Wiedersehen? Zur fünften Auflage von Max Webers *Wirtschaft und Gesellschaft*', *KZfSS*, 2.

——(1992a) 'Interpreting and Translating Max Weber', *International Sociology* 7(4) (Dec.), 449–59.

——(1992b) 'Zur Entstehungs- und Wirkungsgeschichte von Max Webers 'Protestantischer Ethik', in Bertram Schefold et al. (eds), *Vademecum zu einem Klassiker der Geschichte ökonomischer Rationalität.* Düsseldorf: Verlag Wirtschaft und Finanzen.

——(1993a) 'Between Cosmopolitanism and Ethnocentrism: Max Weber in the Nineties', *Telos* 96, Summer 1993.

——(1993b) 'Weber the Would-Be Englishman: Anglophilia and Family History', in Hartmut Lehmann and Guenther Roth (eds), *Weber's Protestant Ethic.* Cambridge: Cambridge University Press.

——(1995) 'Heidelberg-London-Manchester. Zu Max Webers deutsch-englischer Familiengeschichte', in Hubert Treiber and Karol Sauerland (eds), *Heidelberg im Schnittpunkt intellektueller Kreise.* Opladen: Westdeutscher Verlag.

Roth, G. and Schluchter, W. (1979) *Max Weber's Vision of History, Ethics and Methods.* Berkeley: University of California Press.

Ruin Jr, Hans (2000) 'Hägerström, Nietzsche och den svenska nihilismen', *Tidskrift för Politisk Filosofi* 1, 5–30.

Runciman, W. G. (1972) *A Critique of Max Weber's Philosophy of Social Science.* Cambridge: Cambridge University Press.

——(2000) 'Can there be a Nietzschean Sociology?', *Arch. Europ. Sociol.* 41(1), 3–21.

Rutkoff, P. and Scott, W. B. (1986) *New School: A History of the New School for Social Research.* New York: Free Press.

Sadri, A. and Sadri, M. (1988) 'Intercultural Understanding: Max Weber and Leo Strauss', *IJPCS* 1, 392–411.

Sahay, Arun (ed.) (1971) *Max Weber and Modern Sociology*. London: Routledge and Kegan Paul.

Salomon, A. (1934) 'Max Weber's Methodology', *Social Research* 1, 147–68.

——(1935a) 'Max Weber's Sociology', *Social Research* 2, 60–73.

——(1935b) 'Max Weber's Political Ideas', *Social Research* 2, 368–84.

——(1945) 'German Sociology', in Gurvitch and Moore 1945: 586–614.

Samuelsson, Kurt (1957) *Religion and Economic Action*. Stockholm and New York: Basic Books, 1961; orig. in Swedish, Stockholm: Scandinavian University Books, 1957.

Sanderson, Stephen K. (1988) 'The Neo-Weberian Revolution: A Theoretical Balance Sheet', *Sociological Forum*, 307–14.

Scaff, Lawrence A. (1973) 'Max Weber's Politics and Political Education', *APSR*.

——(1984) 'Weber before Weberian Sociology', *British Journal of Sociology*, 190–215.

——(1988a) 'Culture, Philosophy, and Politics: The Formation of the Sociocultural Sciences in Germany', *History of the Human Sciences* 1, 223–43.

——(1988b) 'Weber, Simmel, and the Sociology of Culture', in *Sociological Review*, 1–30.

——(1989) *Fleeing the Iron Cage. Culture, Politics, and Modernity, in the Thought of Max Weber*. Berkeley, Los Angeles and London: University of California Press.

——(1993) 'Life Contra Ratio: Music and Social Theory', *Sociological Theory*, 234–40.

Schelting, Alexander von (1922) 'Die logische Theorie der historischen Kulturwissenschaften von Max Weber und im besonderen sein Begriff des Idealtypus', *Archiv* 49, 623 *et passim*.

——(1934) *Max Webers Wissenschaftslehre*. Tübingen.

Schluchter, W. (1981a) 'Einführung in die Max Weber-Gesamtausgabe'. *Prospekt der Max Weber Gesamtausgabe*. Tübingen: Mohr.

——(1981b) *The Rise of Western Rationalism: Max Weber's Developmental History*. Berkeley: University of California Press.

——(1984) 'Max Weber's Religionssoziologie. Eine werkgeschichtliche Rekonstruktion', *KZfSS*, 342–65.

——(1989) *Rationalism, Religion, and Domination. A Weberian Perspective*. Berkeley and Los Angeles and Oxford: University of California Press; orig. in German 1988.

——(1994) 'Max Webers Religionssoziologie. Eine werkgeschichtliche Rekonstruktion', *KZfSS* 2, 342–65.

——(1996a) *Paradoxes of Modernity. Culture and Conduct in the Theory of Max Weber*. Stanford: Stanford University Press.

——(1996b) *Unversöhnte Moderne*. Frankfurt am Main: Suhrkamp.

——(1998) 'Max Webers Beitrag zum "Grundriss der Sozialökonomik". Editionsprobleme und Editionsstrategien', *KZfSS* 3, 327–43.

——(1999) ' "Kopf" oder "Doppelkopf" – Das ist hier die Frage. Replik auf Hiroshi Orihara', *KZfSS* 51(4), 735–43.

Schmidt, Gert (1980) 'Max Webers Beitrag zur empirischen Industrieforschung', *KZfSS*, 32.

Schmitt, Carl (1923) *The Crisis of Parliamentary Democracy*, tr. Ellen Kennedy. Cambridge, Mass.: MIT; orig. publ. 1923.

Schmoller, Gustav (1883) 'Zur Methodologie der Staats- und Sozialwissenschaften', *Schmollers Jahrbuch*.

Schnädelbach, H. (1983) *Philosophie in Deutschland 1831–1933*. Frankfurt am Main: Suhrkamp.

Schroeder, Ralph (1992) *Max Weber and the Sociology of Culture*. London: Sage.

Schroeder, R. (ed.) (1998) *Max Weber, Democracy and Modernization*. London: Macmillan.

Schroeter, Gert (1980) 'Max Weber as an Outsider: His Nominal Influence on German Sociology in the Twenties', *Journal of the History of the Behavioural Sciences* 16, 317–32.

——(1985) 'The Marx-Weber Nexus Revisited', *Canadian Journal of Sociology* 1, also in Antonio and Glassman (1985), 2–19.

Schulze, Winfried (1974) *Soziologie und Geschichtswissenschaft: Einführung in die Probleme der Kooperation beider Wissenschaften*. Munich: Fink.

Schumpeter, Joseph (1954a) *Economic Doctrine and Method. A Historical Sketch*. New York: Oxford University Press (esp. ch. 4, 'The Historical School and the Theory of Marginal Utility').

——(1954b) *The History of Economic Analysis*. New York: Oxford University Press.

Schutz: see Schütz.

Schütz, Alfred (1944–5) 'On Multiple Realities', *Philosophy and Phenomenological Research* 5, 533–76.

——(1960) 'The Social World and the Theory of Social Action', *Social Research* 27, 203–11.

——(1962–6) *Collected. Papers*, vols I–III. The Hague: Nijhoff.

——(1963) 'Concept and Theory Formation in Social Sciences', in Natanson 1963: 231–49.

——(1964) 'Don Quixote and the Problem of Reality', in *Collected Papers*, vol. II; orig. in Spanish 1955.

——(1967) *The Phenomenology of the Social World*. Evanston, Ill.: Northwestern University Press, 1967 (Engl. version of *Der sinnhafte Aufbau*).

——(1974) *Der sinnhafte Aufbau der sozialen Welt. Eine Einleitung in die verstehende Soziologie*. Frankfurt am Main: Suhrkamp; orig. 1932.

—— (1988) *Neue Beiträge zur Rezeption seines Werkes*, ed. Elisabeth List and Ilja Srubar. Amsterdam: Rodopi.

Schutz, Alfred and Luckmann, Thomas (1963) *The Structures of the Life-World*. Evanston: Northwestern University Press.

Schwinn, Thomas (1993) *Jenseits von Subjektivismus und Objektivismus. Max Weber, Alfred Schutz und Talcott Parsons*. Berlin: Duncker & Humblot.

Scott: see Rutkoff and Scott.

Segady, Thomas W. (1987) *Values, Neo-Kantianism, and the Development of Weberian Methodology.* New York, Berne, Frankfurt am Main and Paris: Peter Lang.

Seyfarth, Constans (1980) 'The West German Discussion of Max Weber's Sociology of Religion since the 1960s', *Social Compass* 27, 9–25.

Sharlin, Allan N. (1974) 'Max Weber and the Origin of the Idea of Value-Free Social Science', *Archives Européenes de Sociologie 2.*

Shils, Edward (1965) 'Charisma, Order, and Status', *ASR* 30, 199–213.

——(1974) 'Introduction' to Max Weber: *On Universities.* Chicago and London: University of Chicago Press.

——(1982) *The Constitution of Society.* Chicago: University of Chicago Press.

——(1987) 'Max Weber and the World since 1920', in Mommsen and Osterhammel 1987: 547–73.

——(1989) 'Arnaldo Momigliano and Max Weber', *Hist. Historiographie,* 54–64.

——(1990) 'Tradition, Ecology, and Institution in the History of Sociology', *Dædalus,* 99.

Sica, A. (1988) *Weber, Irrationality, and Social Order.* Berkeley and Los Angeles: University of California Press.

Skinner, Q. (1969) 'Meaning and Understanding in the History of Ideas', *History and Theory* 8.

——(1978) *The Foundations of Modern Political Thought. Vol. One. The Renaissance.* Cambridge: Cambridge University Press.

Smelser, Neil and Warner, R. Stephen (1976) *Sociological Theory: Historical and Formal.* Morristown, NJ: General Learning Press.

Smith, Michael Joseph (1986) *Realist Thought from Weber to Kissinger.* Baton Rouge: Louisiana State.

Snizek, William E., Fuhrman, Ellsworth R. and Miller, Michael K. (eds) (1979) *Contemporary Issues on Theory and Research: A Metasociological Perspective.* London: Aldwych Press.

Sombart, W. (1915) *Händler und Helden.* Munich and Leipzig: Duncker & Humblot.

Speier, Hans (1935) 'Max Weber', in *Encyclopedia of the Social Sciences.* New York: Macmillan.

Sprondel, Walter M. and Grathoff, Richard (eds) (1979) *Alfred Schütz und die Idee des Alltags in den Sozialwissenschaften.* Stuttgart.

Sprondel, Walter M. and Seyfarth, Constans (eds) (1981) *Max Weber und die Rationalisierung sozialen Handelns.* Stuttgart: Enke.

Srubar, Ilja (1984) 'On the Origin of "Phenomenological" Sociology', *Human Studies.*

——(ed.) (1988a) *Exil, Wissenschaft, Identität. Die Emigration deutscher Sozialwissenschaftler 1933–1945.* Frankfurt am Main: Suhrkamp.

——(1988b) *Kosmion. Die Genese der pragmatischen Lebenswelttheorie von Alfred Schütz und ihr anthropologischer Hintergrund.* Frankfurt am Main: Suhrkamp.

——(1990) 'Wertbeziehung und Relevanz. Zu Schütz Weber-Rezeption', *Critique and Humanism* (Special Issue), 38–53.

——(1993) 'On the Limits of Rational Choice', in 'The Rationality of Everyday Behavior: A Rational Choice Reconstruction of the Theory of Action by Alfred Schutz' (exchange with contributions from H. Esser, I. Srubar, H. Prendergast, R. Collins, A. Wetterlin and T. Luckmann), *Rationality and Society*, 5, 7–31.

Stammer, Otto (1965) *Max Weber und die Soziologie heute. Verhandlungen des 15. deutschen Soziologentages.* Tübingen: Mohr. Engl. trans. Kathleen Morris, Oxford, 1971.

Stark, Jerry A. (1982) 'Weber and Husserl on Social Science and Crisis: An Outline for Inquiry', *Current Perspectives in Social Theory*, 225–41.

Stauth, G. and Turner, B. S. (1986) 'Nietzsche in Weber oder die Geburt des modernen Genius im professionellen Menschen', *ZfS* 15, 81–94.

Steinvorth, Ulrich (1978) 'Wertfreiheit der Wissenschaften bei Marx, Weber und Adorno. Ein Nachtrag zum Methodenstreit zwischen Kritischer Theorie und Kritischem Rationalismus', *Zeitschrift für allgemenine Wissenschaftstheorie* 9(2), 293–306.

——(1982) 'Max Webers System der verstehender Soziologie', *Zeitschrift für allgemeine Wissenschaftstheorie* 12(1), 48–69.

Steding, Christoph (1932) *Politik und Wissenschaft bei Max Weber.* Diss. Breslau.

Stern, Fritz (1972) *The Failures of Illiberalism.* London: Allen and Unwin.

Strauss, Leo (1953) *Natural Right and History.* Chicago: University of Chicago Press.

Strzelewics, Willy (1931) *Die Grenzen der Wissenschaft bei Max Weber.* Frankfurt am Main: Diss. Goethe-Universität.

Swatos, Jr., William H. (1982) 'Sects and Success: Missverstehen in Mt. Airy', *Sociological Analysis*, 43(4), 375–80.

Swedberg, Richard (1990) 'Introduction' to Gunnar Myrdal: *The Political Element.* New Brunswick, NJ: Transaction.

——(1998) *Max Weber and the Idea of Economic Sociology.* Princeton: Princeton University Press.

Szacki, Jerzy (1979a) *History of Sociological Thought.* Westport, Conn.: Greenwood.

——(1979b) 'On So-called Historicism in the Social Sciences', in Jerzy J. Wiatr (ed.) *Polish Essays in the Methodology of the Social Sciences.* Boston Studies in the Philosophy of Science 29. Dordrecht, Boston and London: Reidel.

Szakolczai, Arpád (1998) *Max Weber and Michel Foucault. Parallel Life-Works.* London: Routledge.

Tarcov, Natan (1982) 'Quentin Skinner's Method and Machiavelli's *Prince*', *Ethics*, 693–709.

Tenbruck, Friedrich H. (1959) 'Die Genesis der Methodologie Max Webers', *KZfSS*, 573–630.

——(1975a) 'Das Werk Max Webers', *KZfSS* 27, 663–702.

——(1975b) 'Wie gut kennen wir Max Weber. Über Massstäbe der Weber-Forschung im Spiegel der Massstäbe der Weber-Ausgaben', *Zeitschrift für die gesamte Staatswissenschaft* 131, 719–42.

——(1977) 'Abschied von "Wirtschaft und Gesellschaft". Zur Besprechung der 5. revidierten Auflage mit textkritischen Erläuterungen herausgegeben von Johannes Winckelmann, Tübingen 1976', *Zeitschrift für die gesamte Staatswissenschaft* 133, 703–36.

——(1980) 'The Problem of Thematic Unity in the Works of Max Weber', *British Journal of Sociology* 31, 313–51.

——(1986) 'Das Werk Max Webers: Methodologie und Sozialwissenschaften', *KZfSS* 38, 13–31.

——(1987) 'Max Weber und Eduard Meyer', in Mommsen and Osterhammel 1987: 234–67.

——(1989a) 'Abschied von der "Wissenschaftslehre"?', in Johannes Weiss (ed.), *Max Weber heute*. Frankfurt am Main: Suhrkamp.

——(1989b) 'The Cultural Foundations of Society', in Haferkamp 1989: 15–35.

——(1999) *Das Werk Max Webers. Gesammelte Aufsätze zu Max Weber*, ed. Harald Homann. Tübingen: Mohr Siebeck.

Therborn, Göran (1974) *Science, Class, and Society. On the Formation of Sociology and Historical Materialism*. Göteborg: Revo Press (also New Left Books 1976).

Tibbetts, Paul (1980) 'The Issue of Human Subjectivity in Sociological Explanation: The Schutz-Parsons Controversy', *Human Studies*, 357–66.

Tiryakian, Edward A. (1975) 'Neither Marx nor Durkheim . . . Perhaps Weber', *AJS* 81(1).

Topitsch, Ernst (1965) 'Max Weber und die Soziologie heute', in Stammer 1965.

Topolski, Jerzy (1976) *Methodology of History*. Dordrecht: Reidel.

Torrance, John (1974) 'Max Weber. Methods and the Man', *Archives Européenes de Sociologie* 15(1).

Treiber H. (1985) ' "Elective Affinities" between Weber's Sociology of Religion and Sociology of Law. On the Adequacy Relation between Explanatory Models with the Help of which Weber Reconstructs the Religious and Legal Rationalization Process', *Theory and Society*, 809–61.

——(1992) 'Wahlverwandtschaften zwischen Nietzsches Idee eines "Klosters für freiere Geister" und Webers Idealtypus der puritanischen Sekte. Mit einem Streifzug durch Nietzsches "Ideale Bibliothek", *Nietzsche-Studien*.

Tribe, Keith (1989) *Reading Weber*. London: Routledge.

Troeltsch, Ernst (1922) *Der Historismus und seine Probleme*. Tübingen: Mohr.

Tully, J. (ed.) (1988) *Context and Meaning. Quentin Skinner and his Critics*. Princeton, NJ: Princeton University Press.

Turner, Bryan S. (1990) 'Max Weber's Historical Sociology: A Bibliographical Essay', *Journal of Historical Sociology*, 192–208.

—— (1991) 'Neofunctionalism and the "New Theoretical Movement": The Post-Parsonsian Rapprochement Between Germany and America', in Robertson and Turner 1991.

—— (1992) *From History to Modernity*. London: Routledge.

Turner, Charles (1992) *Modernity and Politics in the Work of Max Weber*. London: Routledge.

Turner, S. P. (1983) ' "Contextualism" and the Interpretation of the Classical Sociological Texts', *Knowledge and Society: Studies in the Sociology of Culture Past and Present. A Research Annual* 4, 273–91.

—— (1985) 'Explaining Capitalism: Weber on and against Marx', in Antonio and Glassman 1985: 167–88.

—— (1986a) *The Search for a Methodology of Social Science*. Boston: Reidel.

—— (1986b) 'Weber Agonistes', in *Contemporary Sociology* 15, 47–50.

—— (1990) 'Weber and his Philosophers', *IJPCS* 3, 539–53.

Turner, Stephen (ed.) (2000) *The Cambridge Companion to Weber*. Cambridge: Cambridge University Press.

Turner, Stephen P. and Factor, Regis (1981) 'Objective Possibility and Adequate Causation in Weber's Methodological Writings', *Sociological Review* 29(1), 5–28.

—— (1984a) *Max Weber and the Dispute over Reason and Value*. London: Routledge and Kegan Paul.

—— (1984b) 'Weber, the Germans, and "Anglo-Saxon Convention": Liberalism as a Technique and Form of Life', in Glassman and Murvar 1984.

—— (1987) 'Decisionism and Politics: Weber as Constitutional Theorist', in Whimster and Lash (eds) *Max Weber, Rationality and Modernity*, London: Allen and Unwin.

—— (1990) 'The Disappearance of Tradition in Weber', *Midwest Studies in Philosophy* 15, 400–24.

—— (1994) *Max Weber: The Lawyer as Social Thinker*. London: Routledge.

Twenhöfel, Ralf (1986) 'Interesse und Forschung. Der Beitrag Alfred Schutz' zur qualitativen Methodologie. Bedeutung, Grenzen und eine Kritik aus der Sicht Max Webers', *Schweizerische Zeitschrift für Soziologie*, 373–96.

Tyrell, Hartmann (1991) 'Religion and "Intellectual Uprightness". On the Tragedy of Religion as Seen by Max Weber and Friedrich Nietzsche; Religion and "intellektuelle Redlichkeit" ', *Sociologia Internationalis*, 159–77.

Udéhn, Lars (1981) 'The Conflict between Methodology and Rationalization in the Work of Max Weber', *Acta Sociologica* 24, 131–47.

—— (1996) *The Limits of Rational Choice*. London: Routledge.

Üner, Elfriede (1992) *Soziologie als 'geistige Bewegung'. Hans Freyer System der Soziologie und die 'Leipziger Schule'*. Wertheim: VCH.

Urry, John (1973) 'Thomas S. Kuhn as Sociologist of Knowledge', *British Journal of Sociology* 24.

Valone, James J. (1980) 'Parsons' Contributions to Sociological Theory. Reflections on the Schutz-Parsons Correspondence', *Human Studies*, 375–86.

Veblen, Thorstein (1915) *Imperial Germany and the Industrial Revolution.* London: Macmillan.

Vidich, Arthur and Lyman, Stanford (1985) *American Sociology. Worldly Rejections of Religion and their Directions.* New Haven and London: Yale University Press.

Voegelin, Eric (1952) *The New Science of Politics.* Chicago: University of Chicago Press.

Wagner, G. (1987) *Geltung und normativer Zwang. Eine Untersuchung zu den neukantianischen Grundlagen der Wissenschaftslehre Max Webers.* Freiburg im Breisgau: Alber.

Wagner, G. and Zipprian, H. (1985) 'Methodologie und Ontologie. Zum Problem kausaler Erklärung bei Max Weber', *ZfS* 14(2), 115–30.

—— (1987) 'Tenbruck, Weber und die Wirklichkeit. Ein Diskussionsbeitrag', *KZfSS* 39(1), 132–49.

—— (1990) 'Oakes on Weber and Rickert', *IJPCS* 3(4), 559–63.

Wagner, G. and Zipprian, H. (eds) (1994) *Max Webers Wissenschaftslehre.* Frankfurt am Main: Suhrkamp.

Wagner, Helmut (1980) 'Reflections on Parsons' "1974 Retrospective Perspective" on Alfred. Schutz', *Human Studies,* 387–402.

—— (1983) *Alfred Schutz. An Intellectual Biography.* Chicago and London: University of Chicago Press.

—— (1984) 'Schutz's Life Story and the Understanding of his Work', *Human Studies* 7, 107–16.

Wagner, Peter, Wittrock, Björn, Whitley, Richard (eds) (1991) *Discourses on Society. The Shaping of the Social Science Disciplines. Sociology of the Sciences. Yearbook 1991.* Dordrecht and Boston and London: Kluwer.

Wallace, Walther (1990) 'Rationality, Human Nature, and Society in Weber's Theory', *Theory and Society,* 199–223.

Wallerstein, Immanuel (1991) *Unthinking Social Science: The Limits of Nineteenth-Century Paradigms.* Cambridge: Polity.

Weber, Marianne (1950) *Max Weber. Ein Lebensbild.* Heidelberg: Mohr (reprint of orig. edn 1926. Engl. transl. by Harry Zohm (New York, London, Sidney, Toronto: Wiley and Sons, 1975)).

Weber, Max: *GARS, GAW, GPS, MWG, WuG,* etc. (See List of Abbreviations, p. vii).

—— (1903) 'Roscher und Knies und die logischen Probleme der historischen Nationalökonomie. (Erster Artikel), Vorbemerkung u. I.', *Jahrbuch für Gesetzgebung, Verwaltung und Volkswirtschaft im Deutschen Reich* 27(3), 1181–221. [In *GAW:* 1–42.]

—— (1904) 'Die "Objektivität sozialwissenschaftlicher und sozialpolitischer Erkenntnis', *Archiv für Sozialwissenschaft und Sozialpolitik* 19(1), 22–87. [In *GAW:* 146–214.]

—— (1905) 'Die protestantische Ethik und der "Geist" des Kapitalismus', *Archiv für Sozialwissenschaft und Sozialpolitik* 20(1), 1–54; 21(1), 1–110.

—— (1906) 'Roscher und Knies und die logischen Probleme der historischen Nationalökonomie. (Dritter Artikel). II. Knies und das

Irrationalitätsproblem (Fortsetzung)', *Jahrbuch für Gesetzgebung, Verwaltung und Volkswirtschaft im Deutschen Reich* 30(1), 81–120. [In *GAW*: 105–42.]

——(1907) "R. Stammlers "Ueberwindung" der materialistichen Geschichtsauffassung', *Archiv für Sozialwissenschaft und Sozialpolitik* 24(1), 94–151. [In *GAW*: 291–359.]

——(1908a) Erhebungen über Auslese und Anpassung (Berufswahl und Berufsschicksal) der Arbeiterschaft der geschlossenen Grossindustrie [Exposé zur Methodik der Erhebungen]. Altenburg: Pierersche Hofbuchdruckerei Stephan Greibel & Co. [In *GASW*: 1–60, with the title 'Methodologische Einleitung für die Erhebungen des Vereins für Sozialpolitik über Auslese und Anpassung (Berufswahlen und Berufsschicksal) der Arbeiterschaft der geschlossenen Grossindustrie'; incomplete.]

——(1908b) 'Die Grenznutzlehre und das "psychologische Grundgesetz"', *Archiv für Sozialwissenschaft und Sozialpolitik* 27(2), 546–58. [In *GAW*: 384–99.]

——(1908c) 'Zur Psychophysik der industriellen Arbeit', *Archiv für Sozialwissenschaft und Sozialpolitik* 24(1), 94–151. [In *GASW*: 61–109.]

——(1913) 'Über einige Kategorien der verstehenden Soziologie', *Logos. Internationale Zeitschrift für Philosophie der Kultur* 4(3), 253–94. [In *GAW*: 427–74.]

——(1916) 'Die Wirtschaftsethik der Weltreligionen. Religionssoziologische Skizzen. Einleitung; Der Konfuzianismus I-IV; Zwischenbetrachtung. Stufen und Richtungen der religiösen Weltablehnung', *Archiv für Sozialwissenschaft und Sozialpolitik* 41(1), 1–87; 41(2), 335–421.

——(1917) 'Der Sinn der "Wertfreiheit" der soziologischen und ökonomischen Wissenschaften', *Logos. Internationale Zeitschrift für Philosophie der Kultur* 8(1), 40–88. [In *GAW*: 489–540.]

——(1947) *The Theory of Social and Economic Organization*. Ed. with an Introduction by Talcott Parsons. New York and London: Free Press and Macmillan.

——(1949) *Methodology of the Social Sciences*. Tr. Edward Shils and Henry Finch. London and New York: Macmillan and Free Press.

——(1954) *Max Weber on Law in Economy and Society*. New York: Simon and Schuster.

——(1975) *Roscher and Knies. The Logical Problem of Historical Economics*. Transl. with Introduction by Guy Oakes. New York and London: Free Press and Macmillan.

——(1977) *Critique of Stammler*. Tr. with Introduction by Guy Oakes. New York and London: Free Press and Mcmillan.

——(1988) *The Agrarian Sociology of Ancient Civilizations*. Tr. F. I. Frank. London: Verso.

——(1990) *Grundriss zu den Vorlesungen über allgemeine ('theoretische') Nationalökonomie (1898)*. Tübingen: Mohr (Siebeck).

——(1994) *Political Writings*, ed. Peter Lassman and Ronald Speirs. Cambridge: Cambridge University Press.

Wegener, Walther (1962) *Die Quellen der Wissenschaftsauffassung Max Webers und die Problematik der Werturteilsfreiheit der Nationalökonomie*. Berlin: Duncker & Humblot.

Wehler, Hans-Ulrich (1985) *The German Empire 1871–1918*. Tr. Kim Traynor. Leamington Spa: Berg.

Weiss, Johannes (1981) *Max Weber and the Marxist World*. London and New York: Routledge and Kegan Paul.

——(ed.) (1989) *Max Weber heute*. Frankfurt am Main: Suhrkamp.

Wertheim, W. F. (1971) *Evolution and Revolution*. Amsterdam: Van Gennep (also Harmondsworth: Penguin 1974).

Whimster, Sam (1987) 'The Secular Ethic and the Culture of Modernism', in Lash and Whimster 1987: 259–90.

——(ed.) (1999) *Max Weber and the Culture of Anarchy*. London: Macmillan.

Whimster, Sam and Lash, Scott (eds) (1987) *Max Weber, Rationality and Modernity*. London: Allen and Unwin.

Wiley, Norbert (ed.) (1987) *The Marx–Weber Debate*. Beverly Hills and London: Sage.

Willer, David (1967) 'Max Weber's Missing Authority Type', *Sociological Inquiry* 37, 231–9.

Willey, Thomas E. (1978) *Back to Kant*. Detroit: Wayne State University Press.

Winch, Peter (1958) *The Idea of a Social Science and its Relation to Philosophy*. London.

Winckelmann, Johannes (1952) *Legitimität und Legalität in Max Webers Herrschaftssoziologie*. Tübingen: Mohr.

——(1986) *Max Webers hinterlassenes Hauptwerk*. Tübingen: Mohr.

Windelband, Wilhelm (1903) *Präludien*. Freiburg and Tübingen; orig. 1884.

Wrong, Dennis (ed.) (1970) *Max Weber*. Englewood Cliffs, NJ: Prentice-Hall.

——(1982) 'A Note on Marx and Weber in Gouldner's Thought', *Theory and Society*, 899–905.

Wuthnow, R. (1989) *Communities of Discourse. Ideology and Social Structure in the Reformation, the Enlightenment, and European Socialism*. Cambridge, Mass.: Harvard University Press.

Zabludowsky, Gina (1989) 'The Reception and Utility of Max Weber's Concept of Patrimonialism in Latin America', *International Sociology* 4, 51–66.

Zaret, David (1980) 'From Weber to Parsons and Schutz: The Eclipse of History in Modern Social Theory', *AJS* 85(5), 1180–201.

Zeisel, Hans (1981) 'Paul Lazarsfeld und das Wien der Zwanziger Jahre', *KZfSS*, 395–403.

Zeitlin, Irving (1968) *Ideology and the Development of Sociological Theory*. Englewood Cliffs, NJ: Prentice-Hall.

Zingerle, Arnold (1974) 'Die verspätete Rezeption. Neuere Literatur zu Max Weber', *Der Staat* 13(4).

——(1981) *Max Webers historische Soziologie. Aspekte und Materialien zur Wirkungsgeschichte.* Darmstadt: Wissenschaftliche Buchgesellschaft.

——(1989) 'Max Weber: Klassiker der Soziologie?', *Soziologische Revue* 12, 377–83.

Index